COMMUNICATION
IN LEGAL ADVOCACY

Studies in Communication Processes

COMMUNICATION IN LEGAL ADVOCACY

by
Richard D. Rieke
Randall K. Stutman

University of South Carolina Press

Copyright © 1990 University of South Carolina
Second Printing 1995

Published in Columbia, South Carolina, by the
University of South Carolina Press

Manufactured in the United States of America

Library of Congress Cataloging-in-Publication Data

Rieke, Richard D.
    Communication in legal advocacy / by Richard D. Rieke, Randall K.
Stutman. — 1st ed.
        p.   cm.
    Includes bibliographical references.
    ISBN 0-87249-639-2. — ISBN 0-87249-681-3 (pbk.)
    1. Trial practice—United States.   2. Forensic oratory.
  I. Stutman, Randall K., 1957– .   II. Title.   III. Series.
KF8915.R54   1990
347.73'7—dc20
[347.3077]   89-16759
                                                                          CIP

Our love and appreciation to
Mary Lou and Sara

CONTENTS

PREFACE

Cicero adapted rhetorical theory to legal advocacy and established himself as a significant contributor to our understanding of both. In the more than two thousand years since Cicero wrote, the relationship between research in rhetorical/communication theory and the practice of trial advocacy has waxed and waned, but it is probably as vital today as it has ever been.

Since the replacement of the apprenticeship system of studying law, the practicing bar has sought to balance the emphasis of law schools on case law with a body of practical guides to such lawyering behaviors as trial advocacy. Great advocates have written their memoirs, and special workshops and projects have published practical guides. They have proven invaluable to young attorneys who find themselves admitted to practice with little understanding of how to go about it.

As valuable as these efforts have been, they share an inherent weakness: They must assume that what was successful for one advocate or what has worked in some trials can be applied generally. They are bound to the presumption that if a trial was won or if an attorney had a successful career, every practice associated with the success was equally responsible. This is an inevitable result of the separation of theory and practice, of mistaking experience for research, of treating a science as if it were an art.

But there is also an inherent danger in granting too much credence to scientific research at the expense of practical experience. The scientists can too easily drift off to the study of issues that have no immediate urgency, or arrogantly assume to have a better understanding of how a justice system should function than those who daily work within it. This can lead researchers to propose utopian solutions to practical problems.

What follows in this book is an effort to return to the Ciceronian ideal: to produce a work that brings our best scholarship to bear directly upon practical problems in such a way that science will inform practice and practice will inform science. We operate from the premise that good advice is generated by good explanations, and there is no shortcut. We presume that theory and research in trial advocacy complement the assumptions of effective advocates and compete only with those assumptions that are the products of hasty or unsystematic generalization and prejudice.

The book is structured according to our analysis of key elements in the process by which lawyers help people resolve their disputes: an overall discussion of dispute resolution followed by a focus on the trial in terms of the environment of the courtroom, legal procedure, fairness, and trial venue. Then we examine individually the elements of the trial, including jury selection, opening statements, the process of negotiating credibility, evidence and testimony, witnesses, closing arguments, and the ways in which juries decide.

In each chapter we have sought to report the best theory and research now available and present that content in terms of the practical concerns of trial advocates. We do not presume to say how the process ought to be constituted. Instead, we try to share our best understanding of how trial advocacy can be practiced consistent with practical experience and scholarship.

COMMUNICATION
IN LEGAL ADVOCACY

Chapter 1

DISPUTE RESOLUTION

From time to time we read of successful people who close out their affairs and escape to some isolated location on a ship, desert island, or mountaintop. When asked, they frequently reply that they just had to get away from the daily grievances that come with living in the modern world. They have found their resolution, but the rest of us cannot get away that easily. We need to learn to deal with grievances and go on living with other people.

Our society has created a variety of ways of dealing with grievances in acceptable ways, and the trial at law is probably the most formal and well developed. Trials, viewed in terms of the communication processes they involve, constitute the focus of this book. However, in order to understand trials, it is first necessary to look at some of the other ways our culture allows us to resolve our disputes with other people. The purpose of this chapter is to examine the basic nature of human disputes and the processes of negotiation, mediation, and their variations.

Just what do we mean by the term "grievance"? First, we need to call to your attention some common situations that could constitute the start of a grievance. For example, have you ever had someone shove ahead of you in the check-out line at a store? Did you ever feel the flush of anger as you were pushed aside on the sidewalk so that someone else could pass? What would you do if your neighbor's dogs barked day and night and kept you awake?

These incidents seem trivial to you, perhaps. So, think of some that might arouse your attention. For example, would you be upset if the dump truck in front of you hit a bump, causing a rock to fly off and drive a deep crack in your windshield? Or maybe you would begin to feel a sense of grievance if you saved up and bought a new car only to have it go wrong every two weeks so that you constantly have it back in the shop. Is it any of your business if your neighbors, the same ones who own the dogs, get drunk every Saturday night, yell at one another, and occasionally get into a fight on the front lawn?

Now, maybe you begin to see what we mean by grievance. Things can get worse. What do you believe should be done if your

1

boss installs a new office machine and tells you to use it without giving you safety precautions, and you almost cut off your finger using it? Or should something be done when you have an operation on one finger only to discover that you have lost the sensation in the entire hand? If you know it was the neighbors' thirteen-year-old son who broke into your garage and took your bicycle, but they deny it, what do you do? Or, what if a fire truck comes into the intersection against the red light so that you hit it, and you feel it should have gone more slowly; is there any way to seek relief?

Each of these situations presents the possibility of a grievance, "a circumstance or condition thought to be unjust and ground for complaint or resentment" (*Webster's New World Dictionary* 1965). But would you issue a complaint in each one? Under what circumstances would you just feel resentment but do nothing?

In many cases people choose to ignore, shrug off, or otherwise refuse to make a complaint. Most of us would let the man shove us aside on the street without saying or doing a thing. Many would just continue to wait quietly while the clerk served the rude woman. Surprisingly, many Americans would not make a formal complaint about the barking dogs, the chip in the windshield, and even the fighting neighbors, although they might talk among themselves about the dogs and the fighting, and ultimately talk with the neighbors.

The fact is that our image of Americans as people who jump to complain about every slight and go to court with any grievance is simply not supported by recent studies. Instead, the research describes people who advocate talking directly to each other and taking care of problems themselves (Merry and Silby 1984).

However, sometimes grievances do become disputes (in labor-management practice disputes are called grievances). Think of a dispute as any situation in which someone (plaintiff) asserts a claim for some injury against someone else (defendant) (Priest and Klein 1984). Or a dispute could be defined as a matured controversy, in contrast to a grievance, which may remain inchoate and unexpressed (Sander 1985).

Once you determine to do something about a grievance—once you choose to define it as a dispute—it becomes necessary to select some means to resolve it. Now, of course, the other person or persons become involved. You are not free to resolve the dispute by yourself if you have chosen not to let it remain merely a grievance. Society and culture influence the range of dispute resolution mechanisms available to you.

Violence and communication compete as basic methods of dispute resolution. Violence, while considered a relic of less civilized times and places, is still employed with frightening regularity in the United States. Drivers on Los Angeles freeways are shot at and sometimes killed by other drivers who are aggrieved by some driving experience. Fights still occur over disputes and people are killed and wounded. Killing is still chosen as a means of removing annoyances both canine and human. Some loans are collected with the help of brute force.

Communication, however, is the socially approved medium of dispute resolution. It presents itself in a variety of systems, which will be the focus of the rest of this chapter.

METHODS OF DISPUTE RESOLUTION

In contemporary parlance the range of dispute resolution mechanisms is divided into two categories: adjudication, or the use of courts on the one hand, and what are called alternative dispute resolution methods (ADR) on the other. Since formal trials occupy such an important place in our society, all other methods of working out disputes fall in the category of alternatives. This probably reflects more the fact that the concept ADR is a creation of lawyers whose primary orientation is adjudication than the frequency with which the methods are used or their importance to ordinary people. Nevertheless, that is the system we will employ. Since this book is devoted to a detailed discussion of communication in adjudication, we will begin with the alternatives and work our way toward adjudication.

To start, consider the various methods of dispute resolution in relation to each other. Sander (1985) considers the two extremes of dispute resolution to be adjudication at one end and avoidance at the other. Goldberg, Green, and Sander (1985) use the colloquial expression "lump it"—as in "like it or lump it"—to refer to the process of avoidance, leading to a rephrasing of Sander's extremes as lump it or litigate it. Either shrug off your feeling of grievance and go your own way or find a lawyer and file suit.

There are, however, other alternatives to litigation than avoidance. Next to avoidance is negotiation. Following that as we move toward litigation is mediation or conciliation. The use of an ombudsman or some other fact-finding or investigation agency does not fall along this continuum, but falls below it as an adjunct to many of the resolution mechanisms in Sander's scheme. There are, as we approach even closer to adjudication, such methods as administrative agencies which serve to resolve disputes, and finally there are various forms of arbitration.

What are the criteria of the continuum we have suggested? In what way do we explain the relationship we have just suggested among the various approaches to dispute resolution? Let the trial set the criteria, and let the continuum indicate a gradual movement away from those criteria.

In a trial disputing individuals are assured of a socially sanctioned public dispute resolution process which will involve the opportunity to present proofs and arguments in their own behalf and a third party with coercive power who will determine a winner by focusing narrowly on immediate matters at issue without regard to the underlying relationship between the parties (Sander 1985). So the criteria we use are these:

1. A socially sanctioned process of dispute resolution
2. Open to public scrutiny
3. Communication of proofs and arguments
4. A third party
5. Coercive power held by the third party
6. The determination of winners and losers
7. A focus on issues immediately in dispute
8. No concern for underlying relationships

These are the elements of adjudication at one extreme of the continuum; avoidance, at the other end, has only the one characteristic of being a socially acceptable if not sanctioned means of resolving disputes.

Negotiation is a socially sanctioned process of dispute resolution that presents an opportunity to communicate proofs and arguments. It is not open to the public; it does not involve a third party or coercive power; and it does not allow for a declaration of winners and losers. It may or may not be focused on issues immediately at hand, and it may or may not address underlying relationships.

Mediation/conciliation is also a socially sanctioned process of dispute resolution that presents an opportunity to communicate proofs and arguments. It is not open to the public, nor does it involve coercive power. It does, however, bring into the dispute a third party, who will not determine winners and losers but who will assist those in dispute to address either the issues immediately at hand or underlying relationships or both.

Administrative hearings are public, socially sanctioned dispute resolution methods that involve third parties with some coercive power and the ability to address to some extent the issues at hand as well as other issues the hearing officers may initiate. Hearings do not consider underlying relationships and typically declare winners and losers after hearing proofs and arguments. They will also involve the consideration of other facts, proofs, and arguments than those presented by the immediate disputants.

Arbitration is a socially sanctioned dispute resolution method that gives disputants the opportunity to present proofs and arguments to a third party, who may or may not have coercive power. It is typically not open to public scrutiny, and it will consider immediate issues as well as some underlying relationships and finally declare a winner.

We will discuss and illustrate each of these alternatives to the use of the courts, and close the chapter with an overview of the trial process.

AVOIDANCE: "LUMPING IT"

Merry and Silby (1984) wanted to know why people use alternative methods of dispute resolution so infrequently. Their previous research had suggested that people in small towns prefer to handle interpersonal problems by themselves, either by talking or avoidance. So they studied people in small towns on the theory that disputes are cultural events with clear rules about what is worth fighting over.

They found that different communities with different cultural rules will respond to disputes differently. They learned that people in general prefer to handle disputes themselves with such avoidance tactics as building fences and looking the other way. When neighbors do enter into a dispute, they are likely to be criticized as troublemakers; they tend to be seen as violating the sense of privacy in the neighborhood. On the other hand, those in lower-income towns with more transient residents feel freer to bring disputes to the courts, even though they report no more grievances than those in other towns.

Some cultural patterns include avoidance of disputes as desirable, respectable behavior. Other cultures seem to value dispute behavior per se. At the University of Utah part of the faculty had been trained as debaters and others as therapists. When a disagreement emerged in department meetings, the debaters would begin an argument that would frighten and embarrass the therapists. The therapists felt that the vigorous arguments were in bad taste, while the debaters could not understand the objection. If a debater disagreed with a therapist, the therapist would seek to avoid further discussion.

Even though a clearly damaged product can easily be returned to the store for replacement, many people will avoid that course simply because they do not relish an interaction with the clerk that may involve disagreement. Many of us have loaned money or other items to friends who fail to return them, but we will not raise the issue lest it turn into a disagreement that might damage our friendship or be embarrassing.

Lumping it, then, is perhaps the most common form of dispute resolution, at least among some cultures. But even in those cultures some disputes demand another tactic, and the one to which people will most frequently turn is some form of negotiation.

NEGOTIATION

Negotiation is the preeminent mode of dispute resolution (Goldberg, Green, and Sander 1985). If you say to the woman who has pushed in front of you at the cashier's desk, "Excuse me, but I believe I was in line ahead of you," and she says, "I beg your pardon," and steps back, you have negotiated. She might also reply, "I'm sorry, I know you were ahead of me but I am desperate to pay for this and get outside before I get a parking ticket. Will you let me go on?" She is negotiating, and you might willingly allow her in front of you, feeling better about the whole situation than before your interaction.

In times past, negotiation has been seen as a rather stylized process of offer and counteroffer leading to a mathematically predictable, mutually acceptable settlement (Siegal and Fouraker 1960). The assumption was that of game theory: Each party to a negotiation perceives the other as an opponent who has a rational goal (maximum payoff/minimum loss) and a limited and knowable set of moves by which to obtain that goal. Thus each player knows fully in advance of negotiation where the other is going and how they can get there. Given this situation, each player can plan moves and countermoves within a range of acceptable settlements and come to a point in which the joint payoff is maximized. In this view communication is unnecessary, and is even an impediment to the discovery of the best settlement.

Take for an example your complaint about your car which you believe to be a lemon. In contact with the manufacturer you want a new car without further payment (maximum payoff/minimum loss), and the car company wants you to accept the car as is without further obligation on their part. In a game theory view you two make moves: you ask for a new car, they offer nothing; you ask for a new engine, they offer to fix the present one; you ask for repairs on the present one with an extended twelve-month warranty, and they accept. Negotiation is thus completed without communication beyond offer and counteroffer, and the outcome is predictable in the sense it involves the best gain with least cost for both parties.

Today scholars are more likely to see negotiation as the way in which people come to their understanding of themselves, each other, and their environment. It is common to hear the suggestion that we negotiate or socially construct reality (Berger and Luckman 1967; Putnam and Bullis 1986). Walton and McKersie (1965) argue that people are not as objectively rational as the game theory model suggests. For example, if the woman at the store had merely glared at you and continued to shove ahead, you may have insisted on your place in line even though you were in no hurry. Your need to go ahead or let her go first was not determined in advance but was instead a product of the interaction. Thus your payoff and costs could not have been calculated in a game theoretical manner.

In actual negotiations people consistently violate what would be objectively rational minimum or maximum acceptable settlements (Smith 1983). Fairness, for example, is an important concept that cannot be quantified in terms of dollars and cents. Anger, friendship, the desire to maintain good feelings, and other equally abstract motives play a part in negotiation. Smith (1983) views negotiation as a process of mutual exploration during which people seek definitions of issues and experiences. It is a process through which values and meanings emerge so that they can be shared by those negotiating.

Parties in negotiation communicate in order to interpret the other's position and future moves, and in so doing construct a new collaborative social reality. Shared meanings develop through revised expectations and interpretations coming from two or more distinct realities (Putnam and Bullis 1986).

To enter into negotiations means that you have chosen not to lump the dispute. You want some resolution, and presumably you want it to work in your favor. However, keep in mind that the very act of negotiation itself may be all you seek. You want the satisfaction of having presented your position to someone who understands and respects it. You want a clear settlement of the dispute—it is too important to ignore—but you may only want it clear that the resolution required your participation. The woman at the cashier's counter was shoving ahead of you and you really were in no great hurry, but you at least wanted her to understand that it was your turn and you were willingly letting her go first.

Negotiation is an interaction in which participants want to cooperate so that a settlement is reached, but at the same time they are competitors with regard to the specific nature of the agreement

(Coleman 1980). Because of the competitive elements in negotiation the use of bargaining agents has grown common for a number of reasons. First, in spite of the fact that we apparently engage in ongoing negotiation as we socially construct our meanings or reality, not many of us feel competent to engage in serious negotiation. This becomes particularly true, second, when one side has an experienced and competent negotiator. Even fewer of us feel able to hold our own in the face of a professional, even though we continue to try to negotiate with merchants who are professional negotiators. Third, effectiveness in negotiation is enhanced if you are not negotiating for yourself. For these and other reasons lawyers spend a good deal of their time acting as professional negotiators.

LAWYERS AS PROFESSIONAL NEGOTIATORS. If it were measured in terms of amount of time spent, negotiating would probably constitute the primary activity of lawyers. It is the responsibility of lawyers to resolve their clients' disputes in the most simple and economical way, and that usually means some form of settlement achieved through negotiation. Although they are not typically trained in the process, lawyers have become professional negotiators through identification with dispute resolution and practical experience.

Williams (1983) surveyed practicing lawyers and learned that about half considered themselves to be effective negotiators. Almost 90 percent of those who felt competent characterized their approach as cooperative, listing these criteria in order of importance: (1) conducting self ethically; (2) maximizing settlement for client; (3) getting a fair settlement; (4) meeting client's needs; (5) avoiding litigation; and (6) maintaining or establishing a good personal relationship with the opponent. Those who perceived themselves as competitive listed this order of criteria: (1) maximizing settlement for client; (2) obtaining a profitable fee; (3) outdoing or outmaneuvering the opponent.

Jacker (1982) has written and lectured extensively on lawyers negotiating, and he provides rather specific advice. For example, the location in which the negotiation is to be held, the number of people on each negotiating team, the amount of authority they have to make binding agreements, the time of day at which negotiation occurs, and the nature of the agenda all receive comment in terms of advance planning. Prior to actual negotiations Jacker recommends that practice sessions or simulations should be conducted. Identifying the issues, with the possibility of putting focus on potentials for settlement through the preparation of an agenda, is a powerful move early in the interactions, he says.

Coleman (1980) surveyed the literature on successful steps in negotiating and generalized four rules.

1. Make a high initial demand and yield from it. Since the objective of distributive (competitive) bargaining is to discover the other party's best offer without revealing your own, it makes sense to start high lest you fail to ask for the maximum possible. Of course, the other party knows this is what you are doing, so a good deal of deceptive communication will occur while each side tries to learn without revealing. From a communication perspective, careful listening and attention to analysis of the interpersonal situation seem appropriate.

2. A balanced pattern of concessions should be employed. The pattern of concessions communicates to the other side, and like bidding in bridge or other card games we sometimes want to reveal and sometimes conceal. If you begin by asking for $1,000,000 and your first concession is $50,000 and the next is $100,000, the other party will be cued to continue pushing for concessions. On the other hand, if your first concession is $100,000 and the second is $50,000, you will send a signal that within a few steps you will probably reach your resistance point after which no further concessions can be expected. However, if your next concession returns to the $100,000 figure, a mixed message will be sent. If confusion is your goal, you will have succeeded. With the exception of hard-ball tactics under the label of commitment, discussed shortly, most negotiators are expected to provide some concession from the initial position to communicate a good faith approach to the process.

3. Retraction of concessions is not allowed. In practice lawyers read each offer as binding. They will not consider you an ethical negotiator if you try to withdraw an offer once it is made.

4. Bargain in good faith. Essentially lawyers expect that everyone involved will play the game, which is to obtain the settlement of a dispute to the overall best interests of their respective clients. If a lawyer seems to be bargaining more for personal gain or other motives not considered proper, the legal community will begin to refuse to negotiate with that person at all. Since negotiation constitutes so much of a lawyer's work, there are codes of ethical conduct that have been published to guide the process (Goldberg, Green, and Sander 1985).

COMMITMENT.   Communicating commitment is crucial to success in negotiating (Schelling [1960]1980). Except in the most open and cooperative of situations, as long as the other parties believe you will make further concessions they will continue to push for them. Once they believe you have truly stated your best and final offer, they will probably stop or dramatically reduce their demands, assuming you have reached a point that is within their range of acceptable settlement. Children, says Schelling, have the marvelous communication device of "cross my heart and hope to die." When the other kid says that, we know there is commitment. Too bad adults lack that.

Adults need to work out other ways of communicating commitment. When the lawyer can say, "My client may be crazy but I am simply not authorized to offer one cent more," commitment may be communicated. More commonly lawyers actively prepare for trial and establish a reputation as a person who willingly goes to trial and frequently wins. Then they can achieve commitment by saying, "Accept this offer or meet me in court."

This and similar statements may at times be nothing more than a bluff designed to learn what is truly the other side's best offer (Putnam and Jones 1982a). But lawyers do not rate deceptive communication as a highly valued practice (O'Rourke and Sparrow 1983), and society typically condemns deception in spite of continued use (Knapp and Comadena 1979). So even though bluffs and other deceptive techniques may be used and may sometimes be effective, as often as not deception by one side will be answered by deception from the other, yielding no progress toward resolution. On the other hand, honesty by one side may secure honesty in return, leading more directly to integrative resolutions (Putnam and Jones 1982b).

A lawyer who is known to be rarely in court and to be relatively ineffective as a litigator cannot use the "see you in court" form of communication. However, even that lawyer may communicate commitment by refusing a substantial offer. This may have the same effect as that made by a notoriously bad poker player who suddenly bets the limit; the others may believe this time he or she is holding a pat hand.

At any rate, one major communication task is to learn how to communicate what will be perceived as an honest commitment in each situation. There are no rules that can be presented because perceived commitment will depend upon the specifics of each case and the people involved.

Having said that communicating commitment is central to successful negotiating, we must now note that achieving flexibility is also a major goal. Jacker (1982) argues that there is value in leaving the bargaining agent free to develop creative solutions to the dispute. This will be particularly valuable in achieving an integrative agreement that addresses mutual needs and satisfaction and seeks a mutually desirable resolution.

ARGUMENTATION.   Argumentation is a central element of any negotiation situation (Keough 1987; Walker 1986). When people sit down to negotiate, they will proceed by generating reasons in support of their claims, and the resulting argumentation will play a key role in the final resolution.

Arguments involve assertions, or claims with reasons attached to justify them. According to Bacharach and Lawler (1981) bargaining is an interaction involving the management of impressions, manipulation of information, and generation of perceived power, and argumentation is the mechanism by which that work gets done.

Arguments can alter others' preferences and perception of the consequences of agreement or disagreement. They are used to make clear the constraints impinging upon the parties. If you are alone in the car when the rock flies off the truck and breaks your window, you will have a hard time arguing the issue of fault. If a passing driver sees the rock fly and motions you over to say she will be a witness to what happened, you suddenly have a strong argument.

Trying to blame the fire truck for being in the intersection when you hit it presents a tough problem in argumentation. Without more to go on, you will probably be ignored. However, if you have a police report saying skid marks indicate the truck was going 40 miles per hour through the intersection and a copy of Fire Department Policies and Procedures that says no truck may pass through an intersection against the red light at more than 15 miles per hour, you have an argument.

Bacharach and Lawler's (1986) dependency theory of power says one-sided dependence creates one-sided power relationships. You must create arguments to change power relationsips in order to increase the chances of a negotiated settlement. Negotiation frequently involves one-sided dependence, such as between you and the city government or a big business. You depend upon them totally to get satisfaction, but they need nothing from you. Without arguments that can command a response, you may not even get the powerful party to enter negotiations, much less come to some resolution other than telling you to go away.

Argument does not necessarily suggest a competitive or antagonistic situation. The word may mean either an angry, competitive exchange or reasoned discourse in the spirit of a cooperative search for solution (O'Keefe 1977, 1982). While negotiation is often seen as a competition to get the largest share (distribution) of a limited amount of goods, it can also mean the joint search for integration of interests (Fisher and Ury 1981). Integrative solutions are more likely to result if you (1) separate people from the problem; (2) focus on interests not positions; (3) invent options for mutual gain; (4) insist on objective criteria; and (5) know your best alternative to a negotiated agreement, or BATNA.

Pruitt (1983) sets out some other techniques of negotiating integrative agreements. (1) Expanding the pie is a process of arguing that there are more resources to be distributed than seem apparent at the outset. (2) Nonspecific compensation is including in the settlement some payment that is not part of the actual costs of the dispute. (3) Logrolling involves agreement on low priority issues in exchange for concessions on more important issues. (4) Cost cutting involves finding some form of specific compensation that can help one side make a concession. (5) Bridging is the process in which neither side gets what it initially demands, but rather a new set of options is found that will satisfy everyone's basic interests.

MEDIATION

Until the latter half of the twentieth century, when a dispute became formal enough to involve lawyers there were two principal modes of dispute resolution: negotiation and litigation. Indeed, the two modes were used together. Often neither party would initiate settlement discussions lest they appear weak and afraid of trial. So the approach of the trial date served as the eleventh-hour force to bring them together. At times the trial judge would serve as an initiating factor, suggesting that the opponents meet to discuss settlement and thus providing an excuse that would not leave either side appearing too anxious to avoid trial. They could say, "The judge has urged us to talk and we want to accommodate the judge, so let's talk."

The approach of the trial also served to alert the sides to the realities of a trial outcome. The closer the trial date came, the more clearly the litigants were likely to assess their chances of winning. A sober evaluation of a case regularly led one side to conclude that a negotiated settlement held more promise than the chances of losing altogether at trial. This process could take place, according to the cliché, on the courthouse steps, in the corridor, and even during a recess of the trial. There are instances of settlement coming after a jury had retired to consider a verdict. The uncertainty of trial outcome and the absolute nature of verdicts, with one winner and one loser, are potent forces behind the fact that almost all disputes taken to lawyers are resolved without a trial.

The complexities of late-twentieth-century dispute resolution demanded some intervening steps between negotiation and litigation. The 1960s were a time of unusual turmoil as blacks intensified their movement for equal rights, women asserted their feminist beliefs and demands, gay and lesbian groups called for acceptance within society, opponents of the U.S. involvement in Vietnam pushed for an end to fighting, environmentalists turned their attention to saving the earth for future generations, consumers spoke out for protection from unsafe products, and so on. The usual methods of dispute resolution were overloaded, and a search for ways to divert disputes away from the courts began.

The Civil Rights Act of 1964, which forbade discrimination in employment or public accommodations on the basis of race, sex, national origin, age, physical handicap, or veteran status, established a Community Relations Service to aid in the settlement of racial and community disputes. Other forums of diversion were explored, including the use of ombudsmen, media problem solvers, mediation panels, no-fault auto insurance and divorces, application of techniques used in mediating and conciliating in labor disputes to a wider range of problems. The Federal Law Enforcement Assistance Administration supported model programs in neighborhood justice, small claims courts mediation alternatives, and mediators working with police to resolve problems rather than issue criminal citations (Johnson 1977; Goldberg, Green, and Sander 1985).

In truth, there had always been mechanisms for dispute resolution other than negotiation and litigation. Throughout recorded history there is evidence of people in dispute turning to some family member, respected friend, religious counselor, elder, or leading citizen to serve as a mediator. Mediation was regularly used in colonial New England (Auerbach 1983).

A 1975 report, *The New Justice: Alternatives to Conventional Criminal Adjudication,* identified three hundred programs designed to resolve criminal problems short of trial (Aaronson et al. 1975). Most of these were methods of changing police or prosecution practices, decriminalization, or diversion to social service agencies, and therefore did not involve mediation. But the report included citizen complaint evaluation centers to deal with potential criminal problems. An earlier report (*Citizen Dispute Settlement* 1974) described the night prosecutor program of Columbus, Ohio, which used law students to hear complaints and try to settle them short of formal prosecution. In 1977, when U.S. Attorney General Griffin Bell announced the establishment of the neighborhood justice center program, designed to make justice faster, fairer, and more accessible to the people, there were estimated to be twenty-nine existing community mediation centers located in ten states.

By the time the American Bar Association Special Committee on Dispute Resolution published its 1986–1987 *Dispute Resolution Program Directory* (Kestner), there were more than three hundred programs and an increasing number of private practitioners who provided mediation services. Half of those programs were developed after 1980 and about one-quarter of them since 1983.

Mediation is truly a step between negotiation and litigation. People in dispute often are unable to resolve their problems through interpersonal negotiation interaction. When they attempt to negotiate for themselves, they suffer from lack of experience and too much personal involvement in the dispute, and they experience the problems that come from not having a bargaining agent working for them. When they select lawyers to bargain for them, it often comes down to the fact that lawyers are trained in litigation, which is a natural alternative to unsuccessful negotiations. Lawyers are rarely trained to serve as mediators, and since they are usually retained to represent one client in a dispute, they cannot easily assume the neutrality required to do mediation.

Mediation is defined by the ABA Special Committee on Dispute Resolution as an

> informal, voluntary process which is frequently used when there is an ongoing relationship whether family, neighborhood or community. A mediator is a neutral party who assists disputants in communicating issues of a dispute and aids them in reaching a mutually-acceptable agreement.

Jones (1986a, 4) provides a more detailed definition of mediation as

> the involvement of an impartial third party in an existing dispute between two or more parties in which the mediator engages in negotiation, both procedurally and substantively, for the purposes of facilitating communication between the parties and promoting resolution of conflict through the development of an agreement that is acceptable to the disputants without the imposition of an agreement from the mediator.

When people are unable to come to an agreement on their own, it is often helpful to find another person who has the respect of all the disputants who can (1) set an atmosphere that is conducive to agreement; (2) assist the disputants in communicating by gathering information from each side and releasing it to the other side when it will help agreement; (3) helping the disputants clarify their objectives for solution; (4) breaking the common logjam that comes from excessive or unrealistic expectations; (5) turning attention toward an integrative solution; (6) managing to keep the disputants talking together; and (7) crystallizing the rationale on which an agreement can be made and implemented (Raiffa 1982).

Mediators, then, are not simply neutral third parties. They take an active or interventionist role. People who seek mediation have probably already tried negotiation and failed, and they will carry into the mediation their roles as adversaries. So the mediator serves actively to facilitate the process of information exchange among disputants. Donohue, Allen, and Burrell (1986) defend a theory of communicator competence in mediation that says successful mediators know when to interrupt the interaction and how to select an appropriate intervention that will improve the information exchange and decision making.

Mediators, according to Donohue, Allen, and Burrell (1986), intervene to *structure the process of mediation* by using such tactics as (1) identifying or enforcing interaction rules such as who speaks when; (2) ending the discussion; (3) setting and enforcing an agenda; (4) setting roles such as who has what task; (5) giving orienting information such as background knowledge. A mediator can intervene to *reframe the disputants' statements* by (1) suggesting alternatives; (2) reacting critically to unproductive statements; (3) restating and clarifying what has been said; (4) noting and reinforcing points of agreement; (5) being a good listener. Finally, the Donohue group says that mediators can *expand the information resource* by (1) seeking opinions and evaluations from disputants; (2) seeking proposals or offers; (3) requesting clarification of proposals; (4) asking disputants to express their feelings; and (5) asking disputants to explain themselves more clearly. Research to date suggests that the mediators who provide insight by identifying issues, translating them into proposals, and focusing on points of agreement may be the most effective (Donohue, Allen, and Burrell 1986).

Jones (1986b) has examined mediation in terms of its flow from one phase to another until a satisfactory conclusion is found. Noting that many observers have inferred phases or stages in negotiation and mediation, she generalizes that successful divorce mediation (which was the object of her study) moves from a competitive focus on individual needs and goals to concentration on common goals and points of potential agreement. Specifically she concluded that there is ample research support for at least a three-phase analysis of mediation: (1) an agenda-building and information-exchange stage; (2) a negotiation phase in which the general range of possible solution is located; and (3) a resolution phase in which the final agreement is settled.

Based on Jones's research, a picture of mediators associated with successful dispute resolution emerges. Mediators in successful sessions spent more of their time than did mediators in unsuccessful sessions during early phases (1) talking about how the process of mediation would proceed, (2) summarizing what others said, and (3) engaging in self-disclosure. And the same mediators spent more of their time than did those in unsuccessful mediations in the latter phases (1) talking about points of agreement and (2) discussing solutions. Of course, it would be rash to assume that success was totally a function of mediator communication. The spouses in successful and unsuccessful mediations also differed significantly. Specifically, spouses in successful mediations concentrated on integrative information exchange at the start of the process and spent a good deal of time talking about solutions toward the end.

Studies of mediation at the University of Massachusetts at Amherst have employed coordinated management of meaning theory as a basis for describing mediator behavior (Littlejohn et al. 1986). Specifically the theory calls our attention to the process of coherence, or sense-making in human interaction, and coordination, which involves meshing actions within a social group. The researchers are particularly interested in the ways individuals view actions and utterances as logical or congruent with their own interpretations of the situation. Mediation, they say, is an exercise in which a third party facilitates the coordination of disputant behaviors so that a favorable agreement becomes possible.

According to the Massachusetts theory mediators become competent to the extent they can make appropriate interpretations of what the parties in dispute understand and expect, and to the extent they can make appropriate explanations and choices by which to influence the disputants' understandings and expectations. But mediators must not suggest solutions.

Littlejohn and his colleagues report the objectives of mediation in a step-by-step procedure prepared by Davis and Orenstein. This procedure employs two mediators who (1) make opening remarks to build trust, establish common expectations, and demonstrate a balance and fairness; (2) then hold a first full session involving both mediators and the parties in dispute where they demonstrate good listening and give the parties a full chance to express themselves; (3) then the mediators caucus apart from the disputants to build a team plan for resolution. The next part of the procedure involves (4) a private session in which the mediators meet with only one of the disputing parties to establish a clear communication link, after which (5) the mediators caucus once again to make plans based on what has been learned in the private session; then (6) a second private session is held with the other disputant. The mediators caucus once again (7) to put together the work from two private sessions and begin tentative drafting of a possible agreement. Finally the process of private sessions, full sessions, and mediators' caucuses continues until a resolution is found.

Throughout the United States an increasing number of neighborhood justice or dispute resolution centers have now been established. Generally they use volunteer mediators who provide resolution services without charge. The Institute for Mediation and Conflict Resolution was created in 1969 by labor-management specialists who felt that collective bargaining and other labor mediation techniques could help solve personal and community conflicts (Stanford 1980). Between 1974 and 1980 they resolved more than 5,000 disputes ranging from family assault to neighborhood nuisance complaints. They developed two settlement centers, a training program with a full-time staff of 25, and more than 150 trained volunteer mediators.

By 1987 The American Bar Association Special Committee on Dispute Resolution *Directory* of dispute resolution programs listed over forty states, the District of Columbia, Guam, and Puerto Rico as having some form of program involving either mediation or arbitration. They dealt with disputes arising from worthless checks, divorce/custody/support/visitation, domestic violence (both children and elderly), juveniles, landlord/tenant, neighborhood disputes, consumer, small claims, ordinance violations, and employer/employee problems. They received referrals from courts, district/state attorneys and prosecutors, police, community agencies, government agencies, bar associations, advertising, previous clients/word of mouth, self-referrals, and churches (Ray 1987).

The Citizens' Settlement Program of Miami, Florida, is a typical program that has been operating since 1975. Studies of its operations give a picture of how mediations commonly occur (Rieke 1976; Rieke and Zundel 1984). Located in the Metro Justice Building in Miami, the Citizens' Settlement Program has intake officers on duty during the day to talk with those presenting disputes. People come to the center on the referral of essentially those sources listed above, and often they believe they are still involved in some official government agency such as the police or prosecutor. It is not uncommon for the first statement to an intake officer to be a request for an injunction or warrant.

Intake officers explain that they are not associated with the courts or police in an official capacity, but if the dispute involves people in such continuing relationships as marital couples, neighbors, landlord-tenant, or employer-employee, the center may be a good place to work out the problem. The intake person may do some counseling with the complainant and end by sending her or him to some other agency such as social service or therapy. If the dispute seems appropriate for the center, a brief summary of the problem is placed on a legal-length form that also includes names and addresses of those involved.

A date and time is set for a hearing, as the mediation sessions are called. In fact, the center wraps itself in many symbols of officialdom—dockets, hearings, notices. Its stationery bears the seal of the State of Florida and the letterhead carries the eleventh judicial circuit of Florida and sometimes the name of the presiding judge or the state attorney. Persons against whom a complaint is made receive what is called a "notice to appear," with the announcement that a complaint has been made and they are hereby notified to be at the Metropolitan Justice Building at a time specified. They are warned that failure to appear may result in the filing of criminal charges. An even stronger notice sent from the state attorney's office makes the threat more obvious.

The center administrators believe that if they did not have the symbols of official power, they would be significantly less able to secure cooperation from both parties in a dispute. The mediation sessions are held in vacant courtrooms at night, and again the administrators feel that talking within the aura of the court increases motivations for settlement. In 1987 they reported 3,500 complaints, of which 60 percent went to hearings; 70 percent of the disputes for which hearings were held were resolved, while the rest were no-shows or withdrawals. Of the 40 percent that did not go to hearings, 30 percent were resolved after the initial talk with the intake officer and 10 percent were canceled or had unknown outcomes. Even serious, potentially criminal cases such as wife beating have been resolved in a way that center officials believe is superior to litigation.

The mediators, of which there are seven, are paid professionals in law, sociology, psychology, or similar fields. The disputants appear at a set time, and the mediator receives a file that contains nothing more than the brief paragraph summary written by the intake officer and the names. The mediator leads the disputants into a vacant courtroom, where they sit around one of the counsel tables. The mediator opens by explaining briefly what a mediation is (a voluntary interaction with the hope of resolution) and sets minimum ground rules such as one person at a time will talk. Even though disputants often bring witnesses and other evidence to support their side of the story, it is possible the mediator will not look at documents and ask witnesses to remain outside to see if the matter can be resolved without them. The mediator is not seeking truth or justice, just a resolution. The object is to allow the people to find a resolution they can live with, and the mediator will allow settlements to emerge without interference. Sometimes mediators leave the room momentarily to allow the resolution to develop spontaneously.

By the time people come to the hearings, say the center administrators, they are ready to talk. The police didn't want to listen, and the state attorney was only interested in seeing if a good criminal case might be involved. The people want someone to listen to their story, and the mediator serves that function. While they may talk to the mediator as they would to someone who will decide their case, the mediator carefully avoids judgment and simply replies in ways that show interest and understanding.

Most of the reasoning used by disputants consists of arguments based on their own authority; they tell what they experienced firsthand and offer themselves as witnesses. They make occasional references to some documentary evidence, and, except in those hearings destined to failure, they consistently seek to propose solutions and reach closure (Rieke and Zundel 1984). They do not demand that all issues be resolved. In one case where a man was accused of (and did not actually deny) spraying an entire family including their dog with mace, a resolution was reached without ever directly addressing the charge. In another case one person was accused of casting a voodoo hex on a neighbor by sprinkling a white crystalline substance all around the house. The neighbors left arm in arm with a happy solution without ever talking further about the hex.

ADMINISTRATIVE HEARINGS

We now turn our attention to modes of dispute resolution that reflect the basic procedures of litigation, and the administrative hearing is the first we will address. Administrative hearing is a concept that applies to a wide range of settings and appears in a variety of forms. We will discuss the process in general as one that offers a socially sanctioned means of dispute resolution, sometimes but not always open to public scrutiny, in which a third party hears the communication of proofs and arguments with the coercive power of decision that determines winners and losers, based on a focus on issues immediately in dispute but often with a concern for underlying relationships.

Since they include so much that is typical of the trial, we will speak only briefly of administrative hearings. By contrast with litigation, administrative hearings do not require fulfillment of all the rules of due process and formal procedure characteristic of litigation. For example, a student at the University of Rhode Island was suspended after a disciplinary hearing in which he was not allowed to have a lawyer present or to tape-record the proceedings of the University Board on Student Conduct which had ordered his suspension. He appealed his case to the U.S. Court of Appeals claiming his constitutional rights had been denied, and the court rejected his claim. The court said, "In fostering and insuring the requirements of due process, courts should not require that a fair hearing be one that necessarily must follow the traditional commonlaw adversarial method. . . . The key is whether the individual has had an opportunity to answer, explain and defend." The court further said, "The undue judicialization of an administrative hearing, particularly in an academic environment, may result in an improper allocation of resources and prove counterproductive" (Fields 1988).

This does not mean, however, that administrative hearings are necessarily more simple than trials. They may involve extensive work by attorneys over long periods of time in highly complex cases. The National Labor Relations Board employed an administrative law judge to consider the problem of university faculty members' rights to organize and bargain collectively in response to a 1980 decision by the U.S. Supreme Court that said the faculty at Yeshiva University were so involved in the management of the institution that the right to bargain through an agent did not apply to them. The hearing before the administrative law judge, involving the Boston University chapter of the American Association of University Professors, which often serves as a bargaining agent, proceeded for 157 days within two years' time. It produced a transcript of 21,000 pages with 1,180 documents entered in evidence and the testimony of 122 witnesses. The decision itself was 126 pages long in deciding against the faculty union (Getman and Franke 1988).

Administrative hearings, as their name suggests, are characteristic of decision making by administrative agencies. Organizations created by legislatures, congresses, and councils to administer laws use hearings as a means of accepting input from interested citizens and groups. Public utility commissions, federal regulatory agencies, licensing boards, zoning commissions, and other similar agencies are locations in which administrative hearings might be employed. While the agency will make the final decision (always subject to possible appeal to the courts), it is usually mandated by law to consider all points of view. As the court said in the University of Rhode Island case, the hearing should guarantee that concerned individuals have a full opportunity to answer, explain, and defend without undue judicialization.

ARBITRATION

Arbitration moves one step closer to the formal adversary process of litigation. Essentially arbitration is a trial with relaxed rules of process and procedure. It involves a third party with decision-making powers that may be binding on the parties involved, or that may be advisory or recommendatory. It is not always open to public scrutiny, nor does it necessarily require lawyers. It does focus on determining winners and losers primarily based on immediate issues. Any concern for underlying relationships tends to be secondary.

Small claims courts, which have become a major television attraction under the direction of Judge Wapner, are essentially arbitrations. When formal labor-management negotiations break down, it is common to have arbitration written into the contract as the next step. One of the most common instances of arbitration in the United States today is that provided by the Better Business Bureaus in more than 150 major metropolitan areas.

According to the Council of Better Business Bureaus, Inc., businesses appreciate the availability of arbitration in that they are pledging to arbitrate consumer disputes with increasing frequency. The automobile and construction industries are two of the most heavily involved. Such government agencies as the Federal Trade Commission, state attorneys general, and local district attorneys and judges are increasingly writing BBB arbitration into consent orders or are referring disputes on a case-by-case basis to arbitration. The American Arbitration Association is equally active in providing this service.

The chief attraction to industry and consumer alike is the quick and inexpensive resolution of disputes that might otherwise go to litigation. The BBB provides more than 15,000 trained community volunteers around the nation who serve as arbitrators. Sometimes they decide a case alone, and sometimes they sit in a three-person panel. Although most of their hearings involve oral, face-to-face presentation of cases, it is possible for the BBB to conduct arbitrations by telephone or in writing.

People come to arbitration from a variety of routes. Many of the programs discussed in the section on mediation also provide arbitration. When mediation fails, voluntary submission to arbitration is a common next step. In such instances the arbitration is probably not binding. On the other hand, "court annexed arbitration" occurs in states and a number of federal courts where, by statute, cases involving claims below a certain dollar amount—such as $15,000 to $20,000 in states and $50,000 to $100,000 in federal courts—must first be tried in arbitration; the loser then has the option to take the case to court. However, there may be a sanction for going to court if the loser has refused to accept what the court finds to be a reasonable arbitration award. In other instances business contracts may contain a clause requiring arbitration of any conflict arising out of the relationship.

For example, the Southland Corporation, which owns and franchises 7-Eleven stores, has a clause requiring arbitration of any conflict arising out of violations of the disclosure requirements of the California Franchise Investment Law. However, that California statute contains a provision that calls for judicial consideration of claims brought under it and therefore seems to override the arbitration agreement. Southland tried to compel arbitration, relying on the Federal Arbitration Act which provides that "a contract evidencing a transaction involving commerce to settle by arbitration a controversy thereafter arising out of such contract or transaction . . . shall be valid, irrevocable, and enforceable." The question was whether the California statute or the federal act took precedence in this case. The U.S. Supreme Court ruled that the Federal Arbitration Act preempts state law:

> Congress declared a clear national policy favoring arbitration and withdrew the power of the states to require a judicial forum for the resolution of claims that the contracting parties agreed to resolve by arbitration. (Southland Corporation v. Keating 465 U.S. 1, 104 S. Ct. 852 [1984])

General Motors, Volkswagen, Porsche-Audi, and Nissan have all written mediation/arbitration clauses into their warranties for all 1984 and later vehicles. The Magnuson-Moss Act, which deals with resolution of consumer disputes, also provides the requirement that before one can turn to the courts to litigate a complaint, efforts to resolve the dispute through arbitration must be exhausted.

The American Arbitration Association and the Institute for Mediation and Conflict Resolution have developed projects to serve the general public in arbitrating a wide variety of disputes. Obtaining their referrals from citizens and agencies, they address both civil and criminal problems. Like the BBB, they employ trained citizen volunteers as arbitrators.

A number of small claims courts have developed arbitration programs. In some New York jurisdictions arbitration is voluntary, inviting disputants to try an attorney's arbitration and thereby waive their right to appeal. In California small claims arbitration within a monetary range is voluntary for the plaintiff but compulsory for the defendant. However, if the defendant is not satisfied with the decision, appeal through a trial is allowed. In Wayne County, Michigan, "advisory arbitration" is employed at the request of either party or the court. A panel of three arbitrators hears the case and issues a decision. Either party may reject that advisory and go to court. However, if the party going to court fails to win a judgment that is at least 10 percent higher than the original advisory judgment, they must pay court costs and attorney fees of their opponent. Some jurisdictions in Pennsylvania, Ohio, and New York employ compulsory arbitration for disputes involving limited amounts of money. A panel of attorneys serves as the arbitrators and the disputants may still request a trial de novo (a trial that proceeds as if nothing had been done previously).

The construction industry has used arbitration for some time, and the American Arbitration Association has a nationwide panel of arbitrators with construction expertise in such areas as architecture, engineering, contracting, and law. Arbitrators, who are chosen by mutual agreement of parties in dispute, serve without charge for two days but are paid for longer cases.

In 1982 a Daytona Beach, Florida, police officer shot and killed a man at a 7-Eleven store. The officer, who was white, claimed the victim, who was black, had a knife and the shooting was in self-defense. The officer was indicted for unnecessary killing to prevent an unlawful act, but the charges were ultimately dismissed. While the charges were still being considered, the *Daytona Times,* a weekly newspaper that serves the black community, published a story in which it quoted a former official who said, "If in fact the charge is incorrect, it does not dismiss the fact that the officer is guilty of murder."

The officer sued the paper for libel, and the litigation proved to be expensive and frustrating to all involved. The case dragged on for over three years, and the costs and anxieties became excessive. The parties finally met to see if some alternative resolution was possible. Both sides wanted to settle, but neither would bargain away the question of whether what was said in the newspaper was true or not. Finally in 1987, at the suggestion of participants at the Florida media conference, an impartial panel of seven persons consisting of journalists, lawyers, and law enforcement officials was convened to hear arguments. Both sides agreed to accept the decision of this panel regarding the truth or falsity of the article as binding. They further agreed to suspend the rules of evidence, reduce time of argument, and make no appeal or ask for any further litigation. The complicated decision, which did not simply find one winner and one loser, was accepted with enthusiasm by all involved. This was a most unusual application of the process of arbitration.

LITIGATION

In our survey of dispute resolution methods that serve as alternatives to litigation we have exposed a range of communication processes that clarify the comparisons and contrasts of these methods with the trial itself. At the start we said a trial is a socially sanctioned process of dispute resolution, open to public scrutiny, involving the communication of proofs and arguments before a third party with coercive power to determine winners and losers in terms of the issues immediately in dispute and without concern for underlying relationships.

We have seen the evolution of alternatives, all of which are becoming more and more accepted socially, from those which are more private to those more public; from those in which the disputants retain their own power to decide to those that invest that power in others; from those in which the disputants retain some final discretion to those which are coercive; from those which seek a mutually acceptable compromise to those which pick a single winner; and from those which address both issues and relationships to those which consider only issues.

No matter how much increased activity there is in alternative methods, however, the trial will continue indefinitely to be the key decision-making process. It will not be the key because it is the mechanism by which a greater number of disputes will be decided, nor will it be the key because it is judged the best means. Instead, it will remain the key decision-making process because the trial will continue to provide the benchmarks by which other decisions will be judged, and it will continue as the last resort for those problems not otherwise settled.

Trials are expensive, time consuming, and dangerous. The danger comes from the fact that it is virtually impossible to know with any certainty how they will come out, but the decision comes with the force of law and government behind it. Once you enmesh yourself in decision by trial, you may find yourself being carried along by irresistible forces toward an unknown and frightening end. It makes sense to know as much as possible about those forces, and that is the purpose of the remainder of this book.

REFERENCES

Aaronson, D.; Hoff, B.; Jaszi, P.; Kittrie, N.; and Saari, D. (1975). *The new justice: alternatives to conventional criminal adjudication.* National Institute of Law Enforcement and Criminal Justice, Law Enforcement Assistance Administration.

Auerbach, J. (1983). *Justice without law.* New York: Oxford University Press.

Bacharach, S., and Lawler, E. (1981). *Bargaining: power, tactics, and outcomes.* San Francisco: Jossey-Bass.

Bacharach, S., and Lawler, E. (1986). Power dependence and power paradoxes in bargaining. *Negotiation Journal* 2: 167–74.

Berger, P. and Luckman, T. (1967). *The social construction of reality.* Garden City, NY: Doubleday.

Citizen dispute settlement. (1974). National Institute of Law Enforcement and Criminal Justice.

Coleman, N. (1980). Teaching the theory and practice of bargaining to lawyers and students. *Journal of Legal Education* 30: 170–82.

Donohue, W.; Allen, M.; and Burrell, N. (1986). Mediator communicative competence. Paper presented at the annual convention of the Speech Communication Association, Chicago.

Fields, C. (1988). Court says college panels are not bound by trial rules. *The Chronicle of Higher Education* 34, 20: A2.

Fisher, R., and Ury, W. (1981). *Getting to yes.* Boston: Houghton Mifflin.

Getman, J., and Franke, A. (1988). The "Yeshiva" case revisited: professors' right to bargain is entitled to statutory protection. *The Chronicle of Higher Education* 34, 21: B1.

Goldberg, S.; Green, E.; and Sander, F. (1985). *Dispute resolution.* Boston: Little, Brown.

Jacker, N. (1982). *Effective negotiation techniques for lawyers.* St. Paul, MN: National Institute for Trial Advocacy.

Johnson, E. (1977). *Outside the courts.* Denver, CO: National Center for State Courts.

Jones, T. (1986a). "Breaking up is hard to do": an exploratory investigation of communication behaviors and phases in child-custody divorce mediation. Unpublished doctoral dissertation, Ohio State University.

Jones, T. (1986b). An analysis of phase structures in successful and unsuccessful child-custody divorce mediation. Paper presented at the annual convention of the Speech Communication Association, Chicago.

Keough, C. (1987). The nature and function of argument in

organizational bargaining research. *Southern Speech Communication Journal* 53: 1–17.

Kestner, P. (ed.). (1986). *Dispute resolution program directory.* Washington, DC: American Bar Association Special Committee on Dispute Resolution.

Knapp, M. S., and Comadena, M. E. (1979). Telling it like it isn't: a review of theory and research on deceptive communication. *Human Communication Research* 5: 270–85.

Littlejohn, S.; Pearce, W.; Hines, S.; and Bean, W. (1986). Coherence and coordination in mediation communication: exploratory case studies. Paper presented at the annual convention of the Western Speech Communication Association, Tucson.

Merry, S., and Silby, S. (1984). What do plaintiffs want? Reexamining the concept of dispute. *Justice System Journal* 9: 151–78.

O'Keefe, D. (1977). Two concepts of argument. *Journal of the American Forensic Association* 13: 121–28.

O'Keefe, D. (1982). The concept of argument and arguing. In J. Cox and C. Willard (eds.), *Advances in argumentation theory and research.* Carbondale: Southern Illinois University Press.

O'Rourke, S., and Sparrow, J. (1983). From the communication profession: communication strategies and research needs in legal negotiating and bargaining. In R. Matlon and R. Crawford (eds.), *Communication strategies in the practice of lawyering.* Annandale, VA: Speech Communication Association.

Priest, G., and Klein, B. (1984). *The selection of disputes for litigation.* Santa Monica, CA: Institute for Civil Justice, The Rand Corporation.

Pruitt, D. (1983). Achieving integrative agreements. In M. Bazerman and R. Lewicki (eds.), *Negotiating in organizations.* Beverly Hills, CA: Sage.

Putnam, L., and Bullis, C. (1986). Bargaining as negotiated order: the dialectic interplay between interaction and structure. Paper presented at the annual convention of the Speech Communication Association, Chicago.

Putnam, L., and Jones, T. (1982a). The role of communication in bargaining. *Human Communication Research* 8: 262–79.

Putnam, L., and Jones, T. (1982b). Reciprocity in negotiations: an analysis of bargaining interaction. *Communication Monographs* 49: 171–90.

Raiffa, H. (1982). *The art and science of negotiation.* Cambridge: Harvard University Press.

Ray, L. (1987). *Dispute resolution program directory.* Washington, DC: American Bar Association Special Committee on Dispute Resolution.

Rieke, R. (1976). Citizen dispute settlement. Paper presented at the annual convention of the Speech Communication Association, San Francisco, CA.

Rieke, R., and Zundel, R. (1984). Alternative means of dispute resolution. Paper presented at the annual convention of the Speech Communication Association, Chicago, IL.

Sander, F. (1985). Varieties of dispute processing. In L. Riskin (ed.), *Divorce mediation: readings.* Washington, DC: American Bar Association.

Schelling, T. [1960] (1980). *The strategy of conflict.* Cambridge: Harvard University Press.

Siegal, S., and Fouraker, L. (1960). *Bargaining and group decision making: experiments in bilateral monopoly.* New York: McGraw-Hill.

Smith, D. (1983). Review of research on negotiating and bargaining: problems with the economic model as a basis for theory and research on negotiation. In R. Matlon and R. Crawford (eds.), *Communication strategies in the practice of lawyering.* Annandale, VA: Speech Communication Association.

Stanford, B. (1980). Gentle art of settling family disputes. *Parade,* Sept. 14: 8.

Walker, G. (1986). Bacharach and Lawler's theory of argument in bargaining: a critique. Paper presented at the annual convention of the Speech Communication Association, Chicago.

Walton, R., and McKersie, R. (1965). *A behavioral theory of labor negotiations.* New York: McGraw-Hill.

Williams, C. (1983). *Legal negotiation and settlement.* St. Paul, MN: West.

Chapter 2

REALITY IN THE COURTROOM

A glance at any dictionary of the American language for the various meanings of the word "trial" gives a hint of the history of the trial at law. Notice, for example, these alternative meanings: test; being tried by suffering, temptation; a hardship, pain that tries one's endurance; a source of annoyance or irritation; a formal examination of the facts of a case by a court of law to decide the validity of a charge or claim (*Webster's New World Dictionary* 1965). While the last definition is the one that suggests the trial at law, the others tell of the context in which trials emerged.

In a modern sense, think of the term "trials" as used in relation to various sporting events. Preliminary to final races it is common to hold trials, which are races to establish the relative performance of the competitors for the purpose of final pairings, seedings, or selections.

Now turn your thinking back a few hundred years. If you held, as most did, that there were absolutes (absolute truth, reality, destiny, etc.), then when a dispute arose between two or more people, you would expect that one person was absolutely in the right and those who disagreed were wrong. If the dispute concerned which of two horses ran faster, you would put them in a race (trial) and the winner would be declared. If the dispute were between two men (women were not allowed to have public disputes back then), they would test themselves similarly. They could engage in some contest of sport or battle to see who was better.

If you now add to this image the certainty most had that a supreme being, omniscient and omnipotent, served as the overseer of all human activity, you are ready to understand the origin of the trial. Suppose James accused John of stealing, but John denied it. Given the mindset we have just described, everyone was certain that it was either true or not true that John did the stealing. There was an absolute truth, but no one knew what that truth, or fact, was.

Let us interrupt the story of this alleged theft long enough to look again to the dictionary as a guide to the historical use of the word "fact" and how it has come to us today. Among the meanings listed for modern Americans are these: a deed; act; a thing that has actually happened or is true; a thing that has been or is; the state of things as they are; reality; actuality; truth; in law, an actual or alleged incident or condition, as distinguished from its legal consequence (*Webster's New World Dictionary* 1965). There is more to be said about the difference between fact and law mentioned in the last phrase, and that will come later in this chapter. For now, concentrate on the definitions of "fact."

Now, back to the theft. The people *know* (they are absolutely certain) that there is a fact concerning the theft. That is to say, they know there is a truth, reality, actuality regarding James's allegation. The problem is how to learn what is fact, because James and John tell two different stories. We know one is lying, but who?

Since the people believed in an all-knowing and all-powerful being, they could be certain that this supreme being knew who was telling the truth. The problem was how to communicate with this being in order to learn the truth. Surely, under the proper circumstances, God would show who was lying, because in addition to being omniscient God was dedicated to truth and righteousness. The answer, of course, was to put James and John to the test, to a trial, and thereby allow God to identify the villain.

The manner of the test varied according to the time, place, and custom of the people conducting the trial. James and John could be allowed to select arms and fight; they could be required to subject themselves to torture, such as holding a hand in the flame or picking up an object at the bottom of a pot of boiling water, or they could be subjected to the inquisition of a priest. In any event the outcome would be seen as a message from God: The winner of the combat or the survivor of the torture or inquisition would be deemed the truth teller.

But this is hardly the kind of trial we will be dealing with in this book. Over the centuries civilizations gradually developed a system of laws and legal procedures designed to resolve such disputes as that between James and John without resort to such gruesome methods. The focus of this chapter will be the various conceptions or images that have provided the foundation for these trials, which could be seen as alternatives to trial by combat or ordeal.

Three conceptions will be examined. First is the more traditional image of the trial as an engine for the discovery of truth. Second is a transitional concept based on an interpretive model of reconstructing reality in the courtroom. Finally, we will discuss recent analyses that suggest a narrative creative image.

TRADITIONAL CONCEPTIONS OF THE TRIAL

Our concept of law evolved gradually, generally following the pattern set by the classical Greek and Roman writers with the addition of powerful influences from Christianity. As with so many other aspects of legal communication, the story starts with Aristotle.

Aristotle (384–322 B.C.E.) produced ideas first published about four hundred years after his death that led medieval European philosophers and theologians to refer to him simply as "the Philosopher." No other single scholar can claim such strong, lasting, and many-sided importance (Stromholm 1985). Empiricism and rationalism characterize Aristotle's approach to the law. He believed there was a truth to be found through the combination of full examination of facts and the processing of them rationally in the human mind.

A full understanding of Aristotle's concept of forensic rhetoric (legal communication) requires extensive reading in his works on rhetoric. A brief overview will have to serve our purposes here.

EMPIRICISM. Think back to the dispute between James and John. James has accused John of theft, but John denies it. From an empiricist perspective it is possible to examine the facts related to the case and thereby start the process of finding truth and justice. In the forensic situation the question always involves consideration of *past* facts: What actually did happen between James and John? Was there truly something stolen some time ago? A look at the facts should provide the answers. John is accused of taking a gold coin; if it is a fact that James had one, there should be witnesses who can say they saw it. If the coin is truly gone, a search of James's house and other places of possible concealment will fail to reveal it. If John took it, the coin should be found in his possession. If it is indeed James's coin, there should be marks of identification or witnesses who can say it is the same coin.

Aristotle's general view of rhetoric was that of discovering, in each case, what are the available means of persuasion. That is, he would suggest the decision maker be exposed to every point of view, to every argument, to every piece of evidence, to every appeal to passion, and from that exposure it would be possible to discern the truth. In this Aristotle sharply differed with his teacher, Plato. Plato would leave truth finding to the experts or philosophers and would rule out what he considered improper arguments or sophistry.

But in the case of legal questions Aristotle moved closer to Plato in his analysis. Aristotle distinguished forensic rhetoric from deliberative rhetoric (political communication). Deliberative decisions, he said, involve people making choices in relation to their own self-interest. If a bad policy is adopted, they will suffer its consequences, and so they should be highly motivated to scrutinize the opposing arguments carefully for their own sake. Forensic rhetoric, on the other hand, involves people making choices about the interests of others. Having no self-interest to motivate them to scrutinize arguments carefully, they may fall into the trap of making mere choices rather than judgment. They might, for example, let themselves be distracted unduly by sympathy and lose sight of justice.

To control for this problem Aristotle proposed that the decision maker in forensic situations not be exposed to *all* the facts that might be brought up, but only to those facts that are relevant to the particular case, material to the issues at hand, and competent to reveal the truth. He thereby formed the foundation for the extensive rules of evidence that now prevail in our courts. The evidence rules serve as a kind of filter to reject admission of facts that might contribute to poor decisions. For example, in most circumstances the rules deny admission of hearsay evidence or that coming from a witness who learned facts at second hand.

RATIONALISM.   Aristotle believed that human beings, unlike other creatures, are endowed with a rational capacity: the ability to think logically and discern the truth. In his other work he had created a logic pattern called a syllogism, which demonstrated a way of relating known elements in such a way as to lead to certain and absolute conclusions. The only perfect syllogism is an abstract one:

If all A is B, and
if all C is A, then certainly and absolutely
all C is B.

The syllogism could take other forms as well, such as the conditional and disjunctive forms that are discussed in any book on formal logic. Aristotle knew, however, that in law as well as other forms of rhetoric it is neither possible nor appropriate to employ perfect syllogisms. It is impossible because the materials with which law deals simply are not known with the certainty needed for syllogisms. It is inappropriate because the audience addressed by forensic rhetoric does not require the agonizing step-by-step development of every premise required in syllogisms. Rather, the audience brings to the interaction a considerable store of knowledge that will be used to understand logic, so the logic should be built around that knowledge and employ it.

Aristotle conceptualized the enthymeme, or rhetorical syllogism, to serve the needs of legal communication along with other rhetorical tasks. It conforms in many details to the rules of the syllogism and is tested similarly, but it lacks the certainty of conclusion and typically does not include all the steps required of syllogisms. The enthymeme provides the rationale for probable rather than certain conclusions.

In law enthymemes are built around questions of the nature and incentives to wrongdoing, the state of mind of wrongdoers, and the kind of persons who are wronged (Roberts 1946). Wrongdoing is defined as injury voluntarily inflicted contrary to law, and law is either special (written laws) or general (unwritten principles generally acknowledged). The causes of our deliberately intending harmful and wicked acts contrary to law are vice and lack of self-control, said Aristotle; thus, every action with which the law is concerned is due to one or more of seven causes: chance, nature, compulsion, habit, reasoning, anger, or appetite.

Now we can combine the concepts of empiricism and rationalism to suggest a traditional pattern of legal communication in the trial as developed in Aristotle's works. The empirical perspective underlies inartistic (i.e., finding facts rather than creating arguments) forms of legal reasoning, which include laws, witnesses, contracts, tortures, and oaths. They are called inartistic because they are found outside the art or the logic processes of reasoning. They are *found* by looking for facts. Artistic proofs are the enthymemes which are *created* through the art of rhetoric. They include the lines of reasoning and general theory of the case which come from the analysis of the lawyer.

Legal communication involves the processes of accusation and defense, and we can now describe them in the trial of John for the theft of James's gold coin. Aristotle believed that truth and justice are by nature stronger than their opposites, and if arguments for them are allowed to compete fairly with those of all other kinds, truth and justice will inevitably prevail. The only sin the legal system can commit is to prevent a balanced consideration of arguments.

For this reason both James and John will be given equal opportunity to present their side of the case, and it is incumbent on them, said Aristotle, to have the skill in rhetoric necessary to state their case and prove it. James, the accuser, will begin: "If John has my gold coin, then he stole it. He does have my coin, so he is guilty of theft. For, either I gave the coin to him or he stole it. I did not give the coin to him, so he stole it."

Then John may reply: "James's enthymeme is faulty in that it sets up only two alternatives: that he either gave me the coin or I stole it. There is a third alternative that proves my innocence. If John promised to pay me the gold coin in return for my goat, and if I took the gold coin as payment for the goat I had given him, then my taking of the gold coin was merely receiving of proper payment. James accepted my goat, so either he stole my goat or he paid me for it. He did not steal the goat, so he has paid me for it."

We now return to the thorny question of the difference between issues of fact and issues of law. If we accept everything the two men have said, it would appear that John took the gold coin without James having given it to him, but James accepted the goat with the promise to pay John the gold coin in return and for some reason did not make the payment. John took it upon himself to secure payment by seizing the coin. Now, presumably, we know the facts, but do we know yet whether John is a thief? We do not. It will require an entirely new set of enthymemes, aimed at questions of law, to determine whether one can legally seize something of value if the intent is to secure proper payment for goods or services already delivered.

FORMAL TRIAL PROCEDURES.   Over the centuries that followed Aristotle formal trial procedures gradually emerged. The traditional pattern in the United States is mostly a product of developments in Roman and English law, all of them reflecting refinements of Aristotelian thought. While the Romans cannot be given credit for originality of philosophy, they were great organizers. Cicero (106–43 B.C.E.), for example, was an orator and rhetorician who developed systematic advice for lawyers. First, he demanded that the lawyer be thoroughly educated and fully informed on the case; and second, he said that the lawyer must be skilled in speaking and writing (Watson 1855; Caplan 1954).

One of Cicero's lasting influences was the identification of the parts of a case or oration. The traditional pattern of trials still reflects the Ciceronian arrangement, as does the format of appellate briefs.

The *exordium* serves to introduce the audience to the case and make an initial favorable impression on them. Cicero was firm in his belief that what occurs first is particularly important in a trial. It should include an intimation of the whole matter at hand and make clear the essence of the cause. This is accomplished in trials during the selection of the jury and the early portion of the opening statement.

The *narratio,* or statement of the case, tells the story of the dispute. As Cicero said, ambiguity or obscurity during other parts of the trial are minor matters which can easily be corrected, but "obscurity in the narrative part spreads darkness over the whole."

(Thonssen 1942, 83). For this reason, as we shall make clear in chapter 5, the opening statement is considered a crucial portion of the trial.

The *confirmatio* involves the proof of our case. In trials this includes the presentation of witnesses, authorities, and other evidence such as documents and physical objects that will tend to prove the facts that were set out in the opening statement. In contemporary trials, this is generally called presenting the case in chief and would characterize the presentation by the plaintiff or prosecutor.

The *refutatio* brings forth refutation from the defense through the presentation of counterwitnesses and evidence and cross-examination of witnesses called by the other side. It also includes the opportunity for the plaintiff or prosecutor to cross-examine witnesses called by the defense.

The *peroration* corresponds with the closing argument or summation in modern trials. The task here is to bring the entire case together in clear summary form and drive it home persuasively with the nearest thing to oratory that still occurs in trials.

In essence, then, the impact of the Romans in the development of what has become a traditional concept of reality in the courtroom was to add a sense of rhetorical strategy. They were concerned not just with the procedures for finding truth and justice; they cared about being effective advocates for a cause. In doing this, they made clear a conflict which continues to this day. To what extent are the procedures of finding truth and justice weakened by the process of advocacy? Can, as Plato argued, an effective advocate win even with an unjust cause? If so, how can the trial be said to be an engine for the discovery of truth and justice? Or, as Aristotle argued, will truth and justice emerge because of their inherent strength and the rational abilities of human beings so long as the skill of advocacy is shared among all those arguing the case?

Clearly, answering the issues about the potential conflict between inquiry and advocacy rests on our philosophical beliefs regarding the nature of law and its procedure as well as our conception of reality. This debate brings out some of the most fundamental issues of philosophy. Again there is too little space to present that debate in detail, but a brief review is necessary.

THE CONCEPTS OF LAW.   Having established the position of the Greek and Roman writers, we must now consider the impact of the emergence of Christianity and several hundred years of philosophical debate on questions of law. St. Augustine (354–430 C.E.) attempted to resolve the conflict between truth and advocacy. From a rhetorical perspective he extended the influence of Cicero by essentially restating Ciceronian ideas in the fourth book of *De doctrina Christiana*. In so doing Augustine made three major contributions toward dealing with our issue of inquiry versus advocacy.

First, Augustine rejected what came to be called the second sophistic interpretation of rhetoric, which placed full attention on the persuasiveness of advocates through the use of techniques of style and delivery and had little regard for the intellectual merits of the cause. Second, he combined Ciceronian rhetoric with Christian theology, thereby giving rhetoric the solid basis of truth on which to be persuasive. In fact, he was most interested in rhetoric as a means of persuading Christians to lead a holy life (Corbett 1965). Third, Augustine broadened the meaning of rhetoric to include exposition or instruction as well as persuasion. In this perspective, which ultimately came to form the traditionalist foundation for legal advocacy, the advocate seeks not to persuade the audience as much as to lay the truth before them so that they can perceive it clearly.

This rhetorical point of view was similar to that originally set out by Plato in his *Phaedrus* when he admitted that even philosophers need rhetoric to make truth and justice prevail. A true rhetoric, Plato claimed, is concerned with the discovery of truth, the nature of justice, clear definition of terms, the structure of discourse, and the various "souls" or types of men together with the arguments that would appeal to each type (Hostettler 1967).

Augustine's most important contribution to a concept of law came in his *De civitate Dei (On the City of God)*. The classical idea of natural law, essentially the concept of rationalism through which human beings are able to discern truth and justice, is modified by Augustine to become a doctrine of omnipotent divine will. Cicero's eternal law theories are thereby modified without much distortion to become *lex aeterna,* or divine reason, or God's will. It is this law that is accessible to human reason through trial advocacy. Even the lowest level of law in Augustine's system, worldly law, must conform to divine law. Thus, in a trial the outcome cannot be forced through sophistic advocacy toward falsity or injustice, for that would be in violation of God's eternal will (Stromholm 1985).

Thomas Aquinas (1225–1274) had profound influence on the development of concepts of law, working from an essentially Aristotelian rationalist point of view. He believed along with Aristotle that all in nature has a goal and purpose, and human beings, the only creatures endowed with reason, have the goal of striving for self-perfection. He held that *lex aeterna* is identical with God's wisdom, only a fraction of which is accessible to humans by means of their rational capacities. The part which is accessible Aquinas called natural law, and that sets out the goals humans are pursuing. Human reason, according to Aquinas, is guided by the use of syllogisms defined by Aristotle.

Aquinas's idea of syllogistic requires some comment. Earlier we said that the only perfect syllogism is an abstract one. Once ordinary language is inserted into the process, we claimed, the syllogism becomes an enthymeme, which can produce at best only probable conclusions. Aquinas's Christian interpretation of the syllogism did not accept that point. Instead, the syllogism was held to retain its capacity for absolute and certain conclusions even when ordinary language is employed. In making this claim, Aquinas provided the logic for legal discourse along with all other formal discourse.

Thus, the syllogism became the tool of legal advocacy, and it was tested according to the rules originally set forth by Aristotle. Rhetorical skill could not make an invalid syllogism valid, and justice was found through valid syllogisms and the human rational capacity to discern that portion of truth and justice that God chooses to reveal.

By the start of the twelfth century, with the establishment for the first time of university teaching in law in such places as Bologna, Paris, Oxford, and Cambridge, attention came to be focused on law as a system of rules. Rules gained their power by coming either from God or authority. Law came from the Godgiven human rational capacity to discern truth and justice, or from authority found in God's revealed words in the Bible, or from Roman law. The starting point was the *Corpus juris civilis* of Justinian, which came to hold a place of authority almost equal to the Bible.

No longer were law scholars interested in rhetoric. They were interested in the rules of law under the expectation that if rules could be made explicit enough, there would be no room for persuasion in the trial. It would be a matter of reasoning through the appropriate rules. Intense effort was given to stating the rules with greater precision, locating their authority, and identifying in each case what would be the appropriate rules. From this work comes our idea of *essential elements* in a case, and that requires explanation if we are to understand the traditional view of reality in the courtroom.

ESSENTIAL ELEMENTS OF THE CASE.   The object of the legal philosophers' work was to discover the essence or inherent being of a case and then set out that essence in a set of statements that would guide the decision makers. The essence is to be "found" by a search of the rules of law that had been extrapolated by authorities and applied in prior cases.

In any trial a major consideration for counsel and the judge is to determine the arguments needed in order to make out a prima facie case. That is a case which contains basic arguments and evidence necessary to warrant a decision in favor of the claim being made if no counterargument is presented. In other words, it is a case which on its face argues to the essence of the cause and thus at first face justifies a continuation of the trial. In order to know if a prima facie case is made, the lawyers must know what is the essence of the cause, what are its essential elements.

Consider a modern example. Mr. and Mrs. Frank Jinks have lived at their home at 2870 Jefferson Avenue for twenty years. Two years ago they had an outdoor swimming pool installed in their backyard. They often kept a small raft by the pool, and the pool and raft were visible from the sidewalk by looking through the six-foot-high cyclone fence that surrounds the pool. An evergreen hedge approximately three feet high surrounds the fence on the outside.

During construction of the pool Jimmie James, who lived at 2865 Jefferson Avenue, had watched the work with excitement. He had asked Mrs. Jinks if he could swim in the pool when it was done, and she had said he could if his parents approved and if he learned how to swim. Jimmie's parents promised to start him in swimming lessons as a tenth birthday present. The James family had lived in their home for about two years.

On July 10, just two weeks before his birthday, Jimmie James was found floating face down in the pool by Mrs. Jinks as she came home from work at 5:30 P.M. Jimmie was dead. The raft was floating upside down in the pool. It had been left out of the water by the last person to use the pool. The pool cover had been left rolled up at one end of the pool. There was no evidence of how Jimmie got into the yard; the gate was closed and locked.

The James family wants to sue the Jinks family for causing Jimmie's death. What do they have to prove if they are to make out a prima facie case? What is the essence of the cause?

The American Law Institute has done the work of studying the vast array of legal rules that have been employed in deciding tort cases, which involve civil wrongs as opposed to criminal violations (American Law Institute 1965). Among the hundreds of causes reviewed is one labeled "Artificial Conditions Highly Dangerous to Trespassing Children" (Sec. 339, p. 197). The rule cited is as follows:

A possessor of land is subject to liability for physical harm to children trespassing thereon caused by an artificial condition upon the land if
(a) the place where the condition exists is one upon which the

possessor knows or has reason to know that children are likely to trespass, and

(b) the condition is one of which the possessor knows or has reason to know and which he realizes or should realize will involve an unreasonable risk of death or serious bodily harm to such children, and

(c) the children because of their youth do not discover the condition or realize the risk involved in intermeddling with it or in coming within the area made dangerous by it, and

(d) the utility to the possessor of maintaining the condition and the burden of eliminating the danger are slight as compared with the risk to children involved, and

(e) the possessor fails to exercise reasonable care to eliminate the danger or otherwise to protect the children.

Where does this rule come from? Probably hundreds of years of legal thought seeking to promulgate such rules, but specifically the American Law Institute traces the rule back to 1873 in the case of Sioux City & Pacific R. Co. v. Stout, 84 U.S. (17 Wall.) 657, where a child was hurt while playing with a railroad turntable, and so the rule is called the turntable doctrine. In an 1875 case, Keffe v. Milwaukee & St. Paul R. Co. 21 Minn. 207, 18 Am. Rep 393, the court argued that a child had been allured or enticed onto the premises by the condition created by the defendant, so that the defendant was responsible for the trespass. From this theory the rule came to be called by what the American Law Institute calls a misnomer of "attractive nuisance."

The Institute tells us that in most cases in which this rule has been applied, the child has been no more than twelve years old, although older children have been successful plaintiffs. In all, this comment on one rule occupies almost eleven pages of discussion defining and commenting upon each important phrase in the rule.

From this, the lawyer for the James family can expect to be successful in this case if the following questions can be answered affirmatively:

1. Did the Jinks family know or have reason to know that their pool was a place children were likely to trespass upon?
2. Was the swimming pool such that the Jinks family knew or had reason to know and realized or should have realized that it involved an unreasonable risk of death or serious bodily harm to Jimmie James?
3. Was Jimmie too young to realize the risk involved in getting into the swimming pool alone and without permission?
4. Was the value of the pool to the Jinks family and the burden of eliminating the danger slight as compared with the risk it proved to be to Jimmie James?
5. Did the Jinks family fail to exercise reasonable care to eliminate the danger or otherwise to protect Jimmie?

If the lawyer can provide arguments and evidence to support an affirmative answer to each of these questions, and if the court is one that recognizes this rule as set out, then the lawyer will be judged to have made out a prima facie case.

Of course, presenting such a case does not mean the James family will certainly win. It only means that the trial can go on and the lawyer for the Jinks family will be obliged to reply. That reply may take the form of rebutting the affirmative answer to any one of the essential issues, or presenting arguments and evidence to show that there are other essential elements that have not been met by the plaintiff.

Suppose, for example, the James family lawyer had provided evidence and argument to prove an affirmative answer to the first four issues but failed to argue the fifth. The defense, representing the Jinks family, could admit that everything claimed by the plaintiff was true but the case still did not, on its face, warrant a reply. Why? Because the defense could say that the Jinks family certainly knew that Jimmie and other children were interested in the pool and might trespass; they clearly knew that children in a pool present a serious risk, and they could admit that Jimmie at ten years of age was too young to appreciate the danger to himself. No one would argue that a pool is worth more than a human life or that taking precautions to protect children who might come into the yard uninvited are too costly in comparison with that life.

But unless the plaintiff can show that the Jinkses did not exercise reasonable care to eliminate that danger or otherwise protect Jimmie, they have no case. The defense would move to dismiss on the grounds the plaintiff had failed to make out a prima facie case. If the judge accepted the rule as set out by the American Law Institute, the case would be dismissed without the defense ever having to argue further.

And so, to summarize, a major thrust of traditional legal thinking, starting in the Middle Ages and continuing to the present, has been to define the essence of every imaginable cause of legal action. By extraordinary specificity in rule statement it is expected that the trial process of discovering facts can be regulated in the direction of finding justice. The dangers of sophistic advocacy distorting justice are thereby reduced if not eliminated.

The dedication to a fixed reality knowable only through formal Aristotelian logic was so great that some thinkers believed that even God was bound in a way similar to human beings. Hugo Grotius (1583–1645) believed that not even God can modify such rules of natural law as contracts should be kept, we must render other's property to them, we must accept penal responsibility. He said, "Just as God cannot make two by two anything else than four, he cannot make that which is intrinsically evil anything else than evil" (Stromholm 1985, 155). To Grotius reason or logic was stronger than God. A characteristic of European life that extended into the United States and continued well into this century was rationalism characterized by mathematical precision. Its impact is reflected to this day in traditional conceptions of reality in the courtroom.

What happened to rhetoric, the rationale Aristotle had set out for forensic expression, in the process of this extreme dedication to formalism and absolute reality? Petrus Ramus (Pierre de la Ramée, 1515–1572), a French philosopher, solved that problem by redefining the seven liberal arts to locate rhetoric solely as the rationale of speaking well, involving only style and delivery. To logic Ramus gave all the processes of invention and arrangement (developing and organizing ideas). Logic was defined as the art of disputing well, and in this way legal argument was seen as consisting of nothing more than formal logic. The Ramist philosophy, published in France by Audomarus Talaeus (Omer Talon) in 1544, and in England by Gabriel Harvey in 1577, rapidly became the standard version that influenced legal thinking well into the twentieth century (Howell 1956).

PRESUMPTION AND BURDEN OF PROOF.   One final element must be explained in order to understand the traditional concept of reality in the courtroom: the concept of presumption and burden of proof. Richard Whately (1787–1863) maintained in his *Elements of Rhetoric* that there are certain presumptions that exist in favor of, for example, existing institutions and innocence. This means that there is a preoccupation of ground that will remain in place unless and until someone or some thing accepts the responsibility or burden to prove this status quo should change. Whately did not mean to say that because we presume, say, that an accused person is innocent until proved guilty this puts any logical force behind the idea of innocence. Rather, he suggested that some home base or starting point needed to be defined in order to determine how a legal case should begin and how it should be decided in the absence of a clear winner (Whately 1963).

Whately believed that there are certain natural presumptions that direct us. Being a theologian, he felt that these presumptions carried the force of natural law or God's will. To return to the example of James vs. Jinks, when Jimmie was found drowned in the swimming pool, it would be natural to presume that the Jinks family was without fault unless and until someone (the James family) undertook the burden to prove otherwise. This presumption comes from the natural presumption in favor of existing states of being. The Jinks family has been without fault in the eyes of the law, and they will remain that way unless the James family satisfactorily presents a prima facie case against this presumption. Then, and only then, will the burden shift to the Jinks family to rebut that case.

What happens if both the James's and Jinks's arguments are strong and the trial seems to be a draw, with no clear winner? How are we to decide? Again, presumption provides the guide. The burden of proof carries the responsibility in this tort case that the James family must show a preponderance of evidence in favor of their side. If it were a criminal case, contemporary rules tend to demand an even higher level: to prove the case beyond reasonable doubt. In baseball the tie goes to the runner; in law the tie goes to the side carrying presumption.

RECONSTRUCTING REALITY IN THE COURTROOM

Well into the development of the legal system in the United States the power of natural law through divine justice continued to be the common perspective. New Englanders had an intense and vivid hatred of sin and its potential for contagion. In Puritan America not only was the supremacy of natural law maintained and identified with the law of God, but the source of the law was found in the Scriptures. Even an opponent of Puritanism in England, Richard Hooker, argued that human law must conform to the general laws of nature and they must not contradict any positive law of Scripture (Tortoriello 1970).

Gradually, however, the American experiment of separation of church and state and the increasing reluctance to define the state-enforced norms of law in terms of God's will led to a search for other sources of authority for the law. As the nineteenth century gave way to the twentieth, such an authority presented itself in the rise of empirical science. Two lines of thought need to be explored here, scientific norms and scientific trial procedures.

SCIENTIFIC NORMS.   Empirical science is based on the perception of a reality that exists apart from human wishes or expectations. Charles Sanders Peirce (1839–1914) said, "There are Real things whose characters are entirely independent of our opinions about them; those Reals affect our sense according to regular laws, and . . . by taking advantage of the laws of perception, we can ascertain by reasoning how things really and truly are" (Peirce 1955, 18).

The problem with this view of reality is the difficulty in finding what *ought* to be merely by observing what *is*. Even such an absolutist as Peirce felt that philosophical considerations of ethics in law and jurisprudence are necessary if law, which consists of ought or normative statements, is to coexist with empirical science. Obviously he felt that logic (including mathematics) continued to hold its place as the rationale through which observations become conclusions.

Scientific sociology described legal norms as societal facts which exert a causal effect upon human behavior. Legal rules function as the motivational factors of human conduct. Through mathematical probability we can scientifically predict the chances of certain behaviors occurring in relation to legal rules (Eikema Hommes 1979). A legal obligation, then, is the existence of the chance that one party will comply with the other's expectations coming from a definite event such as a promise or tort.

Legal realists carried the idea of empirical reality further. They eliminated the normative character of law altogether. Instead they described actual conduct of people in general and judges in particular as the source of law. Oliver Wendell Holmes said that the "bad man" has no interest in normative legal principles. He cares only about what the particular judge will decide in his case. In his lecture "The Path of the Law," Holmes said, "The prophecies of what courts will do in fact, and nothing more pretentious, are what I mean by the law" (Holmes 1920, 173). The realists were among the first to challenge the rationalist theory that had persisted since early in the Christian era. They suggested that legal rules were not found through syllogistic logic, but were instead the product of the psychological forces interacting with empirical reality to produce a judicial state of mind.

To summarize, in modern time the emergence of ideas of empirical reality, a natural world of processes accessible through the human senses but not subject to the influence of human will, gave an authority to law quite apart from the traditional idea of God's will through Scripture. It did not, of course, necessitate denial of God's will, for divine creation was typically seen as the force through which this orderly, law-driven empirical reality had come into existence. The observation of what "is" can be the starting point for what "ought to be" through various conceptions of societal patterns, psychological forces, or natural laws.

SCIENTIFIC TRIAL PROCEDURES.   From the broad idea of natural law traced through the years from Aristotle and Plato come some basic principles of procedural justice to govern trials. They include the following:

1. No person should be judge of his or her own cause.
2. The dispute settler should have no private interest in the outcome.
3. The dispute settler should not be biased in favor of or against a party.
4. Each party should be given fair notice of the proceedings.
5. The dispute settler should hear the argument and evidence of both sides.
6. The dispute settler should hear a party only in the presence of the other party.
7. Each party should be given a fair opportunity to respond to the arguments and evidence of the other party.
8. The terms of the settlement should be supportable by reasons.
9. The reasons should refer to the arguments and evidence presented.

English jurists call these principles a part of natural justice which even acts of Parliament cannot contravene (Golding 1975). Aristotelian rhetorical theory accounts for all of them when these two concepts are considered: (1) human rationality and (2) the inherent strength of truth and justice to emerge when placed in full and fair competition with all possible arguments.

Beyond these long-established principles come those which clearly relate to the presumption that trials reconstruct reality. We will discuss these principles as they apply to three concepts: (1) pleadings; (2) evidence; (3) witness examination.

Pleadings are a branch of legal science dedicated to the exchange of written instruments before a trial, aimed at identifying specifically the issues involved in the dispute and the questions of fact that must be answered. The function of the pleadings as a part of the judicial process is to clarify the controversy so as to make the ultimate decision rest upon the actual points in conflict and not upon irrelevancies (Clark 1947). At the start, then, the object is to establish what reality is to be re-created.

Part of this pretrial process is the announcement of points that will be made and the witnesses and evidence that will prove them true. Discovery procedures allow adverse parties to ask to see the evidence to be used by the other side and to question the witnesses to be called and take their statements down as sworn testimony in depositions. The theory behind this is to reduce the tendency to turn the trial into a contest or game between two attorneys and focus instead on the business of finding what truly was the reality that surrounded the past facts which are the object of the trial. The fact that U.S. lawyers are at once advocates for their clients and officers of the court sworn to participate in the discovery of reality is significant.

Evidence is the focus of the trial under the reconstruction perspective. Even today law professors commonly claim that if an attorney knows the law and is diligent in finding evidence, skills of advocacy are unnecessary. It will be the revelation of what really happened seen through the eyes of legal rules that governs the trial outcome (Miller 1927).

The very use of the term "evidence" reveals the underlying assumption that it serves to give evidence of what really happened. Thus, physical evidence such as fingerprints, bloodstains, and a knife found next to the body are pieces of the reality or artifacts which guide the researchers to an understanding of the whole picture of the past. Documents such as contracts or wills are evidence that people made agreements or determinations.

There should be a positive correlation between the quality of evidence presented in a trial and the quality of decision, in the same way that archaeological observations such as finding charcoal that is carbon dated as three thousand years old may warrant a judgment that the area was inhabited at that time, but finding human bones and tools near the fire ring makes the judgment more sound. Both lawyers and archaeologists are in the business of reconstructing reality according to this way of thinking.

The objective of evidence is to demonstrate fact. The object of the trial is to decide on facts and then apply the law to them. In the trial process there are two steps to be considered when looking at evidence from a reality reconstruction perspective: (1) the admissibility of evidence and (2) the probative value of the evidence.

The theory behind admissibility of evidence has been explained from Aristotle's theory earlier in this chapter. People lacking a vital self-interest in the outcome of the case may choose a winner on some basis other than substantive issues. To prevent this, evidence that might encourage improper choice is simply never brought to the attention of the decision makers. There are many aspects of the law of evidence; we will consider some of them.

First, courts operate under time imperatives. They must decide, and cannot imitate scholars who simply refuse to draw conclusions until sufficient evidence is available. Since courts always deal in past fact, they rely exclusively on artifactual data heavily dependent upon human perception, recall, and reporting abilities. Rules have been established to select only evidence with the probative qualities likely to reveal what the court needs to know given its limitations.

Second, trials, unlike other research situations, always take place within a highly charged competitive context. Adversaries are always tempted to win even if it means distorting the facts. Evidence rules seek to filter out such potential distortion.

Third, the decision makers in trials, unlike other areas of investigation, are laymen with regard to the subject under investigation. In court such problems as those of medicine, psychology, business, and science are often at issue in such complexity as would tax an expert in any of those fields. But jurors are selected at random and typically rejected if they show professional expertise in the topic of the trial. Rules are set up to impose limitations on proof so as to hold the standard of inquiry to a level suitable to a lay judge. Thus, in court some data which would be considered by an expert in the field might be omitted from consideration.

Fourth, the very drama of the courtroom in contrast to the calm of the laboratory demands some control on the evidence. The jurors need to be protected from undue inflammation if they are to do their job of finding fact properly (Wigmore 1937).

The probative value of evidence concerns the likelihood that some testimony, document, or physical object will accurately reflect past fact or reality. The interpretation of science suggesting a fixed reality that can be apprehended by the senses guided developments in the law of evidence. Wigmore's treatises on evidence and judicial proof, which dominated the field during the first half of the twentieth century, became more and more "scientific" in their orientation from edition to edition (see Wigmore 1937). He developed elaborate formulas within which evidence could be inserted to guarantee that the final decision would truly reconstruct reality. He clearly took his cue from the increasingly powerful influence of natural science and the methods of induction and logical positivitism.

Witness examination theories also reflect a commitment to reconstructing reality. The law assumes that people present at the past event which is now the subject of the trial were all witnesses to a common reality. Presumably if the jury were able to travel back in time and thus become witnesses to the accident or contract negotiation which is now disputed, they would be able to see for themselves what truly took place. Lacking this, they look to those who were present to tell them what happened.

Of course, not all witnesses tell the truth or have fully developed faculties for observation, recall, and reporting. So the processes of direct and cross examination are seen as means to assure that the jury becomes exposed to all they need to know in order to judge the veracity of a witness and the extent to which the testimony can be employed in the reconstruction process.

The jury is expected to observe from the demeanor of the witness during testimony if there is a problem of intelligence, or physical impairment in sight or hearing, or a tendency toward dishonesty or bias (Wigmore 1937). Courts of appeal avoid making any judgment about the credibility of witnesses because they were not present during testimony and could not observe the demeanor.

NARRATIVE CREATIVE CONCEPTIONS OF THE TRIAL

At this point in the chapter we can summarize what is, toward the end of the twentieth century, a rapidly emerging view of the trial at law, and look at critical responses that tend to support what we will call narrative creative conceptions of the trial. At the very heart of the common view of a trial is the assumption that the legal process offers a reliable method for putting an accurate picture of an event in the mind of the judge or jury. The source of the event-picture is most commonly the testimony of witnesses supported by documentary and physical evidence and the interpretations of experts. The medium is the questioning of witnesses by opposing counsel.

Underlying this system are a number of assumptions: (1) A witness present at the scene of an event that becomes the subject of the trial is able to perceive it with reasonable accuracy; (2) there is, physically and metaphysically, a single event that existed apart from the perceptions of witnesses; (3) the witness is able to report the perceptions in such a way that personal judgment will not excessively distort the report; (4) a witness's memory is sufficient to allow a complete report (the "whole truth") after a delay that can amount to several years; (5) the accuracy of the report is best obtained through direct questioning by an attorney; and (6) the credibility and accuracy of the witness are best tested by cross-examination by an attorney while the decision makers observe the witness's demeanor (Rieke 1964).

At early as 1909 Hugo Münsterberg (1923) seriously challenged the assumptions of witness accuracy from the perspective of psychology. He demonstrated experimentally that a group of witnesses reporting on the "same" event present significantly different reports. After a half century of active psychological study Münsterberg's concerns were still supported by research findings (Marshall 1966). Contemporary communication research finds no evidence to support the claim that observers can successfully detect deception on the part of witnesses (Cody and O'Hair 1983).

More fundamental reservations about the traditional/reconstructionist view of the trial came from philosophy. We have already noted the legal realists' rejection of human rationality and the power of the syllogism, but their relativism troubled many who saw law as more orderly and "reckonable" if not predictable (Llewellyn 1960).

More serious challenges came from writers who demonstrated that the presumptions of formal logic simply could not hold when applied to legal issues (Toulmin 1958, 1972); Perelman and Olbrechts-Tyteca 1971).

Finally, the assumptions of empirical science which formed the foundation of reality presumed in the trial came under attack. Felix Cohen (1950), writing in *The Yale Law Journal,* argued that instead of a single event existing apart from witness perceptions, there are as many "events" as there are witnesses. Given this, Cohen said it would be better to describe evidence as the basis from which we *construct* an event that most satisfies today's needs. Probert (1972) argued that the concept "fact" is nothing more than a convention in language to describe certain kinds of claims. Facts do not constitute a slice of reality, but are merely words with which we build a claim for reality.

CREATIVE VIEWS.   A creative rather than re-creative view of reality was set out by philosophers of science who made fundamental inroads into the naïve realism held in law. Popper (1962) said scientific theories can never be proved true. At best, he said, they can be refuted. Thus, the science we hold as true at any time is nothing more than conjectures that have not yet been refuted. Kuhn (1970) defined scientific theories in terms of ideas accepted within a paradigm at a given time. What makes one paradigm more powerful scientifically at any time is not its revelation of reality but its survival in a process of scientific revolutions. Toulmin (1972) described science as an evolution within intellectual ecosystems. Riordan (1988) observed that the reality which scientists know is one that communicates or is a shared reality. Ideas that capture the allegiance of a scientific community become for that time the reality of the field. Objectivity, concluded Riordan, is not the way things are but how they are understood and discussed by the majority of scientists.

NARRATIVE VIEWS.   These arguments soon became contagious, and scholars began formulating alternatives to the static view of the trial as a fact-finding inquisition. As a result, a new vision of reality in the courtroom emerged which can be described as a narrative or storytelling view. Taking the perspective of the juror, who is asked to "find" fact by observing the trial, scholars argued that jurors have no special expertise or training either in fact finding or legal reasoning (Bennett 1978, 1979; Bennett and Feldman 1981). Still, they are asked to make sense of the complexities with which they are presented. They do so not by inherent human rationality or by being exposed to a reconstruction of reality. Instead, jurors employ the rules of narrative they have learned through a lifetime of exposure to stories.

After all, what is a trial? It is two parties, each telling its story and asking society to endorse its version of reality. This is not all that much different from two children who scream in dispute and then tell the parent two divergent versions of what happened, each hoping to be accepted.

Anyone, child or adult, who tells a story hoping it will be accepted by listeners as an accurate version of reality must deal with artifacts. If a third-party observer says it didn't happen that way, the storyteller must either adjust to the witness's version or find some way to reject it. This is not to say the witness "knows" better than the storyteller. It is just an artifact that must be accommodated. Similarly, if the dispute involves the charge that a rock was thrown, a toy broken, or a contract signed, the presence of the rock, broken toy, or contract must be dealt with in the story. This does not mean that these prove what "really happened." It merely means that the rules of narrative will require some acknowledgment of their presence now.

In the courtroom jurors confront a complex set of claims which must be interpreted. According to the storytelling perspective, this task would overwhelm jurors if it were not for their reliance on the common organizing tool, namely stories. Through the construction of stories jurors can organize and analyze the vast amount of information involved in making legal judgments. Essentially stories are the systematic means of storing, rearranging, comparing, and interpreting the available information about social behavior. As such, stories translate legal questions into more easily understood forms.

Storytelling assumes that stories have implicit structures which enable people to make systematic comparisons between them. Hence, jurors rely upon the structure of stories to make judgments about their acceptability.

Stories organize information so as to perform three interpretive functions for the juror (Bennett and Feldman 1981). First, jurors locate the central action (the key behavior) in a story so as to make sense of other actions and events. Second, the juror constructs inferences about the relationship of story elements that impinge upon the central action. Third, the network of connections drawn around the central action is then tested for consistency and completeness. In sum, jurors apply narrative tests to the stories they hear in an effort to judge them critically (Fisher 1987). This narrative rationality consists of two subordinate processes: (1) narrative coherence and (2) narrative fidelity.

Narrative coherence calls our attention to patterns we have learned about how stories "hang together," such as acceptable sequences of thought or action (Fisher 1987). When a man approaches you on the street offering to sell a Rolex watch for $30.00, telling you he lost his wallet and needs cab fare home, you may doubt the coherence of his story. The man accused of strangling his wife argues his claim of being at the mercy of his impulses by proving that immediately after the murder and before disposing of the body, he calmly went to work. Here the lack of narrative coherence is used to prove the claim that the killer was out of his mind.

Narrative fidelity identifies the set of tests jurors have learned by which they judge the truth qualities of claims. Our own life experiences combined with vicarious learning have built within us a set of criteria by which we decide whether or not a story accurately portrays the way things "really" happen (Fisher 1987). Children watching weekend cartoons have a verbalized announcement when a story fails in terms of narrative fidelity. It is the "I'm sure" test. When the evil Martian announces that he is only interested in what is good for the innocent victims he has trapped, the children watching the show shout gleefully, "I'm sure." They know that villains care nothing for the good of others and are interested only in selfish gain. In a movie, when the star falls into the ocean and fights for her life against the storm, only to appear in the next scene, on the beach, with her makeup intact and only a few strands of hair out of place, we may challenge the story's narrative fidelity.

Our learned tests of coherence and fidelity, however, may have little to do with what "really" happened if a trial is viewed from the conception of reconstructing reality in the courtroom. Stories are judged in terms of the warrants we have learned and which become salient in a particular case. We judge the stories given in the courtroom by a dual standard of whether it happened the way the lawyers claim and if it could have happened that way (Bennett 1978). A lie told by a good storyteller may be believed over the truth told by a poor one (Bennett and Feldman 1981).

In the murder case involving the man who strangled his wife, he was still convicted of second-degree murder rather than found innocent because of diminished capacity, even though the psychologist testified he was at the mercy of his impulses as demonstrated by his reporting for work with a dead wife still in his home. The jury's choice between second-degree murder, manslaughter, negligent homicide, or innocence will turn, as we shall see in chapter 10, not on a scientific analysis of what truly happened but on a negotiation between the story elements they believe and the legal requirements of various verdicts. The fact that the accused was a black man, his wife a white woman, and the jury consisted of eight white residents of Salt Lake City may have had something to do with their response to the stories told.

REFERENCES

American Law Institute (1965). *Restatement of the law,* second, Torts, 2nd, pamphlet 2. Student Edition (sec. 281–503). St. Paul, MN: American Law Institute.

Bennett, W. L. (1978). Storytelling in criminal trials. *Quarterly Journal of Speech* 64: 1–22.

Bennett, W. L. (1979). Rhetorical transformation of evidence in criminal trials: creating grounds for legal judgment. *Quarterly Journal of Speech* 65: 311–22.

Bennett, W. L., and Feldman, M. S. (1981). *Reconstructing reality in the courtroom.* New Brunswick, NJ: Rutgers University Press.

Caplan, H. (trans.). (1954). *Cicero, ad herennium.* Cambridge: Harvard University Press.

Clark, C. E. (1947). *Handbook of the law of code pleading.* St. Paul, MN: West.

Cody, M. J., and O'Hair, H. D. (1983). Nonverbal communication and deception: differences in deception cues due to gender and communicator dominance. *Communication Monographs* 50: 175–92.

Cohen, F. S. (1950). Field theory and judicial logic. *Yale Law Journal* 59: 238–72.

Corbett, E. P. J. (1965). *Classical rhetoric for the modern student.* New York: Oxford University Press.

Eikema Hommes, H. J. van (1979). *Major trends in the history of legal philosophy.* New York: North-Holland.

Fisher, W. R. (1987). *Human communication as narration.* Columbia: University of South Carolina Press.

Golding, M. P. (1975). *Philosophy of law.* Englewood Cliffs, NJ: Prentice-Hall.

Holmes, Oliver Wendell (1920). The path of the law. In *Collected legal papers.* New York: Harcourt, Brace.

Hostettler, G. F. (1967). Trends in the history of rhetoric. In K. Brooks (ed.), *The communicative arts and sciences of speech.* Columbus, OH: Charles E. Merrill.

Howell, W. S. (1956). *Logic and rhetoric in England 1500–1700.* Princeton, NJ: Princeton University Press.

Kuhn, T. S. (1970). *The structure of scientific revolutions.* 2nd ed., Enlarged, Vol. II, No. 2 International Encyclopedia of Unified Science. Chicago: University of Chicago Press.

Llewellyn, K. (1960). *The common law tradition.* Boston: Little, Brown.

Marshall, James (1966). *Law and psychology in conflict.* Indianapolis: Bobbs-Merrill.

Miller, A. H. (1927). Lawyer's treatment of his client. *American Bar Association Journal* 13: 32.

Münsterberg, H. (1923). *On the witness stand.* New York: Clark Boardman.

Peirce, C. S. (1955). The fixation of belief. In J. Buckler (ed.), *Philosophical writings of Peirce.* New York: Dover.

Perelman, Ch., and Olbrechts-Tyteca. L. (1971). *The new rhetoric.* Notre Dame, IN: University of Notre Dame Press.

Popper, K. R. (1962). *Conjectures and refutations: the growth of scientific knowledge.* New York: Basic Books.

Probert, W. (1972). *Law, language, and communication.* Springfield, IL: Charles C. Thomas.

Rieke, R. D. (1964). Rhetorical theory in American legal practice. Unpublished doctoral dissertation, Department of Speech, Ohio State University.

Riordan, M. (1988). *The hunting of the quark: a true story of modern physics.* New York: Simon and Schuster.

Roberts, W. R. (1946). Rhetorica. In W. D. Ross (ed.), *The works of Aristotle,* vol. 9. Oxford: Clarendon Press.

Stromholm, S. (1985). *A short history of legal thinking in the west.* Stockholm, Sweden: Norstedts.

Thonssen, L. (1942). *Selected readings in rhetoric and public address.* New York: H. W. Wilson.

Tortoriello, T. R. (1970). An audience-centered case study in judicial rhetoric. Unpublished doctoral dissertation, Department of Speech, Ohio State University.

Toulmin, S. E. (1958). *The uses of argument.* Cambridge: Cambridge University Press.

Toulmin, S. (1972). *Human understanding.* Princeton, NJ: Princeton University Press.

Watson, J. S. (1855). *Cicero on oratory and orators; with his letters to Quintus and Brutus.* London: Henry G. Bohn.

Whately, R. [1841] (1963). *Elements of rhetoric.* D. Ehninger (ed.). Carbondale: Southern Illinois University Press.

Wigmore, J. H. (1937). *The science of judicial proof.* Boston: Little, Brown.

Chapter 3

FAIRNESS AND BIAS
IN THE TRIAL PROCESS

Individuals new to the trial process are often staggered by the procedural complexity of litigation. Upon gaining exposure to this morass of rules, litigants then become acutely aware of their apparent inflexibility. In the eyes of many litigants, inexperienced and experienced alike, this rigidity is seen as a threat to the fundamental right to a fair trial. Oddly enough, the court views the rules of procedure as exactly those standards that ensure trial fairness. The struggle between these two competing views is often played out in sharp criticisms directed toward the bench. In an attempt to better understand this tension, researchers have spent considerable time examining how litigants perceive the adversarial system.

Research in this area has shown that litigants' reactions to the court are affected not only by case outcomes but also by their judgments regarding the fairness of the process through which the outcomes are reached. Hence, judgments of fairness are thought to be distinct from judgments of personal gain. Indeed, research reveals that the most significant determinant of legal satisfaction is perceived fairness, not case outcome (Tyler 1984). This is not to say the two measures are not related. Judgments of outcome fairness depend upon perceived procedural fairness (Walker, Lind, and Thibaut 1979). Not surprisingly, when participants perceive the procedures for dispute resolution to be fair, they are more likely to judge outcomes produced in that system as fair.

PROCEDURE AND PERCEPTIONS OF FAIRNESS

People hold lucid and forceful views about fair methods for resolving disputes. In general, litigants express greater satisfaction with the legal process when they have substantial control over the form and content of evidence presentation (O'Barr and Conley 1985). Moreover, litigants who have more control believe the process produces fairer verdicts (Walker, LaTour, Lind, and Thibaut 1974). An increase in perceived procedural fairness also carries over to perceptions of the court. Consistently, litigants who rate the procedural process as fair find the court to be more fair (Tyler 1984).

In one study researchers asked subjects to rate twelve legal procedures which varied along three dimensions: the degree of control over the decision by a third party, the presence or absence of the individuals in dispute, and the opportunity for the disadvantaged party to present evidence. Subjects from both the United States and Europe overwhelmingly preferred adversary procedures over inquisitorial procedures (LaTour et al. 1976). In similar experiments subjects repeatedly judged the adversary procedure as more fair (Thibaut and Walker 1975). When compared to the judge-controlled inquisitorial system, similar to the model used in French and many Third World nations courts, the adversary procedure produced greater satisfaction and higher ratings of fairness even when litigants received unfavorable verdicts (Lind, Kurtz, Musante, Walker, and Thibaut 1980).

In a fascinating study examining procedural preference, researchers exposed subjects from four countries to four dispute-resolution procedures which varied in adversariness (Lind, Erickson, Friedland, and Dickenberger 1978). Least adversarial was the inquisitorial model, where a decision maker would question disputants and render a verdict. One step closer to a U.S. trial was the single investigator model, whereby a single professional would investigate the dispute and then report to the decision maker. The third model made this more adversarial by employing two professionals, one for each side. The fourth and most adversarial model specified that an advocate for each side would investigate the dispute and present the evidence before a decision maker. Subjects were asked to rate their preference for the use of each model if they were to become involved in a lawsuit. Subjects from all four countries (United States, England, France, and West Germany) preferred more adversarial procedures to less adversarial models.

A critical question remains: If litigants prefer an adversary system, finding its procedures more fair, more satisfying, and producing better verdicts, then why are litigants so highly critical of these procedures? In other words, why do people often view trial procedure as unfair? The answer to this question involves many intangibles but revolves around the issue of control and restriction. One vital reason that litigants are more satisfied with an adversary system, as opposed to a more judge-controlled system, is exactly that—control. The studies reported so far all share one common finding: litigants favor those procedural models where they possess more control over the presentation and interpretation of evidence.

If one examines the adversary system employed in the United States, two features surrounding control stand out. First, many of the procedural rules enforced by the court grant greater control to litigants. The closing argument is a good example. When presenting the summation of a case, attorneys are encouraged to interpret the facts so that they argue favorably for the client. Yet many other procedural rules operate to restrict litigant control. For example, the opening statement in a case is to be, by rule, void of argument and persuasive appeal. Similarly witnesses, who are sometimes the litigants themselves, are not free to provide testimony beyond the scope of the questions posed by counsel. Perhaps more frustrating for litigants and observers alike is what does not get asked during examination. For these reasons perceptions of fairness, even in a highly adversarial system, will vary from case to case and from person to person.

Ironically, the procedural rules which litigants find most restrictive are in place primarily to prevent bias and ensure fairness. The court recognizes that the adversarial system, despite its successes, also has its shortcomings. Most notably the vigor with which advocates argue for their clients often interjects bias and supplants credible evidence. For example, one study found that when the evidence presented in a case is described as unreliable, jurors depend more heavily on preexisting attitudes (Kaplan and Miller 1978). Of course, a primary responsibility of an advocate in an adversary system is to question the reliability of opposing evidence. Therefore, the nature of the adversary system may encourage the expression of attitudinal bias. Critics also claim that because attorneys in an adversary system want only to present the best case possible, they have no interest in finding and presenting evidence damaging to their clients. Research, however, has not supported this claim. In fact, one experiment reveals that attorneys in the adversary system conduct more complete investigations and uncover more facts when the case leans heavily against their clients (Lind, Thibaut, and Walker 1973). Interestingly, this still results in bias, but of a different kind. Attorneys work so hard to uncover facts in disadvantaged cases that they often make unbalanced cases look more balanced than they actually are.

Danger from advocate enthusiasm does not stop with the facts. Perhaps the most prevalent form of bias fostered by a competitive system is the introduction of inadmissible evidence, evidence judged prejudicial by the court. In the next section we will discuss how lawyers interject evidentiary bias and the effects it has on jury decision making.

BIAS IN THE COURTROOM

A common courtroom scenario is that of an attorney purposely raising inadmissible evidence through questioning and then coyly withdrawing the question. The exchange goes something like this:

Counsel: Isn't it true, Mr. Smith, that you currently have an incestuous relationship with your daughter?

Judge: Counselor, you are out of order.

Counsel: I respectfully withdraw the question, your honor. No further questions of this witness.

That this tactic and others like it are commonplace in courtrooms around the country is certain. What little controversy exists regards the weight such evidence carries. Can jurors ignore testimony once its substance has been offered for consumption?

INADMISSIBLE EVIDENCE.   As early as 1937, research confirmed attorneys' worst suspicions; namely, that jurors consider inadmissible evidence during jury deliberations (Wanamaker 1937). Subsequent research confirms this finding (Sue, Smith, and Caldwell 1973; Simon 1966; Sutton 1979; Wolf and Montgomery 1977). In one study thirty mock juries were exposed to one of three versions of an automobile liability case which heavily favored the plaintiff (Broeder 1959). Jurors exposed to the evidence that the defendant had no liability insurance awarded the plaintiff an average of $33,000. When the defendant disclosed that he had liability insurance, jurors exposed to that message gave an average award of $37,000. Jurors in the final condition, who were instructed to disregard the fact that the defendant possessed liability insurance, awarded the plaintiff an average of $46,000. The instruction to disregard the information concerning the defendant's liability insurance not only failed to eliminate the impact of the evidence but instead sensitized the jurors to the fact, resulting in a substantial increase in the average award.

Although inadmissible evidence considered mundane, unbelievable, or incomprehensible does not influence jury verdicts (Hirsch, Reinard, and Reynolds 1976), scholars generally agree that inadmissible evidence is prejudicial. As one attorney has stated the case, "You can never unring the bell." In fact, one research study found that the entire evaluation of the defendant may be poisoned by inadmissible evidence. In that study jurors who reached guilty verdicts after hearing inadmissible evidence conferred less credibility to the defendants and suggested longer terms of punishment (Reinard 1985). This study also illustrated the importance of testimony source. Results revealed that testimony from nonofficial sources, such as an eyewitness, was more impactful on juror verdicts than was inadmissible evidence presented by official sources, such as a law officer or forensic expert. The author concluded that the role played by official sources makes it easier for jurors to disregard their testimony. Since eyewitnesses have no apparent ax to grind, jurors may have more difficulty forgetting what appears to be honest and important evidence.

In many trials inadmissible evidence and bias can infiltrate the jurors' minds even before the jury is impaneled. By the simple fact that we live in an information-intensive society, jurors, like the rest of us, often fall prey to pretrial publicity.

PRETRIAL PUBLICITY.   In regard to pretrial publicity, a tension exists between the First and Sixth Amendments of the U.S. Constitution. The former guarantees the press the freedom to inform the citizenry of public events, while the latter guarantees the right of an accused citizen to a trial by an impartial jury. This conflict, commonly referred to as the free press–free trial issue, centers on the question of bias and the right to a fair trial. The possibility that pretrial press coverage may prejudice jurors so that a fair and impartial jury cannot be selected is hotly debated. While the legal system assumes that jurors, as unique beings, will possess biases, it also assumes that jurors will admit to and suspend biases that might interfere with the receptivity of trial evidence. Although the jury selection process represents a deliberate attempt to eliminate the intrusion of significant bias, the court has repeatedly conceded that pretrial publicity may undermine faith in voir dire (Davis 1986). As a result this conflict of interests has accentuated the use of gag orders, pretrial hearings closed to the press, and requests for venue changes.

Research on the effects of pretrial publicity is mixed. Several experimental studies have demonstrated that mock jurors exposed to pretrial publicity predispose the guilt of the defendant (Riley 1973; Shaffer 1986; Sohn 1976), consider the information during deliberation (Kline and Jess 1966), and produce a verdict consistent with the publicity (Padawer-Singer and Barton 1975; Tans and Chaffee 1966). Yet other studies have found little or no effect (Davis 1986; Hoiberg and Stires 1973) or an influence that was overcome when jurors were instructed to disregard the information (Simon 1966).

A summary of the research in this area provides practitioners with general guidelines concerning the effect of pretrial publicity on jury decisions. Pretrial publicity most affects perceptions of guilt and verdicts under three conditions: (1) when the evidence in the case is weak or ambiguous; (2) when the pretrial information is considered highly relevant to the case, such as confessions or prior record of the same offense; and (3) when jurors are not confident in their judgments (Kaplan 1982).

PROCEDURES FOR REDUCING BIAS

The influence of inadmissible evidence and pretrial publicity is clear. As a rule jurors find it difficult to ignore information they consider germane to a case. To offset this effect the court is armed with procedures aimed at reducing bias. The most widely recognized of these procedures is the use of objections. Objections function to limit inadmissible evidence before it is heard by the jury. Many attorneys argue that if the evidence is presented, even in abbreviated form, before it is objected to, the jury will have heard the evidence despite its inadmissibility. Whatever else follows, the jury will already be poisoned. For this reason the court allows attorneys to object "in limine," before a trial begins, and attorneys are advised to use this option whenever possible.

In addition to attorney objections judges also possess a substantial weapon for combating bias, namely jury instructions.

JURY INSTRUCTIONS

Because the average juror does not possess a knowledge of law sufficient for rendering legally sound verdicts, the judge provides a set of instructions from which the jury is expected to operate during deliberation. These oral instructions, often lengthy and replete with legal terminology, supposedly enable jurors to apply such concepts as "burden of proof," "reasonable doubt," and "presumption of innocence" to the evidence presented in a case and interpret the law as it applies to the case in question. Many legal experts are skeptical that jurors can fully comprehend the judge's instructions. Researchers claim that because of legal jargon and passive sentence structure, a lion's share of the concepts explained in a judge's instruction will typically be misunderstood (Buchanan, Pryor, Taylor, and Strawn 1978). In one study researchers found that 45 percent of the important instructional elements were misunderstood (Charrow and Charrow 1979).

Instructions are complex for good reason. Judges know that if instructions are inaccurate or imprecise, then an excellent case for reversal at a higher court is possible. As a result, many judges go overboard in providing compound instructions that ensure legal accuracy, often repeating language used in appellate court decisions. This practice exacerbates an already bad problem. To curtail the difficulties associated with convoluted instructions, many states have adopted "pattern" jury instructions, where approved and uniform instructions are issued to a jury before deliberation. But instruction writers, claim critics, continue to pay more attention to legal accuracy than readability. In addition, research has revealed that jurors' attitudes about the law color their understanding of instructions (Pryor, Taylor, Buchanan, and Strawn 1980). Perhaps the worst news is that the attitude a judge conveys when giving instructions can affect jurors. Through the use of postdeliberation questionnaires one study revealed that a judge's demeanor as perceived by jurors can influence deliberations, and jurors often attempt to return a verdict that would satisfy the judge (O'Mara 1972). For these reasons many experts remain skeptical as to the benefits of pattern instructions.

Regardless of whether judges employ process or pattern instructions, judicial instructions serve a range of functions extending beyond the objective of providing legal information relevant to the case. Most important, judges also rely on judicial instructions to expunge inadmissible evidence. Instructions intended to filter out forbidden information are generally termed "cautionary."

Cautionary instructions generally involve appeals to the jury to fulfill their duty to remain fair and impartial, usually by disregarding evidence and information deemed inadmissible or prejudicial. Although research is mixed, more studies have shown that jurors generally do not comply with instructions to disregard inadmissible evidence. This resistance may be particularly strong when evidence against the defendant is weak. For example, one study found that a simulated jury did not disregard inadmissible evidence concerning an illegal wiretap when the evidence against the defendant was weak (Sue, Smith, and Caldwell 1973). In another study subjects exposed to confessional evidence obtained in a coercive manner were found to ignore cautionary instructions to reject as evidence any confession they believed to be coerced (Kassin and Wrightsman 1981). This resistance also applies to instructions regarding how jurors view evidence. In yet another study jurors disregarded instructions concerning witness speaking style and attribution of credibility (O'Barr and Lind 1981). Jurors ignored the instruction that a "powerless" speaking style should not be used to infer judgments of believability, and used speaking style to discredit evidence during deliberation. Ironically, telling jurors to disregard information may sometimes exacerbate the problem of inadmissibility, drawing greater attention to the rule-violating material.

Limiting instructions. A defendant with a criminal record often faces the dilemma of whether to testify and risk that the jury upon hearing of previous crimes may use this information to determine guilt, or to remain silent, as accorded by the Fifth Amendment, and have the jury draw its own inferences. Testifying, of course, gives the examining attorney the chance to parade the defendant's criminal record before jurors. To offset this, when the defendant choses to testify, the court provides a safeguard of a **limiting instruction,** which directs the jury to consider the evidence only for the authorized purpose of impeachment and not for guilt determination. The relative impact of the defendant testifying is discussed in chapter 7. The discussion here focuses on the effectiveness of limiting instructions.

The concept of limiting instructions assumes that jurors have both the ability and willingness to compartmentalize the evidence as directed by court. Common sense tells us this is highly unlikely, and experimental research confirms this. One study found that convictions are more likely when the prior record is introduced than when it is not, regardless of limiting instructions (Hans and Doob 1976), whereas another study revealed jurors given limiting instructions rendered fewer convictions than those jurors not so instructed (Cornish and Sealy 1973). A close examination of these studies suggests that conviction rates are highest under unlimited admission without instruction, lowest under complete exclusion, and somewhere in between with limiting instructions (Loh 1985).

When are instructions effective? Although jurors generally resist cautionary and limiting instructions, several factors contribute to greater obedience. Most notably among these is the timing or placement of the instruction. Some studies have shown that judicial instruction is effective only when it precedes the evidence (Kassin and Wrightsman 1979). For example, one study revealed that presenting instructions on the burden of proof before evidence is heard, rather than after evidence presentation, tends to reduce the rate of convictions (Kerr, Atkin, Stasser, Meek, Holt, and Davis 1976). This timing effect may be due to how jurors interpret new information. When jurors have a reason to view evidence suspiciously before it is made salient by argument, they may process this information differently, generating more negative thoughts as a result of the instruction. In other words, the instruction timing may alter jurors' orientation to the evidence in a trial. Indeed, one study found that jurors' interpretation of a case changed as a result of instruction timing (Elwork, Sales, and Alfini 1977).

Instructions with added commentary may also reduce juror resistance to instructions. In one recent study subjects were exposed to a videotaped burglary case where a questionable eyewitness played a pivotal role for the prosecution's case (Katzev and Wishart 1985). Those subjects who received instructions, a summary of the evidence, and a commentary from the judge concerning the eyewitness testimony spent less time deliberating and did not allow the eyewitness evidence to alter the weak case against the defendant. Consistent with this finding researchers have found that a two-barreled instruction gains greater compliance. For example, in one experiment instructions which emphasized the unfairness of a coerced confession and the unreliability of the evidence were effective in limiting the use of this evidence (Kassin and Wrightsman 1985).

From the growing body of research on jury instructions we can extrapolate several consistent findings and in doing so offer three general rules surrounding the use and abuse of instructions by juries. First, jurors have a general tendency to ignore judicial instructions. As uncomfortable as this thought is to many judges, the evidence is convincing. Second, jurors are more apt to follow instructions concerned with the criteria for decision making than they are to comply with requests to disregard types of information. Third, the timing and elaboration of this instruction will ultimately contribute to its effectiveness. With these rules in mind, we can turn our attention to the final means of reducing bias in the courtroom: changing the location of the trial.

CHANGES OF VENUE.   Traditionally, drawing a jury from the community where a crime or dispute originated was not only geographically practical but reasonable as well. Applying local standards to interpret the deviancy of a defendant's behavior or to determine compensation consistent with community customs has long been considered a necessary ingredient to just and equitable decisions. Today, however, the courts recognize that it is often impossible to obtain an impartial hearing in a particular jurisdiction. When the courts are convinced that it is improbable to impanel an impartial jury, they will grant a motion for a change of venue.

Generally speaking, two sets of circumstances are viewed as grounds for this motion. The most common instance is when the case or its principal agents have attained widespread notoriety. This notoriety and publicity must be thought to infect the minds of a majority of community residents so as firmly to instill negative attitudes. A second reason for a change of venue is the widespread knowledge of inadmissible evidence. For example, a family's history of criminal behavior or mental illness is sometimes exceedingly well known in smaller communities. In either of these situations, according to case law, there exists a justification for a change of venue. Yet courts have displayed a general reluctance to grant motions for changes of venue. As a result, in the last several decades attorneys have turned to opinion surveys as evidence of community bias. Some attorneys have gone so far as to employ independent research firms to conduct these surveys and report on the results in court, but these surveys have met stiff resistance. Sworn affidavits about the state of public opinion in a jurisdiction by persons who are believed to have their fingers on the pulse of the community have been much more successful (Hans and Vidmar 1982). Critics claim that this is due partly to judicial conservatism and partly to the inability of judges to interpret statistical survey data.

Although empirical research examining the effects of venue change on juror bias has not been conducted, researchers assume that the building blocks of impartiality, despite attorney zeal in an adversary system, begin with an impartial pool of jurors. Lawyers generally share this sentiment.

REFERENCES

Broeder, D. (1959). The University of Chicago jury project. *Nebraska Law Review* 38: 744–61.

Buchanan, R. W.; Pryor, A.; Taylor, K. P.; and Strawn, D. (1978). Legal communication: an investigation of juror comprehension of pattern instructions. *Communication Quarterly* 26: 31–35.

Charrow, R. P. and Charrow, V. R. (1979). Making legal language understandable: a psycholinguistic study of jury instructions. *Columbia Law Review* 79: 1306–74.

Cornish, W. R., and Sealy, A. P. (1973). Juries and rules of evidence. *Criminal Law Review* 17: 208–18.

Davis, R. W. (1986). Pre-trial publicity, the timing of the trial, and mock jurors' decision processes. *Journal of Applied Social Psychology* 16: 590–607.

Elwork, A.; Sales, B. D.; and Alfini, J. J. (1977). Juridic decisions: in ignorance of the law or in light of it? *Law and Human Behavior* 1: 163–89.

Hans, V. P., and Doob, A. N. (1976). Section 12 of the Canada Evidence Act and the deliberations of simulated jurors. *Criminal Law Quarterly* 18: 235–53.

Hans, V. P., and Vidmar, N. (1982). Jury selection. In N. L. Kerr and R. M. Bray (eds.), *The psychology of the courtroom*. New York: Academic Press.

Hirsch, R. C.; Reinard, J. C.; and Reynolds, R. A. (1976). The influence of objection to mundane and sensational testimony on attorney credibility. Paper presented at the annual convention of the Rocky Mountain Psychological Association, Phoenix.

Hoiberg, B. C., and Stires, L. K. (1973). The effect of several types of pretrial publicity on the guilt attribution of simulated jurors. *Journal of Applied Social Psychology* 3: 257–75.

Kaplan, M. F. (1982). Cognitive processes in the individual juror. In N. L. Kerr and R. M. Bray (eds.) *The psychology of the courtroom*. New York: Academic Press.

Kaplan, M. F. and Miller, L. E. (1978). Reducing the effects of juror bias. *Journal of Personality and Social Psychology* 36: 1443–55.

Kassin, S. M., and Wrightsman, L. S. (1979). On the requirements of proof: the timing of judicial instruction and mock juror verdicts. *Journal of Personality and Social Psychology* 37: 1877–87.

Kassin, S. M., and Wrightsman, L. S. (1981). Coerced confessions, judicial instruction, and mock juror verdicts. *Journal of Applied Social Psychology* 11: 489–506.

Kassin, S. M., and Wrightsman, L. S. (1985). Confession evidence. In Kassin and Wrightsman (eds.), *The psychology of evidence and trial procedure*. Beverly Hills, CA: Sage.

Katzev, R. D., and Wishart, S. S. (1985). The impact of judicial commentary concerning eyewitness identifications on jury decision making. *Journal of Criminal Law and Criminology* 76: 733–45.

Kerr, N. L.; Atkin, R. S.; Stasser, G.; Meek, D.; Holt, R. W.; and Davis, J. H. (1976). Guilt beyond a reasonable doubt: effects of concept definition and assigned decision rule on the judgments of mock jurors. *Journal of Personality and Social Psychology* 34: 282–94.

Kline, F. G., and Jess, P. H. (1966). Prejudicial publicity: its effect on law school mock juries. *Journalism Quarterly* 43: 113–16.

LaTour, S.; Houlden, P.; Walker, L.; and Thibaut, J. (1976). Procedure: transnational perspectives and preferences. *Yale Law Journal* 84: 258–90.

Lind, E. A.; Erickson, B. E.; Friedland, N.; and Dickenberger, M. (1978). Reactions to procedural models for adjudicative conflict resolution. *Journal of Conflict Resolution* 22: 318–41.

Lind, E. A.; Kurtz, S.; Musante, L.; Walker, L.; and Thibaut, J. (1980). Procedure and outcome effects on reactions to adjudicated resolutions of conflicts of interest. *Journal of Personality and Social Psychology* 39: 643–53.

Lind, E. A.; Thibaut, J.; and Walker, L. (1973). Discovery and presentation of evidence in adversary and nonadversary proceedings. *Michigan Law Review* 71: 1129–44.

Loh, W. D. (1985). The evidence and trial procedure: the law, social policy, and psychological research. In S. M. Kassin and L. S. Wrightsman (eds.), *The psychology of evidence and trial procedure.* Beverly Hills, CA: Sage.

O'Barr, W. M., and Conley, J. M. (1985). Litigant satisfaction versus legal adequacy in small claims court narratives. *Law and Society Review* 19: 661–701.

O'Barr, W. M., and Lind, E. A. (1981). Ethnography and experimentation—partners in legal research. In B. D. Sales (ed.), *Perspectives in psychology and law: the trial process,* vol. 2. New York: Plenum.

O'Mara, J. J. (1972). The courts, standard jury charges—findings of pilot project. *Pennsylvania Bar Journal* 120: 166–75.

Padawer-Singer, A. M., and Barton, A. H. (1975). The impact of pretrial publicity on jurors' verdicts. In R. J. Simon (ed.), *The jury system in America: a critical overview.* Beverly Hills, CA: Sage.

Pryor, B.; Taylor, K. P.; Buchanan, R. W.; and Strawn, D. U. (1980). An affective-cognitive consistency explanation for comprehension of standard jury instructions. *Communication Monographs* 47: 68–76.

Reinard, J. C. (1985). The effects of witness inadmissible testimony on jury decisions: a comparison of four sources. Paper presented at the annual convention of the Western Speech Communication Association, Fresno, CA.

Riley, S. G. (1973). Pretrial publicity: a field study. *Journalism Quarterly* 50: 17–23.

Shaffer, R. A. (1986). Pretrial publicity: media coverage and guilt attribution. *Communication Quarterly* 34: 154–69.

Simon, R. J. (1966). Murder, juries and the press: does sensational reporting lead to verdicts of guilty? *Transaction* 3: 40–42.

Sohn, A. B. (1976). Determining guilt or innocence of accused from pretrial news stories. *Journalism Quarterly* 53: 100–105.

Sue, S.; Smith, R. E.; and Caldwell, C. (1973). Effects of inadmissible evidence on the decisions of simulated jurors: a moral dilemma. *Journal of Applied Social Psychology* 3: 344–53.

Sutton, G. (1979). Effects of inadmissible evidence on jury deliberations. Paper presented at the annual convention of the Speech Communication Association, San Antonio.

Tans, M. D., and Chaffee, S. H. (1966). Pretrial publicity and juror prejudice. *Journalism Quarterly* 43: 647–54.

Thibaut, J., and Walker, L. (1975). *Procedural justice: a psychological analysis.* Hillsdale, NJ: Erlbaum.

Tyler, T. R. (1984). The role of perceived injustice in defendants' evaluations of their courtroom experience. *Law and Society* 18: 51–74.

Walker, L.; LaTour, S.; Lind, E. A.; and Thibaut, J. (1974). Reactions of participants and observers to modes of adjudication. *Journal of Applied Social Psychology* 4: 295–310.

Walker, L.; Lind, E. A.; and Thibaut, J. (1979). The relation between procedural and distributive justice. *Virginia Law Review* 65: 1401.

Wanamaker, L. (1937). Trial by jury. *University of Cincinnati Law Review* 11: 191–200.

Wolf, S., and Montgomery, D. A. (1977). Effects of inadmissible evidence and level of judicial admonishment on the judgments of mock jurors. *Journal of Applied Social Psychology* 7: 205–19.

Chapter 4

JURY SELECTION

Juries function as the voice of the community. In that voice the jury symbolizes freedom from persecution and forms the cornerstone of liberty for the average American citizen. Yet the jury is not without its antagonists. Before and since the time Socrates was condemned to death by a jury of 501 members, critics have called for the abolition of juries. At the heart of the criticisms made by those who oppose juries are nagging doubts that laypersons can render just and equitable decisions concerning highly complex events and ideas. Despite such critical questions Americans hold the jury as sacred, partly due to a history in which trial by jury defended the populace against political repression. In the United states the trial by jury has become a cherished touchstone of democracy.

Ideally juries constitute a representative cross section of the community. The courts have reasoned that representativeness is essential for ensuring the ability to interpret complex facts. By relying on a set of diverse backgrounds and talents, juries composed of members representative of the community are thought to be superior problem solvers, conducting more robust deliberations by generating more arguments for both sides. Moreover, more heterogeneous juries are generally believed to render decisions that are more fair and just than those made by judges.

Beyond the issue of representativeness lies the question of impartiality. The U.S. Constitution guarantees the accused the right to a trial by an impartial jury. To ensure impartiality, attorneys are afforded the right to question prospective jurors. This process is most often referred to as "voir dire," meaning "to speak or say the truth." Lawyers ask potential jurors to speak the truth and reveal any prejudice they hold concerning the case. As the Supreme Court recently stated in its opinion of Rosales-Lopez v. the United States:

> Voir dire plays a critical function in assuring the criminal defendant that his Sixth Amendment right to an impartial jury will be honored. Without an adequate voir dire the trial judge's responsibility to remove prospective jurors who will not be able impartially to follow the court's instructions and evaluate the evidence cannot be fulfilled.

66

The practice of questioning jurors to discover bias originated in the United States following the Revolution. Because of a more mobile and heterogeneous population, information about potential jurors before a trial became increasingly hard to obtain. To combat juror anonymity the courts expanded the right of litigants to question jurors. The turning point of this expansion occurred in the treason trial of Aaron Burr in 1807. Chief Justice John Marshall allowed an extensive voir dire on the grounds that any juror who had formed a firm opinion on any significant point in the case could not be deemed an impartial juror. The Burr case was widely cited by courts of the nineteenth century and allowed for the evolution of what we know today as jury selection (Gold 1984).

Before discussing current research in voir dire, we must first outline the process of selection and define several terms. To begin with, we will discuss the rules surrounding the impaneling process.

After prospective jurors are selected from a community list (such as voter registration) and assembled for selection, lawyers from both sides exercise challenges against the inclusion of particular jurors. This process continues until a jury acceptable to both sides is impaneled. The challenges in this process take one of two forms: challenge for cause or peremptory challenge. During the voir dire jurors are asked questions pertaining to their knowledge of the case and its agents as well as to their ability to remain impartial during the presentation of evidence in the case. If, through questioning, a prospective juror demonstrates to the judge that he or she is biased or prejudiced in any way, the judge will dismiss that individual for cause. Attorneys who wish to challenge a juror for cause must identify for the court the biases which would preclude a juror from rendering an impartial verdict. Age, race, religion, gender, and other general indicators of belief do not constitute adequate reason for cause; attorneys must rely on other means to exclude jurors for any reason other than self-acknowledged bias. Since the turn of the century the courts have increasingly recognized the influence of unconscious prejudices on jurors. To offset such bias, attorneys are afforded the use of peremptory challenges. Peremptory challenges are votes of rejection left solely to the discretion of the attorneys. Each side commonly has a prescribed number of challenges which can be used to exclude any juror for any reason deemed worthy by counsel. The number of peremptory challenges usually varies by jurisdiction and the seriousness of the offense.

Those unfamiliar with jury selection must remember that voir dire is a process of impaneling a jury by exclusion. Lawyers do not decide who serves on a jury, only who is to be prohibited from serving. Lawyers do try to seat jurors likely to favor their cause, but a juror highly favorable to one side will typically be rejected by the other side. In that way opposing lawyers cancel each other out.

Although court rules directing and restricting voir dire vary from jurisdiction to jurisdiction, generally three procedural models are employed throughout the country. Within the "federal" model attorneys are prevented from asking questions directly. Instead, all questions are posed to the judge, who decides upon their merit. The judge then conducts the voir dire with those questions he or she deems appropriate. In the more popular "state" model counsel conducts the questioning with only limited input from the bench. Judges tend to interject only when they deem a questions to be inappropriate because it is offensive or unfairly addresses upcoming evidence in the trial. A third model is commonly called the "struck" method. In this model the critical distinction is in how jurors are retained. Questioning is conducted either in the state or federal model; after each side exercises its challenges, whoever remains serves as the jury. For example, if a six-person jury is to be selected and each attorney has six peremptory challenges, then of the eighteen persons originally called, the remaining six are sworn in and the rest are released.

THE GOALS OF VOIR DIRE

Aside from the obvious objective of discerning juror bias through questioning, three subsidiary goals drive the voir dire: establishing juror rapport, obtaining juror commitment, and previewing the case. Before describing the research surrounding selection criteria, we will first discuss these three goals and the research related to their accomplishment.

ESTABLISHING RAPPORT.   Voir dire represents the only occasion during the trial where jurors have the opportunity to interact with counsel; that is to say, it is the only time jurors can respond to questions posed by counsel. Thus voir dire is the ideal time for attorneys to establish rapport with jurors, ensuring receptivity to the messages they will offer throughout the trial. With established rapport jurors will be more likely to see themselves as similar to the attorney and see counsel as more likable and trustworthy. A wealth of research acknowledges that both perceived similarity and greater affinity enhances the effectiveness of persuasive messages. (We discuss this research in chapter 6.)

Rapport with jurors has other benefits as well. By gaining rapport counsel can elicit increased self-disclosure and honesty during questioning. Not surprisingly, juror dishonesty is a serious problem for lawyers. Potential jurors often conceal pertinent information during voir dire. In one study of 225 jurors who had served in 23 cases, researchers found jurors commonly withheld information reflecting possible bias (Broeder 1965). Despite a pledge or oath to tell the truth, jurors often deceive questioners as a means of positive self-presentation. Under close scrutiny and with the added pressure to perform well under new circumstances, jurors become concerned about their self-image. They experience a strong desire to be believed by attorneys and judges, often resulting in nervousness and embarrassment. This evaluation anxiety sometimes leads to sophistry. The results of one study employing post–jury service interviews revealed that the greater the anxiety reported by ex-jurors, the more dishonest they were during voir dire (Marshall and Smith 1986).

To circumvent juror dishonesty attorneys often turn to humor to elicit a favorable reaction from jurors. Although humor is used by some attorneys throughout the trial, it is most often employed during voir dire because probing questions create visible anxiety in jurors. In an attempt to ease the tension these questions create and to reduce anxiety, attorneys sometimes resort to self-deprecating humor. Since humor is well received only when its timing and content are considered appropriate for a given social context, its use in the courtroom is especially precarious. Although specific advice on the use of humor depends heavily on the situation and people involved, research does allow us to make several useful generalizations concerning its use in the courtroom.

Humor assists speakers in gaining attention and audience interest as well as boosting evaluations of friendliness. By relaxing jurors and establishing similarity in what one finds funny, humor may enable attorneys to quickly establish rapport with venirepersons. Indeed, several researchers have confirmed that humor does aid in establishing and maintaining rapport with an audience (Markiewicz 1974; Gruner 1970; Freedman and Perlick 1979). But although humor may enhance the evaluation of the persuader, humor has not been found to be more persuasive toward a subject or object. That is to say, a humorous message is not more persuasive than a nonhumorous message, all else held constant (Brooker 1981; Gelb and Pickett 1983; Markiewicz 1974). Considering that lawyers, unlike advertisers, generally do not employ humor to persuade, they appear on safe ground when incorporating humor in their messages. Yet researchers cannot agree whether humor facilitates or hinders recall and comprehension of a message. This dispute aside, attorneys must also be wary of the type of humor they use. In particular, self-disparaging humor is sometimes harmful.

Like other speakers lawyers sometimes poke fun at themselves to create a more relaxed climate for a presentation. Such self-disparaging humor uses the self as the object of humorous comment. The use of self-disparaging humor directed at one's occupation or profession increases a speaker's perceived "wittiness" and sense of humor (Chang and Gruner 1981). But when this humor is directed more at the self than one's occupation or profession—such as one's personal shortcomings—research reveals that ratings of competence decrease (Gruner 1985; Hackman 1988).

While no general rules for the use of humor exist, lawyers are cautioned to take both the advantages and disadvantages into account before incorporating humor into their courtroom presentations. Moreover, a general reading of the research underscores the need for attorneys to strategically plan the use of humor in any aspect of the trial. In short, speaking from the cuff might not be very funny in the long run.

OBTAINING COMMITMENTS.   Obtaining commitments from jurors relating to issues crucial to the case at hand is another essential goal of voir dire. Asking a juror publicly to commit himself or herself to a belief is an effective means of increasing resistance to subsequent persuasive appeal (Kiesler 1971). An enormous research literature suggests that once people make a commitment, they tend to behave in a manner consistent with that commitment. And once made public, commitments are even more powerful for ensuring behavioral consistency.

To achieve this public reinforcement lawyers often ask questions of commitment to individual jurors and receive answers that are on the record and heard by other jurors. To further this reinforcement attorneys often remind jurors of their commitments during the summation.

Attorneys have two important directions in which to obtain commitments. First, jury antipathy toward rules of law can jeopardize a defendant's right to an impartial jury. Asking prospective jurors about their willingness to follow specific rules of law is not enough. When the court allows, attorneys are best advised to seek public agreements including the commitment to follow the law, commitment to duty as a juror, and commitment to set aside prejudice (Morrill 1972). The specific case will naturally dictate appropriate commitment topics, such as the right to have no adverse inference drawn when the defendant does not testify. Second, a commitment can be used to enhance reception to one's case. For example, the commitment to remain open-minded throughout the trial or not to judge a defendant based on his physical features can ensure jury compliance and have dramatic effects on jury behavior.

PREVIEWING THE CASE.   A third goal of voir dire is to preview the case so that jurors may orient themselves to the evidence most favorable to counsel's case. Although the court will not permit selection questions that prejudice jurors toward facts in the case, most judges will allow attorneys to question jurors concerning central issues in the case. In the process of this questioning trial manuals advise lawyers to lay the groundwork for the opening statement, employing words and statements that favor counsel's interpretation of the evidence. Although technically lawyers cannot educate the jurors about the case until the opening statement, one study confirmed the pursuit of this goal by attorneys in voir dire practices. That study showed that more than 40 percent of lawyers' communication was directed toward creating positive impressions and laying the foundation for the case (Balch, Griffiths, Hall, and Winfree 1976).

IMPANELING THE JURY

DEMOGRAPHIC AND PERSONALITY FEATURES OF JURORS.   Predicting juror bias is a formidable task, one that requires all the resources at hand. The most popular of these resources are the demographic and personality features displayed by jurors. Limited evidence indicates that lawyers themselves use the factors of gender, race, age, and attitudes toward conviction (whether few or many defendants avoid conviction due to legal technicalities) to predict juror predispositions (Turner, Lovell, Young, and Denny 1986). Unfortunately, the use of these predictors often does nothing more than allay the fears of counsel. Several reviews have concluded that even when armed with current knowledge in this area lawyers can often do no better than to eliminate openly prejudiced persons (e.g., Hans and Vidmar 1982). Taken together, demographic and personality variables do not offer adequate safeguards against bias.

Naturally enough, lawyers often raise the question: Is jury selection just a crapshoot? One innovative study suggests the answer is No. Because it is usually impossible to know how excluded jurors would respond in the jury box, researchers in one study arranged for challenged jurors in twelve criminal trials to serve as mock jurors (Zeisel and Diamond 1978). The challenged jurors witnessed the complete trial and then deliberated and returned a verdict. In comparison to the actual juries, the mock juries returned the same verdict in seven of twelve trials. In the remaining five trials, however, the real jury either returned a different verdict or was less likely to convict than was the mock jury. This aptly illustrates the possible efficacy of jury selection.

Despite this encouragement a more pragmatic question remains: What factors should receive attention during voir dire? The answer is perplexing. The advocate's task, simply stated, is to identify and correct for juror bias. Peremptory challenges are commonly based on presumed links between demographic and personality variables and a tendency for jurors to favor the state or the defendant. A thorough review of this literature, however, reveals that no clear-cut relationship between social categories or individual traits and jury behavior exists. Nonetheless, several interesting relationships have emerged. In this section we will summarize these findings, paying particular attention to those variables lawyers traditionally have relied upon.

Gender differences. As with many other demographic differences, studies examining the relationship between juror gender and verdict predisposition are mixed. Whereas several studies have found males more likely to convict and more punitive in recommending sentences for a defendant judged guilty (e.g., Morrow 1974; Simon 1967; Steffensmeier 1977), other studies show that females are more conviction prone and punitive than males (e.g., Austin, Walster, and Utne 1976; Griffitt and Jackson 1973; Scroggs 1976). This inconsistency is further compounded by a significant number of studies that report no gender differences (e.g., Nemeth, Endicott, and Wachtler 1976). In those cases where differences between the sexes do exist, undoubtedly they rest upon the nature of the offense. This is demonstrated by a consistent finding in rape cases. Predictably, females are more likely to convict and give harsher sentences in cases of rape than are males (Miller and Hewitt 1978; Rumsey and Rumsey 1977). Also not surprising is the finding that males are more likely than females to presume that the victim was partially to blame (Calhoun, Selby, Cann, and Keller 1978).

Racial bias. Attorneys commonly assume that black jurors are more prone to acquit defendants than are white jurors. A study of 121 criminal trials in Louisiana confirmed this belief. Results revealed that prosecutors were indeed more likely to exclude black jurors and defense attorneys were more apt to exclude Caucasian jurors, regardless of the defendant's race (Turner et al. 1986). Although attorneys tenaciously believe in this racial tendency, empirical evidence in support of this bias is not available. Evidence is also lacking for other racial beliefs. For example, many attorneys believe that highly dogmatic and authoritarian persons are more intolerant of minority and ethnic groups in general. They extend this supposition in jury selection, assuming that such rigid thinkers would be racially prejudiced. Again, the absence of research in this area leaves many unanswered questions.

Although more research is desperately needed in racial bias, many general assumptions have been confirmed. In a culture still plagued by racism, it is not surprising that black defendants are commonly judged more harshly than are white defendants (Thornberry 1973). Research also demonstrates that whites and blacks display a bias for their own race. Essentially, whites are more severe when the victim is white, while blacks are more severe when the victim is black (Ugwuegbu 1976). As one would expect, evidence strength moderates racial prejudice. Although it is more likely for jurors to find defendants of another race guilty of rape charges, guilt assessments were found to be dependent upon several factors including evidence type (Ugwuegbu 1979). In one study examining racial bias, when little incriminating evidence existed racial prejudice did not influence assessments of guilt. The same was true when substantial evidence existed against the accused rapist. Only when the evidence was marginal did jurors tend to judge other-race defendants more harshly.

Other work also reveals a race and gender interaction. Although black females tend to perceive crime as less serious than do either white females or all males, limited evidence suggests they are more likely to believe a defendant is guilty before the trial (Mills and Bohannon 1980).

Age, education, status, and occupation. The general scarcity of research in demographic factors easily ascertained from jurors is puzzling. Given the enormous interest in related work during the last three decades, one might surmise that researchers have failed to find relationships between common demographic factors and jury behavior and have therefore foregone publication. Whatever the reason, generalization from the existing research base is risky.

The most studied variable in this group is juror age. Several studies have shown that younger jurors have a greater tendency to acquit than do older persons (Stephen and Tully 1977). This is consistent with the general finding that more liberal people are prone to acquittal. Since older persons are generally found to be more conservative than younger people, they tend to exhibit a greater tendency to convict. In one study, 84 percent of jurors over sixty years old believed that a witness who took the Fifth Amendment was hiding guilt, whereas only 12 percent of the eighteen- to thirty-year-old age group concurred with this belief (Zeigler 1978). Although evidence in support of political affiliation is also scarce, one study supports this finding. In a study of over six thousand jurors, one researcher found that registered Democrats tend to favor the plaintiff in a civil case, rendering more favorable judgments as well as awarding greater compensation (Hermann 1970).

Education is of less help as a predictor. Although education exerts a strong liberalizing effect between age and conservatism, one study found that highly educated persons are more conviction prone (Reed 1965). Nor does juror occupation reveal much, although one civil analysis found that more favorable verdicts were awarded in civil law suits when the occupation of the jurors and the plaintiff was similar (Van Dyke 1977). Similarly, disparity of socioeconomic standing influences ratings of guilt. In one analysis the greater socio-economic disparity between defendants and jurors, the greater was the likelihood of a conviction (Adler 1973). In another study higher status jurors, those who defined themselves as upper class, were found to be more punitive than those of lower status, also defined by their own accord (Rose and Prell 1955).

Authoritarianism and rigidity. Unlike other personality traits, none of which have proven reliable predictors of jury behavior, authoritarianism has yielded fairly consistent results. High authoritarians have a propensity to reach more guilty verdicts than do low authoritarians, especially in murder cases (Bray and Noble 1978). Consistent with the trait, this inclination is known to reverse in cases involving a defendant who is in a position of authority or whose defense involves the justification that she or he was acting under orders (Hamilton 1978). Furthermore, several studies have concluded that highly dogmatic or authoritarian jurors recommend harsher sentences than their low dogmatic or low authoritarian peers (Boehm 1968; Mitchell and Byrne 1973). This punitive tendency is particularly acute when the defendant is perceived to have a low status, negative character, or dissimilar attitudes.

Authoritarianism is characterized by rigidity, moralism, and conservatism (Adorno, Frenkel-Brunswick, Levinson, and Sanford 1950). In other words, authoritarians see the world in blacks and whites. Moreover, authoritarians are exceedingly punitive and intolerant of opposing viewpoints and lower status persons, although they are deferential to authority figures. Consistent with this characterization are findings that high and low authoritarians recall evidence differently, and that high authoritarians are more resistant to persuasive attempts during deliberation (Berg and Vidmar 1975;

Christie 1976). Also congruent is the finding that liberal jurors tend to give more lenient sentences than their conservative counterparts (Nemeth and Sosis 1973).

Similar to authoritarianism, dogmatism is generally described as a more generalized form of authoritarianism that is void of political overtones. Like their authoritarian relatives, dogmatics share an intolerance for the unconventional. In one recent investigation of dogmatism researchers exposed mock jurors to either a conventional (heterosexual) or nonconventional (homosexual) defendant who was on trial for murder (Shaffer and Case 1982). As predicted, dogmatic jurors were more likely to judge homosexual defendants as guilty and more deserving of conviction than were nondogmatic jurors. In another study, which examined the dogmatic tendencies of the total jury rather than individual jurors, researchers also found dogmatic juries to be more punitive than less dogmatic juries (Shaffer, Plummer, and Hammock 1986). In that study investigators uncovered a connection between dogmatism and defendant suffering. Researchers had previously found that jurors exhibit a general leniency toward suffering defendants, especially those whose suffering was related to the criminal action in question (Austin, Walster, and Utne 1976). Highly dogmatic jurors, however, view defendant suffering differently. Whereas nondogmatic juries assigned shorter sentences to defendants whose injuries were crime related rather than unrelated, in contrast dogmatic juries assigned longer sentences to defendants whose suffering was crime related. Researchers claim this finding is indicative of dogmatic beliefs. Since dogmatics believe in a "just world" where people get what they deserve, dogmatic jurors view the crime-related injuries sustained by a defendant as just deserts.

Attitudes toward capital punishment. Until the landmark decision in Witherspoon v. Illinois in 1968, jurors with scruples against capital punishment were challenged for cause and excluded from jury service in capital cases. Only recently, then, have death-penalty attitudes created concern for lawyers in challenging jurors. This anxiety, however, is not without its benefits. Attitudes toward capital punishment have proven a strong indicator of jury behavior. Not only are those who favor capital punishment more likely to choose the death penalty, but they are also more conviction prone. In other words, a favorable attitude toward capital punishment has been found to predict higher conviction rates and more severe sentences when the case involves lesser crimes (Bronson 1970; Cowan, Thomson, and Ellsworth 1987; Goldberg 1969; Jurow 1971). Several scholars have tendered the explanation that attitudes toward capital punishment reflect a deeper proclivity toward conservatism and authoritarianism. This is consistent with claims that individuals who favor capital punishment tend be white, professionals, wealthy, and Republican (Vidmar and Ellsworth 1974).

Locus of control and responsibility. Several scholars have proposed that attribution of responsibility in criminal and civil cases depends heavily on the similarities between the defendant and the jurors. In one study involving attributions of responsibility in a car accident, subjects assigned less responsibility to a behaviorally similar victim than a dissimilar one (McKillip and Posavac 1975). In another study, subjects who were dissimilar to a car owner involved in an accident rated him more responsible than did those who were similar to him (Shaver 1970). Although this defensive attribution generally does not apply to mildly negative consequences, actors judge similar actors as less responsible for serious outcomes, while dissimilar actors are judged more responsible in adversely serious events.

To explain this similarity effect researchers have recently turned to the extensively investigated concept of control (Rotter 1966; Lefcourt 1982). In regard to control over the rewards and punishments in life, people tend to fall into one of two camps. Internals believe that rewards and punishments in life are a direct result of matters internal to themselves, such as hard work, talent, and personal traits. Externals, on the other hand, believe that rewards and punishments are contingent on external forces, such as fate, powerful others, and luck. This "locus of control," as it is known, has proven a promising predictor of responsibility and similarity.

On the whole, internals attribute significantly more responsibility to accident victims than do externals (Sosis 1974). This is even true when the causal relationship between the victim and accident is ambiguous (Phares and Wilson 1972). This effect may be tempered by similarity, however. Limited research has shown that internals assign greater responsibility to agents involved in a severe crime when they were attitudinally similar to the defendant (Kauffman and Ryckman 1979). This attribution did not occur, however, for less severe crimes or with dissimilar defendants. Conversely, externals were found to attribute greater responsibility for a severe crime when they were attitudinally dissimilar to the defendant. It appears as if internals judge similar others harshly but do not extend this severity to dissimilar others. Apparently externals may need to distance themselves from dissimilar others and do so by attributing more responsibility to them.

The severity of an accident may also moderate perceived responsibility. Most notably, when jurors believe the severity of an accident mandates compensation, they are more apt to find fault. The relationship between fault and liability to compensate is not as direct as many believe. Limited evidence suggests that people often believe an accident victim is entitled to compensation even when they do not believe anyone is at fault. An analysis of one thousand accident victims in Great Britain revealed that persons attribute fault as a means of justifying compensation, not the other way around (Lloyd-Bostock 1979). In other words, if people believe a person is entitled to compensation and also, from an awareness of law, believe that compensation must be justified by fault, they will attribute fault to justify compensation. In many cases, then, a belief in compensation entitlement precedes the attribution of responsibility. This is consistent with another study which revealed that greater damages in an accident resulted in great attribution of responsibility (Walster 1966). For practical purposes these findings translate directly to civil litigation. Jurors will vary in their beliefs about outcome severity and the point at which any victim should be compensated. These beliefs may prove useful in predicting attributions of responsibility in civil cases.

Prior jury experience. Many lawyers believe that prior jury experience heavily prejudices a juror's ability to remain impartial. This perceived bias is commonly attributed to jurors' reliance on facts and beliefs acquired in previous trials when interpreting new evidence and information. Limited evidence supports this view.

Research has revealed that attitudes formed through direct behavioral experience are more predictive of later behavior than are attitudes stemming from indirect experience or hearsay (Fazio and Zanna 1981). More importantly, attitudes originating in prior experience have been found to be more resistant to change (Wu and Shaffer 1987). Research also confirms that jurors with prior experience may be more than just intransigent listeners. In one study of 206 criminal cases, although no individual juror's experience was found to affect verdicts, juries containing a high proportion of experienced jurors displayed an increase in conviction rate (Werner, Strube, Cole, and Kagehiro 1985).

Most jurisdictions will allow counsel to discuss prior jury experience, although the depth to which this discussion may be carried varies from state to state. At a minimum lawyers can ascertain if prospective jurors have prior experience and, if so, whether they served in a civil or criminal case.

Alternatives. As a result of the poor record of selecting jurors by focusing upon demographic and personality variables, lawyers have recently turned to alternative strategies to aid them in the jury selection process. Most popular among these strategies is to employ social science methodologies to identify juror bias and to use narrative theory as a foundation for predicting juror receptivity.

SCIENTIFIC JURY SELECTION.   Scientific or systematic jury selection commonly refers to the use of social science methodologies applied to the problem of identifying juror bias. The most popular techniques involve the use of community opinion surveys and the charting of ideal juror profiles. By conducting a survey of local citizens concerning the issues and agents involved in a case, questioners develop demographic profiles of desirable and less desirable jurors. For example, survey researchers might find females under forty who work full-time in the local community to hold more favorable attitudes toward a key aspect or agent in a case. Hence, potential jurors in that demographic group would be favored by counsel during selection.

Attorneys, of course, cannot tamper with the jury by contacting them outside of the courtroom; yet nothing prevents counsel from seeking information indirectly through a juror's friends and associates. Another technique is to interview persons who possess reliable knowledge about a juror or to seek out public documents, such as driving records or financial statements, that can be used to infer status or traits. Research supporting the superiority of these techniques over more traditional approaches to selection is not yet available (Hans and Vidmar 1982). But the recent popularity of scientific jury selection in its many forms compels us to describe an additional procedure and to add a word of warning. Currently more widely employed than either community surveys or reliance on indirect sources is the systematic observation of prospective jurors' courtroom behavior. The popularity of scientific jury selection has prompted lawyers to go so far as to employ social scientists, psychiatrists, soothsayers, and sundry other professionals to observe jurors and expose bias. Unfortunately, much of what passes as scientific observation is a fabrication.

The term "scientific" is a loaded concept in our culture, denoting proofs and the systematic investigation of a phenomenon. When we think of a process as scientific, most of us conceive of a process void of values and free of its own bias. In regard to some "scientific" jury selection, nothing could be further from the truth. Scientific jury selection in its best form is simply community or courtroom research involving systematic attention to the problem of bias. This observation has the potential of yielding valuable insights, since much of the attention brought to bear in this process is grounded in the current state of our knowledge about human behavior. Other systematic approaches, however, have not kept pace. This is especially true of selection based on the detection of bias through nonverbal markers. By exaggerating claims several commercial research firms have attempted to pass off canards of nonverbal behavior as proprietary wisdom. Much like astrologers, these trial consultants attempt to predict jury behavior from stereotypical signs, ranging from particular nonverbal behaviors to the dress or cosmetics worn by prospective jurors. As many scholars have pointed out, the grandiose claims of nonverbal translation rest on a nonexistent foundation (Reinard 1986). Evidence for generalizing from juror idiosyncrasies does not exist, and claims based on this evidence are generally without foundation. However tempting the quick fix might seem, we appeal to the better judgment of lawyers looking for honest answers.

SELECTION BASED ON STORY CONNECTIONS.   Also tempting is the specious premise that personality and demographic factors leading to juror predispositions will override the evidentiary features of a case. Evidence, as will be explained in our chapter on evidence and testimony, is the most powerful predictor of jury verdicts. Although demographic and personality variables enable attorneys to make intelligent challenges, their overall effect in eliminating jury bias is rather small. A promising alternative to this isolated variable approach is jury selection based on the storytelling theory outlined in chapter 2. Not only is this theory heuristic in explaining jury behavior, but a storytelling framework also accounts for evidentiary effects. In this concluding section we will fully explore the implications of storytelling for jury selection.

THE APPLICATION OF STORYTELLING.   If one recalls the central premises underlying the storytelling perspective, the practical application of this theory becomes obvious. Recall that the storytelling perspective operates primarily from three assumptions: (1) When attempting to make sense of the complex information and events presented during the trial, jurors will construct stories for each side by first discerning a central action. (2) Once this central action is identified, jurors then arrange the supporting elements in relation to this action. These elements include the scene, the agency, the agents, and the purposes or motives of the agents. (3) To interpret and judge the stories jurors first assess the structural consistency of the story by identifying missing elements. Fidelity of the story is then assessed when jurors make connections between the elements offered. These connections, which will be either consistent or inconsistent in relation to the central action and each other, depend on personal knowledge based upon experience, social categories, stereotypes, and norms.

A jury selection strategy based on this theory assumes that possible juror bias is a function of the relationship between a juror's knowledge and the story elements presented in the case. In other words, jurors will make negative story connections when their beliefs and values fail to support the intended force of the story elements. A selection strategy from this view is not a question of whether or not a juror possesses bias, but rather is a probability of bias based on the interaction of story elements and juror knowledge. Since counsel knows before a trial what actions and elements will generally be presented on both sides, possible negative interactions can be calculated and used during voir dire. The primary assumption of this strategy lies with identification. Attorneys can assume that when a juror's world knowledge (experience, values, beliefs, etc.) enable him or her to identify closely with a story element or action, then the probability of a consistent connection is either enhanced or diminished, depending on the elements in question. Favorable or unfavorable connections depend, of course, on the desired consistency of the elements. It is important to note that lawyers may sometimes wish to foster inconsistency as a means of exposing the ambiguity of the opponent's story. (For instance, imagine a story where counsel accounts for the defendant's behavior but leaves other agents' actions ambiguous.) Identification and knowledge serve only to intensify the connections made by jurors.

As an example of the story approach, suppose that the constructed story for the prosecution in a fraud case turns on the defendant having driven a motorcycle within range of an automatic teller machine. Further suppose that in this prosecution story the defendant spied on customers from a distance of 30 feet and collected customer identification codes which he later used to his benefit. According to the prosecutor, the defendant depended on his eyesight to identify the code numbers. From the storytelling perspective what juror features might increase the likelihood of consistent or inconsistent connections? First, we must delineate the story elements. The central action for this sequence is the collection of transaction codes. Other elements include the agents (the defendant and miscellaneous customers), the agency (eyesight), and the scene (man sitting on motorcycle 30 feet from teller machine). The purpose is not stated directly but can be assumed to be fraud. The question is not what types of jurors would respond favorably or unfavorably to this story; rather the question is what juror knowledge may affect the probability of favorable or unfavorable connections. The prosecutor wants these story connections to be viewed as consistent; the defense, of course, is hoping for ambiguity leading to inconsistency. When confronted with a problem like this one, the attorney's task is to reason through the knowledge and story element interactions. In this problem several logical questions might be raised by an average person: Can a person identify numbers accurately from a distance of 30 feet? Moreover, can this be done while sitting on a motorcycle? Juror knowledge concerning both eyesight and motorcycles, then, may intensify interpretation. Since identification is the vital link between knowledge and story connections, attorneys may also want to ascertain the answers to two other questions: Which of the jurors frequently use a banking machine? Do any of the jurors use that particular teller machine and know the scene? From these general questions lawyers can compose voir dire questions that logically and theoretically expose juror knowledge and identification concerning the story. While questions like "From what distance can an adult accurately identify telephone buttons?" will be prohibited by the court because of their prejudicial nature, the court will commonly allow such questions as "To what degree does one's eyesight weaken with age?" Or "Have you any knowledge of optometry?"

We can further illustrate this approach with a more complete example. Consider a civil case with the following facts.

The plaintiff, James Jones, was fourteen years old when he sustained serious personal injuries by electricity. The youth had climbed a pole, located on property owned by Southern Telegraph, on which utility wires were strung. Jones was an admitted trespasser on the property, and later told authorities that he climbed the pole to view an insulator which appeared to him to be of ancient vintage. He did not know he was in danger. Damages sought by the plaintiff include medical expenses, physical disability, disfigurement from burns, and loss of earning capacity.

In selecting a jury by means of storytelling theory, lawyers for the plaintiff or the defense would dissect the story and its elements and then compose questions which would enable counsel to infer juror knowledge and possible identification regarding those elements.

The central action for the facts as presented is the youth receiving an electrical charge. Secondary to this action is climbing a utility pole. No information as to how the charge occurred is provided. The agency for this action is the boy's body, and the scene elements include utility wires and an insulator, presumably atop the pole, and the ambiguous space termed "property." The self-acknowledged motive for this action was the boy's interest in insulators. Based on this breakdown, attorneys for either side should attempt to assess juror knowledge of five central areas: (1) identification or experience with children; (2) identification with an accident experience; (3) identification with or knowledge of Southern Telegraph; (4) knowledge of electricity; and (5) identification or experience with trespass. These issues naturally give rise to questions that may reflect this knowledge.

Identification with children. Questions might include: Do you have any children? any sons? how old? How much time do you spend with children? Do you live with or around families with teen-agers? Have you ever had a problem with teen-agers in your neighborhood? Does your occupation require contact with children or youths? How should children be disciplined? Do teen-agers have a malicious tendency?

Identification with an accident experience. Possible questions include: Have you or your children ever been seriously injured? Has anyone you know been in a serious accident? Do you know anyone who works with burn patients? Are any of your children or those you know handicapped? disfigured? Is anyone in your circle of friends in the health profession? Have you ever been in a situation where a child under your care was harmed? Do you require your children to wear seat belts?

Knowledge of Southern Telegraph. Questions might include: Do you know anyone who is employed by Southern Telegraph? Have you or anyone you know ever had a dispute with Southern Telegraph? Do you or anyone you know own stock in Southern Telegraph? Do utility companies have a responsibility to society? to the local community? to customers?

Knowledge of electricity. Questions might include: Have you or anyone you know ever been severely shocked? Have you ever visited an electrical plant? Do you live near an electrical facility? Do you have electrical safety features in your home? Who do you know that works with electricity? electrical wires? high voltage?

Identification with trespass. Lawyers might compose such questions as: Do you own property? Do you have a fence surrounding your property? Have you ever had need to post a no-trespass sign? Have you ever knowingly trespassed on private property?

This list is not exhaustive, nor does it necessarily include the best questions for surmising juror knowledge. What these questions do accomplish is to provide a frame for assessing juror identification with story elements. Many of the questions provided also serve the double duty of verifying demographic and personality factors.

In conclusion, despite its intuitive appeal the storytelling approach to voir dire is not without its weaknesses, most notably that it requires a search and seek pattern based on yet a second set of assumptions, those of the attorney who dissects the story. Nevertheless, its promise is further revealed by pondering what data are most relevant for ascertaining juror knowledge and identification; namely, the demographic and personality variables discussed earlier. Rather than using these variables as fixed numbers in an equation, however, as with traditional approaches (such as excluding all liberals or conservatives), they are used as additional sources for inferring identification in a case-by-case system.

Lawyers may believe they already use this system intuitively. At a general level many do. But even though attorneys are narrative creatures, they rarely organize the facts in a case in an explicit story form. By eschewing the procedure of separating actions and elements, attorneys often overlook exactly what connections jurors must make. In addition, the storytelling framework outlines the reasons why incoherency and inconsistency might exist, which further aids in the questioning process. Although the system is indeed commonsensical, like other heuristic devices its value is in precision, not rules. Because a narrative conception of the trial and juror identification with story elements is easily conceived, we believe this approach is particularly auspicious.

As a final illustration, recall the highly publicized New York subway shooting involving Bernard Goetz in December of 1984. As you may remember, Goetz was accused of using unnecessary force to repel the advances of four teen-agers on a New York subway. According to the testimony offered by several witnesses, the youths surrounded Goetz and demanded $5. Goetz, feeling threatened, drew and fired a pistol, striking all four assailants. After a bitter and dramatic trial, Goetz was acquitted of all the major charges against him. Among many interesting features of this case one stands out, especially in light of our discussion in this chapter. Of the twelve jurors who served in the Goetz case, six had been recent victims of crime. Moreover, three of these six jurors had been victims of crime which took place on a New York subway.

REFERENCES

Adler, F. (1973). Socioeconomic factors influencing jury verdicts. *New York University Review of Law and Social Change* 3: 1–10.

Adorno, T. W.; Frenkel-Brunswick, E.; Levinson, D. J.; and Sanford, R. N. (1950). *The authoritarian personality.* New York: Harper and Row.

Austin, W.; Walster, E.; and Utne, M. K. (1976). Equity and the law: the effect of a harmdoer's "suffering in the act" on liking and assigned punishment. In L. Berkowitz and E. Walster (eds.), *Advances in experimental social psychology,* vol. 9. New York: Academic Press.

Balch, R. W.; Griffiths, C. T.; Hall, E. T.; and Winfree, L. T. (1976). Socialization of jurors: the voir dire as a rite of passage. *Journal of Criminal Justice* 4: 271–83.

Berg, K., and Vidmar, N. (1975). Authoritarianism and recall of evidence about criminal behavior. *Journal of Research in Personality* 9: 147–57.

Boehm, V. (1968). Mr. Prejudice, Miss Sympathy, and the authoritarian personality: an application of psychological measuring techniques to the problem of juror bias. *Wisconsin Law Review* 734–50.

Bray, R., and Noble, A. (1978). Authoritarianism and decisions in mock juries: evidence of jury bias and group polarization. *Journal of Personality and Social Psychology* 36: 1424–30.

Broeder, D. W. (1965). Voir dire examinations: an empirical study. *Southern California Law Review* 38: 503–28.

Bronson, E. J. (1970). On the conviction proneness and representativeness of the death-qualified jury: an empirical study of Colorado veniremen. *University of Colorado Law Review* 42: 1–32.

Brooker, G. W. (1981). A comparison of the persuasive effects of mild humor and mild fear appeals. *Journal of Advertising* 10: 29–40.

Calhoun, L. G.; Selby, J. W.; Cann, A.; and Keller, G. T. (1978). The effects of victim physical attractiveness and sex of respondent on social reactions to victims of rape. *British Journal of Social and Clinical Psychology* 17: 191–92.

Chang, M., and Gruner, C. R. (1981). Audience reaction to self-disparaging humor. *Southern Speech Communication Journal* 46: 419–26.

Christie, R. (1976). Probability v. precedence: the social psychology of jury selection. In G. Bermant, C. Nemeth, and N. Vidmar (eds.), *Psychology and the Law.* Lexington, MA: Lexington.

Cowan, C.; Thomson, W.; and Ellsworth, P. (1987). The effects of death qualification on jurors' predisposition to convict and on the quality of deliberation. *Law and Human Behavior* 8: 53–80.

Fazio, R. H., and Zanna, M. P. (1981). Direct experience and attitude-behavior consistency. In L. Berkowitz (ed.), *Advances in experimental social psychology,* vol. 14. New York: Academic Press.

Freedman, J., and Perlick, D. (1979). Crowding, contagion, and laughter. *Journal of Experimental Social Psychology* 15: 295–303.

Gelb, B. D., and Pickett, C. M. (1983). Attitude toward the ad: links to humor and to advertising effectiveness. *Journal of Advertising* 12: 34–42.

Gold, J. H. (1984). Voir dire: questioning prospective jurors on their willingness to follow the law. *Indiana Law Journal* 60: 163–90.

Goldberg, F. (1969). Toward expansion of *Witherspoon:* capital scruples, jury bias, and the use of psychological data to raise presumptions in the law. *Harvard Civil Rights Civil Liberties Law Review* 5: 53.

Griffitt, W., and Jackson, T. (1973). Simulated jury decisions: the influence of jury-defendant attitude similarity-dissimilarity. *Social Behavior and Personality* 1: 1–7.

Gruner, C. R. (1970). The effect of humor in dull and interesting informative speeches. *Central States Speech Journal* 21: 160–66.

Gruner, C. R. (1985). Advice to the beginning speaker on using humor—what the research tells us. *Communication Education* 34: 142–47.

Hackman, M. Z. (1988). Reactions to the use of self-disparaging humor by informative public speakers. *Southern Speech Communication Journal* 53: 175–83.

Hamilton, V. L. (1978). Obedience and responsibility: a jury simulation. *Journal of Personality and Social Psychology* 36: 126–46.

Hans, V. P., and Vidmar, N. (1982). Jury selection. In N. L. Kerr and R. M. Bray (eds.), *The psychology of the courtroom.* New York: Academic Press.

Hermann, P. J. (1970). Occupations of jurors as an influence on their verdict. *The Forum* 5: 150–55.

Jurow, G. L. (1971). New data on the effect of a death-qualified jury on the guilt determination process. *Harvard Law Review* 84: 567–611.

Kauffman, R. A., and Ryckman, R. M. (1979). Effects of locus of control, outcome severity, and attitudinal similarity of defendant on attributions of criminal responsibility. *Personality and Social Psychology Bulletin* 5: 340–43.

Kiesler, C. A. (1971). *The psychology of commitment: experiments linking behavior to belief.* New York: Academic Press.

Lefcourt, H. M. (1982). *Locus of control: current trends in theory and research.* Hillsdale, NJ: Erlbaum.

Lloyd-Bostock, S. M. (1979). Common sense morality and accident compensation. In D. P. Farrington, K. Hawkins, and S. M. Lloyd-Bostock (eds.), *Psychology, law and legal processes.* Atlantic Highlands, NJ: Humanities Press.

McKillip, J., and Posavac, E. J. (1975). Judgments of responsibility for an accident. *Journal of Personality* 43: 248–65.

Markiewicz, D. (1974). Effects of humor on persuasion. *Sociometry* 37: 407–22.

Marshall, L. L., and Smith, A. (1986). The effects of demand characteristics, evaluation anxiety, and expectancy on juror honesty during voir dire. *Journal of Psychology* 120: 205–17.

Miller, M., and Hewitt, J. (1978). Conviction of a defendant as a function of juror-victim racial similarity. *Journal of Social Psychology* 105: 159–60.

Mills, C. J., and Bohannon, W. E. (1980). Juror characteristics: to what extent are they related to jury verdicts? *Judicature* 64: 22–31.

Mitchell, H. E., and Byrne, D. (1973). The defendant's dilemma: effects of jurors' attributions and authoritarianism on judicial decisions. *Journal of Personality and Social Psychology* 25: 123–29.

Morrill. A.E. (1972). *Trial diplomacy*. Chicago: Court Practice Institute.

Morrow, W. G. (1974). Women on juries. *Alberta Law Review* 12: 321.

Nemeth, C.; Endicott, J.; and Wachtler, J. (1976). From the 50's to the 70's: women in jury deliberations. *Sociometry* 39: 293–304.

Nemeth, C., and Sosis, R. H. (1973). A simulated jury study: characteristics of the defendant and the jurors. *Journal of Social Psychology* 90: 221–29.

Phares, E. J., and Wilson, K. G. (1972). Responsibility attribution: role of outcome severity, situational ambiguity, and internal-external control. *Journal of Personality* 40: 392–406.

Reed, J. P. (1965). Jury deliberations, voting and verdict trends. *Southwestern Social Science Quarterly* 45: 361–70.

Reinard, J. C. (1986). Nonverbal communication research in legal settings: considerations of limits and effects. Paper presented at the convention of the Western Speech Communication Association, Tucson.

Rosales-Lopez v. United States, 451 U.S. 182 (1981).

Rose, A., and Prell, A. (1955). Does the punishment fit the crime? a study in social valuation. *American Journal of Sociology* 61: 247–51.

Rotter, J. B. (1966). Generalized expectancies for internal versus external control of reinforcement. *Psychological Monographs* 80: 1–28.

Rumsey, M. G., and Rumsey, J. M. (1977). A case of rape: sentencing judgments of males and females. *Psychological Reports* 41: 459–65.

Scroggs, J. R. (1976). Penalties for rape as a function of victim provocativeness, damage, and resistance. *Journal of Applied Social Psychology* 6: 360–68.

Shaffer, D. R., and Case, T. (1982). On the decision to testify in one's own behalf: effects of withheld evidence, defendant's sexual preferences, and juror dogmatism on juridic decisions. *Journal of Personality and Social Psychology* 42: 335–46.

Shaffer, D. R.; Plummer, D.; and Hammock, G. (1986). Hath he suffered enough? effects of jury dogmatism, defendant similarity and defendant's pretrial suffering on juridic decisions. *Journal of Personality and Social Psychology* 50: 1059–67.

Shaver, K. G. (1970). Defensive attribution: effects of severity and relevance on the responsibility assigned for an accident. *Journal of Personality and Social Psychology* 14: 101–13.

Simon, R. J., (1967). *The jury in the defense of insanity*. Boston: Little, Brown.

Sosis, R. H. (1974). Internal-external control and the perception of responsibility of another for an accident. *Journal of Personality and Social Psychology* 30: 393–99.

Steffensmeier, D. J. (1977). The effects of judge's and defendant's sex on the sentencing of offenders. *Psychology* 14: 3–9.

Stephen C., and Tully, J. C. (1977). The influence of physical attractiveness of a plaintiff on the decisions of simulated jurors. *Journal of Social Psychology* 101: 149–50.

Thornberry, T. P. (1973). Criminology, race, socioeconomic status and sentencing in the juvenile justice system. *Journal of Criminal Law and Criminology* 64: 90–98.

Turner, B. M.; Lovell, R. D.; Young, J. C.; and Denny, W. F. (1986). Race and peremptory challenges during voir dire: do prosecution and defense agree? *Journal of Criminal Justice* 14: 61–69.

Ugwuegbu, D. C. E. (1976). Black jurors' personality trait attribution to a rape case defendant. *Social Behavior and Personality* 4: 193–201.

Ugwuegbu, D. C. E. (1979). Racial and evidential factors in juror attribution of legal responsibility. *Journal of Experimental Social Psychology* 15: 133–46.

Van Dyke, J. M. (1977). *Jury selection procedures*. Cambridge, MA: Ballinger.

Vidmar, N., and Ellsworth, P. (1974). Public opinion and the death penalty. *Stanford Law Review* 26: 1245–70.

Walster, E. (1966). Assignment of responsibility for an accident. *Journal of Personality and Social Psychology* 3: 73–79.

Werner, C. M.; Strube, M. J.; Cole, A. M.; and Kagehiro, D. K. (1985). The impact of case characteristics and prior jury experience on jury verdicts. *Journal of Applied Social Psychology* 15: 409–27.

Witherspoon v. Illinois, 391 U.S. 510 (1968).

Wu, C., and Shaffer, D. R. (1987). Susceptibility to persuasive appeals as a function of source credibility and prior experience with the attitude object. *Journal of Personality and Social Psychology* 52: 677–88.

Zeigler, D. H. (1978). Young adults as a cognizable group in jury selection. *Michigan Law Review* 76: 1045–1110.

Zeisel, H., and Diamond, S. (1978). The effect of peremptory challenges on jury and verdict: an experiment in federal district court. *Stanford Law Review* 30: 491–531.

Chapter 5

THE OPENING STATEMENT

In chapter 2 we learned that the trial is organized more or less according to the format Cicero set out for an oration. In the Ciceronian scheme, the opening statement fulfills the role of the *exordium* and *narratio*. Three important functions are served: to introduce the jury to the case, to make a favorable impression on them, and to tell the story of the dispute. Two thousand years ago Cicero believed that the audience's first impressions are important to their final judgment, and lawyers and scholars today believe the same thing.

In this chapter we will discuss the opening statement from three perspectives: (1) legal theory; (2) narrative theory; and (3) persuasion theory. Prior to those discussions, though, we will pause to recall some ideas from chapter 2 on the traditional perception of the trial in relation to the opening statement.

The traditional reconstructionist view of the trial places most attention on the presentation of evidence. Over two hundred years of legal education in the United States have been based on the assumption that lawyers need only know the law and research the facts diligently in order to be effective advocates. Leading law professors have been outspoken in their disdain for rhetorical skill and the potential for persuasion in trial (Rieke 1964).

Given this background, it is no surprise that opening statements have been generally downgraded. The U.S. Supreme Court has ruled that the opening statement is limited to informing the jurors concerning the nature of the action and the issues involved, along with an outline of the case. The objective, from the court's perspective, is simply to help the jury understand the important part of the trial, which is presentation of evidence (United States v. Dinitz 1976).

Following this lead, it is common for trial lawyers to present their opening statement with nothing more than handwritten notes on a legal pad hastily set down shortly before trial time. Of all the parts of a trial openings are the most abused by the typical lawyer. They are often dull, tedious, and disjointed presentations of facts. Not only poorly prepared, they are often poorly delivered. Lawyers regularly consider the opening of such little importance that they choose not to present one at all (Starr 1983).

It is common to begin the opening with words guaranteed to fail in Cicero's objective of introducing the jurors to the case and making a favorable impression on them. It may sound like this:

> Now ladies and gentlemen of the jury, this is an opening state-ment, and his honor has told you nothing I say and nothing opposing counsel says is evidence. You must wait until you hear the witnesses we bring before you before you begin to form your opinion of this case. All I will do in this opening statement is lay out the broad outline of the case so that you can follow the evidence when it comes before you. Now ladies and gentlemen, we are dealing here with a negligence action and I represent the plaintiff. It will be my burden to prove to you by a clear preponderance of the evidence that defendant . . .

And so they typically go, ranging from abstract legal references on the one hand to oversimplified statements on the other. The jury will search desperately for meaningful information seeded in among the incomprehensible jargon and patronizing lecturing.

Legal folklore says that it is the closing argument, or summa-tion, that is the key point in the trial. A visit to the library will disclose collections of great summations, but no one has shown interest in collecting great opening statements. As with the Cicero-nian oration, in which the memorable part is the peroration, lawyers have felt that the summation is the point at which trials are won or lost (Starr 1983). They seem to have forgotten that Cicero felt the opening was of vital importance even though sublime rhetoric is reserved for the peroration.

The practicing bar has recognized the need to improve trial practice in this area as well as others. To find legal theory regarding the opening it is necessary to turn to the comments of the practicing lawyers who have discovered, after graduation from law school, that this speech is more important than they were led to believe.

THE OPENING STATEMENT AND LEGAL THEORY

From the juror's point of view the opening statement is vitally important. Jurors have been selected at random, most of them never having served before. They arrived early in the morning, having received a summons that threatened them with punishment if they failed to appear. Sitting in a large room with others like themselves, they have been impersonally ordered to follow a designated person who took them to the courtroom.

They have survived voir dire, often against their wishes, and now face the task, with considerable apprehension, of making a decision. The typical juror will take the job seriously and want to make a proper decision even though he or she would have chosen to avoid the responsibility if given the chance. During voir dire they have been exposed to bits and pieces of the case, just like the tantalizing flashes given in the preview of a movie. The judge has given them some instructions and a general introduction to the case, so they are not completely in the dark when that is combined with the information gained during voir dire. But the jury is now in the mindset of doubt, knowing that decision will eventually come. Human beings find doubt an unpleasant state of mind, much preferring to have a settled opinion.

Think of a time when you came into a room where someone was watching a game on television. You have no knowledge or interest in either team, but you sit and watch. Soon you find yourself rooting for one team without knowing why. In a contest, we are told by our culture, you should favor one side over the other. A trial is seen as a contest between teams about which you have neither knowledge nor interest. You will be looking for cues to help you decide which side to pull for. This is an active search, and the opening statement promises valuable information.

Practicing attorneys perceive the trial as a dramatic event and themselves as actors. The opening statement serves the purpose of substituting for stage settings, lighting effects, backdrops, and the theatrical illusions which are used so effectively in creating an appropriate atmosphere in the theater (Lorry 1959). Even with such a dramatic purpose lawyers do not recommend a flamboyant style because that too often turns into histrionics, which may be all too transparent (Starr 1983). Here is a sample:

> Now that you have been selected to try this case, our practice permits me to make what is known as an opening statement before the witnesses are called. As I told you during your selection, I represent the plaintiff and I am now going to open on behalf of the plaintiff. This opening statement is not evidence and it would not be proper for me to argue. I make this opening statement only in the hope that I might assist you in understanding the evidence as it is produced. In this opening statement I hope I can put our theory in a connected form, giving you the picture which must necessarily come bit by bit from the witnesses (Stewart 1940, 159).

In the opening there is an opportunity to explain terms and materials that will be essential to the case but which the jury may not understand (Wellman 1914).

TIMING THE OPENING.   The jury's attention should be gained and held, and that means that the speech should not run too long. What is

too long varies, but contemporary audiences are familiar with seg-
ments that range up to about fifteen minutes, after which their
attention may wane. In court a judge may interrupt an opening
statement to suggest that it is running too long, and that tends to
diminish the lawyer's standing in the eyes of the jury (Lorry 1959).

Legal practitioners have given thought to the relative power of
the first message the jury is exposed to in contrast with the last one
they hear (primacy versus recency). As we will learn, persuasion
research has considered the same issue with the same results: Both
are important, and their impact varies according to the situation.

The issue is first addressed in the decision about whether to give
an opening statement and how much effort to put into it. Traditional/
reconstructionist thought would suggest that one might as well go
directly to the important part of the trial, the evidence. Following
that advice, lawyers have sometimes chosen to pass up giving an
opening or give only a perfunctory statement. Many practitioners,
on the other hand, argue that the opening statement may be critical
to the decision, should never be bypassed, and should always be
given serious attention (Reed 1912).

A second issue faces the defense: timing. Typical trial practice
allows the defense to open immediately following the prosecution or
plaintiff, or defense can wait until all the witnesses and evidence for
the other side have been presented and they have rested their case.
Generally the defense is advised to open immediately. To wait raises
a serious chance that the opportunity to win a receptive hearing from
the jury has passed. First impressions, say the practitioners, frequently influence jury thinking to such an extent that they color the
way all the evidence is understood. The defense must not allow the
jury to develop a pro-plaintiff mindset, for once they do, it will be
almost impossible to get them to listen to the defense case with
anything approaching an open mind (Lorry 1959).

Timing of the defense's opening statement has been found to
influence perceptions of the case. In one study researchers varied
the timing of the defense attorney's opening statement in an auto
theft case so that it preceded the prosecutor's statement, immediately followed the prosecutor's statement, or was reserved until
after the prosecutor had completed the case in chief (Wells,
Wrightsman, and Miene 1985). Results of the study revealed that
when the defense's opening statement was earlier rather than later,
perceptions of eyewitnesses, attorney effectiveness, and the prosecutor's case favored the defense. When the opening by the defense
was delayed, these perceptions benefited the prosecution.

In another study, conducted by University of Chicago researchers of 3,576 trials, it was found that "the real decision is often made before the deliberation begins" (Kalven and Zeisel 1966, 488). And a summary of research on opening statements and closing arguments led to the conclusion that the prosecution is strengthened by an extensive opening statement while the defense will gain through an extensive open only when the prosecution has been brief (Benoit and France 1983). And, it is helpful to promise to prove even more than the evidence will support, as long as that failure does not become a factor in closing arguments.

While these studies do not support the conclusion that many cases are truly over after the opening statements, they allow that to be a serious possibility. This must be considered in contrast with the traditional/reconstructionist version of the trial. The long-standing view, supported by the practice of judges in counseling jurors, is that the jury must avoid coming to conclusions until the trial is complete and all the evidence has been considered. Furthermore, the jury is repeatedly told that nothing in the opening statements should be considered evidence and lawyers are not allowed to make arguments. Our knowledge of the human desire to avoid doubt and come to decision, when combined with this evidence that apparently some if not many jurors reach a firm point of view following opening statements which eventually becomes their verdict, necessarily supports a rejection of the traditional belief.

In terms of timing, concentration on the presentation of evidence in accordance with traditional advice may simply come too late. The jury may already have made their commitment.

INFORMATION VERSUS ARGUMENT.   The rules of procedure deny the attorney the right to make arguments in the opening statement, but practitioners declare that failure to do so may jeopardize the case. This leads to a discussion of the differences between information and argumentation.

By rule the opening statement is to be confined to an overview of the facts that will be presented. It is not to include talk about how these facts combine to prove a case. The task facing the lawyer is to discover a way to talk about the facts so that their implications for the case will be apparent without direct and pointed claims.

From the perspective of the law a major difference is in tense: in the opening statement the future tense is used. For example: "Ms. Smith, the crossing guard, *will tell* you that the car was moving faster than the 20-mile-per-hour limit in the school zone." In argument the past tense is used: "You *learned* from Ms. Smith, the crossing guard . . . "

Another distinction made in law between opening and closing statements is in language intensity. The opening should be relatively temperate, with language held closely to the concrete and specific. This is very much a matter of judgment, and language may be only one measure. Other measures may be nonverbal and metalinguistic. In law the determination will be made by the judge if opposing counsel chooses to interrupt the opening with the charge that a violation of rules against making an argument in the opening has occurred. If this should happen and the judge reprimands a lawyer, there will be loss of standing in the eyes of the jury. For this reason, those making opening statements tend to control, in addition to language, their voice, intonation, gestures, and movements so that they will be seen as restrained (Hardwicke 1920).

Finally, a subtle distinction between argument and opening center around the explicit drawing of conclusions. The emphasis is on *explicit*. Conclusions will be drawn through the narrative, as we will explain in the next section, but they must be masked so as not to appear to be conclusions. One commentator said that few people appreciate the force there is in a clear, succinct, orderly narrative of facts (Donovan 1927).

THE OPENING STATEMENT AND NARRATIVE THEORY

Preparation for trial involves balancing two processes that lead to the same point following different avenues: traditional analysis and narrative analysis. Traditional analysis, which we have explained in chapter 2, involves identifying the essential elements of the case and locating a theory of the case that will allow persuasive arguments acceptable within the confines of the law.

It is through traditional analysis that lawyers satisfy themselves that they are operating within legal expectations. Failure to know, for example, what will count as a prima facie case could lead to dismissal. Failure to know that the theory of the case is consistent with common law or statutory limits could have similar results. It is through traditional analysis that the search for evidence is guided. The essential issues and the arguments that will be made relative to them dictate what testimony must be obtained from each witness and locate the role of documentary or physical evidence. It is also through traditional analysis that the value of expert testimony is determined.

It is through narrative analysis, however, that a story is created that will communicate effectively to the judge or jury and play a vital role in the decision. In chapter 2 we learned that a creative vision of the trial has emerged from narrative theory. In chapter 10 we will learn that jury decision making can best be understood from a story or narrative model. At this point we will concentrate on the contention that it is in the opening statement that the case is presented in a narrative fashion.

To return to the two processes that lead to the same point via different paths, in pretrial preparation a traditional analysis based on essential elements must be performed. This analysis will guide both the discovery of evidence and the conduct of its presentation. It may well return to help organize the closing argument. But it is through narrative processes that the case can be set before the audience with clarity and force that will hold throughout the presentation of evidence and into decision. So the opening statement must be, above all, one that meets the needs and critical tests of the jury.

Three approaches to the construction of an effective narrative in the opening statement will be reviewed: (1) Fisher's narrative rationality; (2) Bennett's storytelling model of social judgment; and (3) Pennington and Hastie's story model. These are not competing points of view. They are simply different ways of characterizing the same concept. Any one or a combination of them can be used to guide the construction of an opening statement.

FISHER'S NARRATIVE RATIONALITY.   Fisher (1987) has presented a theory of narrative rationality, consisting of two principles: coherence and fidelity. The story of the case must be told in such a way as to pass the jury's tests of coherence and fidelity if it is to satisfy their sense of rationality.

Narrative coherence concerns whether a story hangs together and is assessed, according to Fisher, in three ways. A story must have argumentative or structural coherence; it must have material coherence, which involves comparison and contrast with stories from other discourses that may raise problems, counterarguments, or missed issues; and the story requires characterological coherence. The latter element deals with the central feature of all stories, character. A character in a story is defined by decisions and actions that reflect values. The character is an organized set of actional tendencies. If the tendencies are contradictory or change significantly from one story point to another, the jury will tend to doubt the character.

Recall the impact on the character of Richard Nixon when the transcripts of conversations in the Oval Office of the White House were published. Nixon had presented himself to the people as a man of high principle and good moral character. He even criticized former

President Harry Truman for swearing in public. Then people learned of a President Nixon who used foul language regularly and acted in a most common and self-serving manner. When, later, he tried to defend himself from the posture of this high moral character—"I'm no crook"—many found it hard to believe because of characterological incoherence.

Nixon's defense against Watergate charges was also lacking in the other areas of narrative coherence. For example, it was learned that substantial amounts of money had been given to the men accused of breaking into the Democratic National Headquarters by men who were in the President's cabinet or were his closest advisers. Nixon, however, claimed that the money had nothing to do with payments to keep their mouths shut but was merely given in the spirit of friendship. The story lacked material coherence, and many refused to believe it because of their general knowledge of hush money.

In the opening statement, from Fisher's perspective, the first obligation is to compose a story that has an internal logic, seems materially consistent with the jury's expectations of stories in general, and develops clearly defined and consistent characters.

Narrative fidelity is demonstrated through what Fisher calls the logic of good reasons. Good reasons are the means by which the jury members will decide if the story of the case is accurate in terms of their sense of reality. The good reasons involve five components:

1. Are the statements in the opening that purport to be facts truly facts, and what are the values embedded in them?

2. Have relevant facts been omitted, or are there distortions in those included, and are the values implied appropriate to the case?

3. Are the connections of facts to conclusion reasonable, and can the jury adhere to that rationality without violation of their sense of self?

4. Is the reasoning implied in connecting facts to conclusions all that should be considered in this case, and are the values implied confirmed and validated by the experience of the jurors?

5. Does the story address the real issues in the case, and do the values involved constitute the ideal basis for human conduct?

Clearly Fisher is concerned not only with the surface story elements but with the value implications as well. Think back to chapter 1 and the problem with the collision between the auto and the fire truck. Suppose that case came to trial and the plaintiff and defense each told their story. First, look at portions of each opening statement, then consider the value implications of each.

Opening for the plaintiff, Mary Louise Scott, might include this.

A cold rain was falling at 3:00 P.M. on March 3, 1988, as Mary Louise Scott drove north on State Street. She had the windows closed and the radio on. As she approached the intersection with 8th Avenue the light was green, so she went on at her usual 30-mile-per-hour rate. To her left was the high school and beyond it 8th Avenue dropped sharply down the hill.

Suddenly, she heard a siren. She looked quickly but before she could even turn her head a fire truck leaped into her left peripheral vision. She smashed her brake pedal to the floor. The car veered slightly before it hit the right rear tire of the truck.

Officer Don Little, who conducted the accident investigation, measured her skid marks and confirms that she was going about 30 miles per hour. He checked the marks left by the fire truck, which traveled on virtually through the intersection before coming to a stop, and noted it was moving about 35 to 40 miles per hour. He also included in his report that the high school and the hill on 8th Avenue may have blocked vision and hearing that would have warned Mary Louise of the coming truck.

Fire Department regulations caution drivers who are about to enter an intersection against the light to slow, look for oncoming traffic, and proceed cautiously, never faster than 15 miles per hour.

Mary Louise believes the driver of the fire truck was at fault for not slowing and for going too fast. Because of that, she believes the city should compensate her for the accident.

Opening for the city could give this version of the accident and imply a different set of values.

The law obliges the Fire Department to reach the scene of fires and other appropriate emergencies in the least possible amount of time. Every minute that passes between a call and the arrival of the fire truck can mean the loss of lives and property. We can lose what has taken a lifetime of work to build; we can cause disastrous increases in insurance rates; we can destroy our image as an efficient and caring city if we cannot manage to get help promptly to those in need.

Toward this end the law requires citizens driving or walking to give way when emergency vehicles sounding their sirens and flashing their lights approach, even if they would ordinarily have the right of way. The image of fire trucks having to wait patiently at stoplights is as ridiculous as that old story of Nero fiddling while Rome burned.

Yes, the city has rules that we use to guide the actions of our emergency personnel, and these include the admonition to be careful before moving through a red light. The driver of our fire truck, George Davis, looked and saw no traffic. In his determination to meet the demands that he reach the scene of emergency in the shortest possible time, he went through the intersection and was struck by a driver who clearly did not believe it was necessary to give the right of way or who

simply did not pay proper attention. It was her mistake and she will
have to live with it.

Which of these two stories are you most inclined to believe? Can
you say why? The surface facts are not very much in conflict, with
the exception that the driver of the fire truck claims not to have seen
Mary Louise approaching the intersection and she claims he was
driving faster than he should have. The basis on which the jury will
judge the stories will probably be the values they bring to the task.

Fisher discusses values in terms of hierarchies which form the
basis for assessing the elements in reasoning. Consider these two
stories in terms of values. The basic datum—that Mary Louise ran
into the fire truck—is not contested. It is the attached warrants, or
values, that will guide decision.

For example, (datum) Mary Louise hit the truck. Since (warrant) the rules require the truck not to go against a light if traffic is
present, and (backing) departmental policies and procedures constitute the operating principles that are to be obeyed, and (value) our
theory of civic duty demands that civil servants carry out their duties
consistent with the rules, for (transcendent value) responsibility and
duty in fulfilling a public trust are essential to the very being of a
democratic state, then (claim) the Fire Department should compensate Mary Louise. (For a discussion of the pattern of reasoning used
by Fisher, which includes data, warrant, backing, and claim, see
Toulmin, Rieke, and Janik 1984.)

For the contrary example, (datum) Mary Louise hit the truck.
Since (warrant) law requires citizens to give right of way to emergency vehicles displaying lights and siren, and (backing) the state law
establishes precedents that preempt any subordinate rules or procedures, for (value) to have a functioning government the ordinary
rights and privileges must give way to overarching societal interests
in emergency situations, for (transcendent value) we are committed
to a social/political community that places survival of order over
individual transient interests, then (claim) Mary Louise will have to
live with the consequences.

Finally, Fisher discusses the fact that it is in the audience that
argument is to be judged. "Rationality is grounded," he says, "in the
narrative structure of life and the natural capacity people have to
recognize coherence and fidelity in the stories they experience" (p.
137). It does not do to ask which of the two stories is true. Rather, it
is appropriate to ask how do members of the jury critically react to
the stories.

In our two samples jurors could side with Mary Louise and

accept her version of what "actually happened" to the extent they felt her story was internally coherent and was faithful to their values of the way things are. If, for example, they believed that civil servants must follow the rules if citizens are not to be victimized by their behaviors, jurors would be more inclined to accept the assertion that the driver of the fire truck was careless in entering the intersection.

On the other hand, jurors could side with the city if they did not accept Mary Louise's story. If, for example, they believed that civil servants have a higher duty to serve society, then they might even doubt the coherence of Mary Louise's version and think she was simply not paying attention and carelessly drove into the intersection ignoring the oncoming truck.

Today lawyers sometimes gather together sample juries that are drawn from the same population as the actual jury will be and present their statements to them. Then they observe the jury deliberating to see how, in fact, the jury evaluates the competing stories. Stories are revised within the constraints of the artifacts to improve the jury's critical evaluation.

BENNETT'S STORYTELLING MODEL OF SOCIAL JUDGMENT.   Bennett (1978) developed his theory of storytelling and social judgment by observing trials and puzzling about how jurors with no training can make sense of legal issues. He notes, first, that disputes that lead to any form of adjudication tend to involve two parties talking to a neutral judge by telling their side of the story. Important storytelling episodes emerge during examination of witnesses and during the opening and closing remarks. "From earliest childhood on," claims Bennett, "we . . . are encouraged to explain our side of things in a story form that organizes relevant information in the service of a defensible definition for the disputed action" (p. 5). Through the years children learn storytelling skills by being exposed to stories in many forms, by playing all the roles themselves during play, and by justifying themselves to adult adjudicators. By the time they become adults, they have a well-developed method of social judgment through the rules and procedures of storytelling.

Bennett identifies three interpretive operations through which jurors judge the stories in trials: (1) identification of central action; (2) construction of inferences about the relationships among surrounding elements of the story; and (3) testing the story for internal consistency and descriptive adequacy or completeness.

Central action is identified as the focal point of the story, the behaviors around which the dispute centers. We learn various linguistic conventions of stories that highlight central actions and allow us to keep track of them through all the devices of stories such as flashbacks and multiple themes. In the opening statement it is critical that central action be identified and that the story conventions not be violated by incoherence. In the case of the fire truck, the central action is this: Mary Louise ran into a fire truck.

Interpreting the central action is accomplished by connecting it to the surrounding narrative elements. This involves what Bennett calls a "symbolic triangulation," in which certain symbols are placed in structural proximity and their relationship is set up to clarify the significance of the central action. The interpretation tends to follow five types of social understanding: (1) empirical knowledge, (2) language categorization, (3) logical operations, (4) norms, and (5) aesthetic criteria. Each of these can serve as a powerful means of relating social knowledge to the action of any story, leading to judgment.

Empirical connections consist mostly of the artifacts of the dispute. They may be contracts, physical objects, or the product of any observation. In our fire truck story empirical artifacts include the position of the car and the truck, the location of the damage to the car and truck, the black skid marks on the pavement, the physical location of the high school, the hill on 8th Avenue, the weather on that day, the report of the investigating officer, the testimony of Mary Louise and the truck driver.

When there is inconsistency between testimony, empirical connections can make the difference. For example, it would be difficult for Mary Louise to claim the truck hit her car when the physical damage to her car is on the front but the truck was damaged on its side. Bennett posits a listener's maxim: Descriptions are taken literally. If they involve terms that have to be changed in order to produce a sensible version of an incident, listeners tend to conclude the story is made up.

Language categorizations are, according to Bennett, among the most powerful means of establishing relationships among symbols in stories. How we characterize people and actions linguistically can support the basis of judgment. Jurors will use such characterizations to form their judgments. For example, if we characterize Mary Louise as a careful and responsible driver who typically drives about 30 miles per hour even when the limit would allow more speed, it would lead to a different judgment than if we described her as a careless driver more concerned with what was playing on the radio and asserting her right of way than with what was going on around her.

Logical connections involve making inferences in an everyday sense. For Bennett they involve categorizing two symbols so that some invariant empirical properties always accompany the categorization. For example, it is not logical that Mary Louise saw the truck in time to stop and simply drove right into it. People do not assert their right of way at the risk of their lives. So the truck must have been coming too fast.

Normative connections form the foundation for logical chains and categorizations. We used one in the example above. How fast is too fast? If the truck moved into the intersection so fast that Mary Louise had no choice but to hit it, then it was going too fast. Our sense of what ought to be may well cause us to believe false accounts or disbelieve true ones. Think of times you are forced to tell a story that you knew violated norms. You may have used the common opening, "You may find this hard to believe, but . . ."

Aesthetic connections involve relationships that go beyond the others mentioned and involve a sense of what is perfect, familiar, pleasing. Lawyers want to present their clients in terms of aesthetics: innocent, attractive, careful. They know that attractive litigants tend to receive more favorable treatment at the hands of juries, and so they wish to make their clients as attractive as possible through their choice of language.

Evaluating the interpretation involves the jurors' decision that enough connections have been established to make a consistent and confident interpretation. This sense of completeness will depend upon the learned social judgment techniques the jurors bring to the task. Human beings will complete stories by filling in gaps left in the telling. The processes we use in reading a book, in which we supply descriptions not given by the writer, illustrate this. Or, in movies and television when two people walk out the door in one scene and are driving in a car in the very next scene, we easily fill in the "facts" of them walking to the car, opening doors, getting inside, closing doors, starting the car, moving into the street.

The evaluation rests on whether the stories told provide as many connections as we require to fill in the gaps without feeling as if there is distortion involved. The driver of the fire truck says he saw no cars approaching the intersection, and so entered in what was a safe manner. Mary Louise says she entered the intersection without hearing or seeing a fire truck until it was upon her and she could neither stop nor swerve. Neither story gives all the details. Does either one provide enough connections to satisfy you that you can safely fill in the details and select it as the version of what really happened?

Bennett concludes that justice may have little to do with what "really" happened. Jurors, like other story audiences, "judge the plausibility of a story according to certain structural relations among chosen symbols, not according to direct perception of the actual events in question" (p. 21). For this reason the writer of an opening statement should consider the way in which the story is told, its plausibility in terms of structural relations.

PENNINGTON AND HASTIE'S STORY MODEL.   Because Pennington and Hastie's story model is discussed in detail in chapter 10, our discussion here will be brief. We will try to include what information they add to the other story concepts in relation to the needs of the opening statement.

Pennington and Hastie (1986) reason that "jurors impose a narrative story organization on trial information, in which causal and intentional relations between events are central" (p. 243). There are three components to their story model: (1) evidence evaluation through story construction; (2) decision alternative representation (verdict category establishment); and (3) story classification (selecting the verdict category that best fits the story).

Story construction involves assigning meaning to trial evidence by incorporating it into a plausible account of what happened. Jurors bring to their task general knowledge about human action (episode schema) which serves to help them organize events according to cause or intent. Narrative discourse in general is understood through conceptual schema that describe most human action sequences whether in the "real" world or in stories. Episode schema help us build a story by calling attention to (1) initiating events, which involve (2) physical states, which combine to initiate (3) psychological states and (4) goals. All these together provide the reason behind (5) actions which result in (6) consequences.

The story can be seen as a hierarchy of embedded episodes, with those that represent the most important features of "what happened" being at the highest level. These bear a direct relation to verdict alternatives. These high-level episodes are elaborated by more detailed event sequences in which casual and intentional relations among subordinate story events are given.

Verdict category establishment comes from information about what the law allows in relation to alternative story constructions. This is explicitly given in the judge's instructions to the jury at the end of the trial, but it is possible to include it in the opening statement by calling attention to what the judge "will instruct you at the end of the trial." It is, of course, made even more a part of the presentation in the closing argument.

For example, to be guilty of first-degree murder, the accused must have killed with a resolution to kill and a purpose formed to do so, with insufficient provocation, and with an interval of time between resolution and killing. The killing must have been in pursuance of the resolution without efforts to escape or avoid excessive force.

To be guilty of second-degree murder the accused must have killed with intent to inflict injury likely to result in death as a deliberate cruel act with insufficient provocation, using a deadly weapon without attempting to escape or avoid excessive force. Each of these verdict categories requires a different set of behaviors, causes, intentions, and so on.

Story classification involves matching the story with the verdict category. The decision categories suggested in law—identity, mental state, circumstances, and actions—correspond to the features of the story model of initiating events, goals, actions, and accompanying states. Jurors have little or no background in the verdict categories and must take them as given. They do have extensive experience with the components of stories. For this reason, say Pennington and Hastie, the jurors are likely to classify the story into an appropriate verdict in a deliberate manner.

The jury will have the story in mind as they turn to the verdict alternatives. If they are inclined to find the defendant guilty of second-degree murder rather than first, they will probably revise their understanding of the story to allow that verdict. They might, for instance, decide that there really was not an interval of time between the point at which a resolution to kill was made and the time the killing was committed. Without that interval the killing has not satisfied the verdict requirements of first degree but still satisfies second degree.

Evaluations of plausibility, on the basis of story completeness and coherence, are preliminary, claim Pennington and Hastie. "If an incriminating story is deemed plausible, then a general evaluation of goodness-of-fit of story to verdict category determines the final verdict decision" (p. 245). The basic claim of their story model, then, is that stories enable critical interpretive processing and organization of the evidence so that it can be evaluated meaningfully against various judgment dimensions represented in legal rules.

Knowing this, the writer of the opening statement will first consider what the judge's final instructions to the jury will be. Then the verdict alternatives will be examined in relation to the outcome sought by the side preparing the opening. Finally, the story constructed in the opening will be tailored to the desired verdict alternative in such a way as to assist the jury in reaching that conclusion.

If the artifactual constraints on the story make it impossible or difficult to construct a plausible story which fits a chosen verdict alternative, the writer may well consider arguing for a different verdict that will be a better match with the story that can be constructed.

OPENING STATEMENT AND PERSUASION THEORY

From the perspective of persuasion theory the entire trial is a campaign. Just as in politics or advertising, the trial functions as an interrelated series of messages occurring in sequence so as to be instrumental in producing intermediate and ultimate goals. One trial lawyer observed that as far as he was concerned, the trial begins the moment he puts his foot out of the car after parking at the courthouse. The person parking next to him or passing him on the sidewalk or court steps could be a potential juror. If he is rude or makes a bad impression, he has already damaged his campaign.

The campaign continues during the informal milling about while waiting for the judge and getting things organized. Those future jurors are sitting in the courtroom, feeling the anxiety of doubt and future challenges, and they are already searching actively for information that will help them form their judgments. If they see attorneys behaving in objectionable ways, they will begin to root for the other side. If they overhear comments around the drinking fountain that communicate cynicism, arrogance, lack of feeling, or some other negative trait, they will begin to root for the other side. If they perceive lawyers who communicate incompetence by their dress or manner, they will begin to root for the other side.

In chapter 4 we discussed how the campaign continues during the voir dire. It is not only that negative behaviors repel jurors; positive behaviors attract them.

From a campaign persuasion point of view the opening statement falls at about the middle stage. The early steps of planning, which involved determining the theory of the case, setting basic strategy through traditional analysis, gathering evidence through research and deposition, and the audience analysis of voir dire and the preparation that preceded it, are complete. Now comes the opening statement, which will relate the audience (jury) on the one hand and the traditional analysis of essential issues on the other through the medium of narration.

The instrumental goal of the opening statement is clear: It must establish a narrative with such power of coherence and fidelity that it will provide the framework within which the jury will hear and evaluate the evidence to come. Instead of listening to all the disjointed testimony with an open mind, the jurors will be striving for closure throughout. They will be seeking ways in which to make sense of the evidence, and the opening narrative should provide that.

The opening statement serves as the "invitation to the drama" of the courtroom (Larson 1983). It is the dramatic that moves jurors, and that includes plot, character, action, and purpose. The drama includes that peculiar and powerful relationship between communicator and audience that has been the object of interest since Aristotle called it variously ethos, source credibility, or communicator acceptability. There is a bond that can form between juror and attorney that leads to increased trust and belief.

Cronkhite and Liska (1980) claim that the bond comes with lawyers who seem most likely to satisfy the needs of the jurors and help them achieve the goals that are most salient and important at that moment. As we have said earlier, the jurors are filled with anxiety over doing a good job in an awesome task and they are quite uncomfortable about being in a state of doubt. Their goal is to reach a fair and reasonable decision as soon as possible, and their needs center on clear and cogent information to support a decision.

The opening statement that makes it clear that this will be an easy job because the case is so clear-cut and one-sided will probably set the lawyer up to establish a bond with the jury that will serve for the rest of the trial. There is no single trait or behavior that can guarantee this relationship, in spite of years of searching for it. There are, however, some behaviors that seem likely to assist in the process. Zimbardo (1972) suggests the following, which we have adapted to the legal setting: (1) impress the jury with your expertise, concern, and dedication, being forceful without being overbearing; (2) willingly admit some points against your interest; (3) minimize your manipulative intent by claiming interest only in truth and justice; (4) show enthusiasm and concern for your issues.

Persuasion is often defined as one person working some power on another for selfish purposes, and this has led to widespread distrust of the process. More recent theories, however, reject this concept. Instead, persuasion is seen as an interpersonal process in which people interact to form some common identities and understandings. Larson (1983) defines persuasion as the co-creation of a state of identification or alignment between a source and a receiver that results from the use of symbols. Stiff and his colleagues (1988) find evidence to support the idea that if the lawyer can effectively take the perspective of the jurors in the opening statement, there is greater likelihood the jurors will generate an empathic concern for the lawyer's client. Empathic concern, in turn, tends to stir in jurors' minds feelings similar to those reported felt by the client. And such emotional contagion is accompanied by communicative responsiveness and a desire to help.

INOCULATION.   Since the opening statement will invariably be followed by opposing evidence and argument, a persuasion goal is to inoculate the jury against that opposition. Persuasion theory has drawn this idea through a medical metaphor. In medicine it has been discovered that a person can be inoculated against a disease by exposure to weakened forms of the virus toward which immunity is to be generated. Following that metaphor, inoculation in persuasion deals with providing messages which help immunize the jury against the opposition's case.

Miller and Burgoon (1973) suggest some steps through which inoculation can be accomplished in the opening statement. High self-esteem tends to be associated with resistance to persuasion, so in the opening lawyers can identify with the jury and assure them that they have the ability to do their job well. Sharing success with the jury—allowing them to join the cause—by letting them see how they can further justice in association with the lawyer will help immunize. Generating some hostility toward the opposition by suggesting they are greedy and self-serving can be effective.

Generating commitment in the jurors tends to immunize them (Fontes and Bundens 1980). In the opening statement the lawyer can stress the importance of following the rules and living up to the expectations of the legal process, and setting aside prejudice. Repeating commitments obtained during voir dire may be useful.

Anchoring techniques also tend to induce resistance to counterarguments. The use of anchoring techniques involves linking new beliefs to beliefs, attitudes, values, and goals already held by the jury or those whom they respect. Anchoring rests upon solid information about the jury gained before and during the voir dire. Preparation of the opening statement should be done with this specific jury in mind; anchoring can be accomplished by relating important trial elements with ideas that are potent to the jurors.

Analogies and metaphors thus become powerful tools in the opening statement. Members of the jury can understand and anchor an idea if it can be linked with one close to them. For example, in the opening statement about Mary Louise's unfortunate collision with the fire truck, attorney for the plaintiff might recognize that all the jurors are experienced drivers and say,

How many times have you driven with the windows closed and the radio playing? How many times have you heard a siren and still needed to look long and hard to find out where it was coming from? Expecting drivers to hear and locate immediately a fast-moving truck going against a red light is unreasonable. We might as well throw a baseball at you when you are looking away and then shout at you to catch it just as it reaches your face.

POWER. Power is an important concept in the process of compliance gaining, and the opening statement is seeking compliance from the jury. Jurors will probably grant power to the lawyer who addresses them in terms of (1) expectancies/consequences; (2) relationships/identification; and (3) values/obligations (Wheeless, Barraclough, and Stewart 1983). In the first category the opening statement would include comments on how the jury can be helped to finish their onerous task with minimum difficulty, and that will partly come from their recognition of the expertise of the lawyer. It might also include some threat of the consequences of failure to do their duty. The second category involves the lawyer establishing some relationship or identification with the jury, and that has already been discussed. It would suggest that the opening include statements that would flatter the jury, build their self-esteem, and generally try to get the jury to like the lawyer and the client. In the third instance the opening statement would seek to engage the values and sense of obligation already well established in the minds of the jurors, and this has been discussed in relation to the narrative. However, in addition, we can mention that engaging the moral obligations of duty to family, nation, equity, and formal law are substantial elements in the reasoning people ordinarily use along with acknowledgment of legitimate authority (Willbrand and Rieke 1986). Power and persuasion are discussed in more detail in chapter 5.

PRIMACY. Primacy and recency must be discussed in relation to the opening statement. While persuasion research has failed to show that the first statement heard is more potent than the last, there is evidence showing the importance of the opening statement in terms of primacy and impression formation (Fishbein and Ajzen 1975). Although primacy effects are not alwlays significant, there is reason to expect that when a person is introduced by being described with a number of adjectives, those adjectives heard first will determine the impression a listener forms about the person.

If the first description you receive about a person is favorable, then it is likely you will form a favorable impression. If your introduction is through negative adjectives, you will likely form a negative impression. It may be that adjectives heard early establish an expectancy that colors what is heard later.

A major function of the opening statement is to introduce the leading characters in the drama. The jury is eager for information, and the first characterization of leading players may well build an expectation in their minds for all that follows. Think of the times you have read a novel and realized after a few chapters that you like one character and dislike another without knowing why. No action has happened so far to cause your feelings, yet you already know who the villain will be. If you were to look back in the novel to see what words were used to introduce those characters, you would probably see why you formed the impressions you did.

It is in the opening statement, then, that the first description of leading characters occurs. It is possible to establish positive and negative impressions in the minds of jurors just as the novelist does.

REFERENCES

Bennett, W. L. (1978). Storytelling in criminal trials. *Quarterly Journal of Speech* 64:1–22.

Benoit, W. L., and France, J. S. (1983). Review of research on opening statements and closing arguments. In R. Matlon and R. Crawford (eds.), *Communication strategies in the practice of lawyering.* Annandale, VA: Speech Communication Association.

Cronkhite, G., and Liska, J. R. (1980). The judgment of communicant acceptability. In M. E. Roloff and G. R. Miller (eds.), *Persuasion: new directions in theory and research.* Beverly Hills, CA: Sage.

Donovan, J. W. (1927). *Modern jury trials.* New York: G. A. Jennings.

Fishbein, M., and Ajzen, I. (1975). *Belief, attitude, intention and behavior.* Reading, MA: Addison-Wesley.

Fisher, W. R. (1987). *Human communication as narration.* Columbia: University of South Carolina Press.

Fontes, N. E., and Bundens, R. T. (1980). Persuasion during the trial process. In M. E. Roloff and G. Miller (eds.), *Persuasion: new directions in theory and research.* Beverly Hills, CA: Sage.

Hardwicke, H. (1920). *The art of winning cases or modern advocacy, a practical treatise on preparation for trial, and the conduct of cases in court.* 2nd ed. New York: Banks.

Kalven, H., Jr., and Zeisel, H. (1966). *The American jury.* Boston: Little, Brown.

Larson, C. U. (1983). *Persuasion: reception and responsibility.* 3rd ed. Belmont, CA: Wadsworth.

Lorry, W. R. (1959). *A civil action—the trial.* Philadelphia: American Law Institute and the American Bar Association.

Miller, G. A., and Burgoon, M. (1973). *New techniques in persuasion.* New York: Harper and Row.

Pennington, N., and Hastie, R. (1986). Evidence evaluation in complex decision making. *Journal of Personality and Social Psychology* 51:242–56.

Reed, J. C. (1912). *Conduct of lawsuits.* Boston: Little, Brown.

Rieke, R. D. (1964). Rhetorical theory in American legal practice. Unpublished doctoral dissertation, Ohio State University.

Starr, V. H. (1983). From the communication profession: communication strategies and research needs on opening statements and closing arguments. In R. Matlon and R. Crawford (eds.), *Communication strategies in the practice of lawyering.* Annandale, VA: Speech Communication Association.

Stewart, W. S. (1940). *Stewart on trial strategy.* Chicago: Flood.

Stiff, J.; Dillard J.; Somera, L.; Kim, H.; and Sleight, C. (1988). Empathy, communication, and prosocial Behavior. *Communication Monographs* 55:198–213.

Toulmin, S. E.; Rieke, R. D.; and Janik, A. (1984). *An introduction to reasoning.* 2nd ed. New York: Macmillan.

United States v. Dinitz 424 U.S. 600, 96 S. Ct. 1075, 47 L. Ed. 2d 267 (1976).

Wellman, F. (1914). *Day in court or the subtle arts of great advocates.* New York: Macmillan.

Wells, G. L.; Wrightsman, L. S.; and Miene, P. K. (1985). The timing of the defense opening statement: don't wait until the evidence is in. *Journal of Applied Social Psychology* 15:758–72.

Wheeless, L.; Barraclough, R.; and Stewart, R. (1983). Compliance-gaining and power in persuasion. In R. N. Bostrom (ed.), *Communication Yearbook 7.* Beverly Hills, CA: Sage.

Willbrand, M. L., and Rieke, R. D. (1986). Reason giving in children's supplicatory compliance gaining. *Communication Monographs* 53:47–59.

Zimbardo, P. (1972). The tactics and ethics of persuasion. In B. T. King and E. McGinnies (eds.), *Attitudes, conflict, and social change.* New York: Academic Press.

Chapter 6:

CREDIBILITY

If, in the words of one writer, a person's life is dyed the color of his imagination, then surely a person's influence is reflected in the hue of his image. The creation and maintenance of a good image is an incessant process and goal, one that plays a vital role in determining success or failure in social situations. A speaker's image represents the aggregate of responses to all possible questions about the speaker. The Greeks termed this portrait "ethos," signifying the character of the speaker. Today we commonly refer to this quality as credibility. This chapter outlines the relevant research concerning how receivers, such as jurors, confer ethos, what factors contribute to a favorable image, and what problems courtroom actors confront when attempting to capitalize on a credible image or overcome a demurring one. We begin this review at the fountainhead of image: namely, the process of impression formation.

IMPRESSION FORMATION

To form an initial impression is both natural and a break from the grand adage not to judge a book from its cover. But with so many books in the world and so little time, impression forming is the most efficient method by which to judge the qualities and character of those who confront us.

From our very first contact with another person, we immediately develop a sense of whether we like or dislike the person. We do this by first collecting as much information as possible, either directly or indirectly, and then structuring this information into an organized form. This cognitive representation of another denotes our impression. Because much of the information we obtain is incomplete, we fashion our impression by making inferences and relying on stereotypes. When trying to make sense of the behavior of others, we scrutinize the environment, the setting, and people's actions in an attempt to search for reasons behind their behavior. Upon discovering a plausible reason or cause, we attribute the other's behavior to it. These reasons fall into two categories: (1) situational factors or (2) dispositional factors. For example, ability, mood, effort, and knowledge are dispositional causes arising from the individual, whereas task difficulty, interference, and luck are causes considered to be situational in nature and stemming from external sources. All factors internal to the individual are considered dispositional, and all factors external to the individual are deemed situational. The interesting feature of attribution is that we commonly attribute others' behavior to dispositional factors and our own behavior to situational factors (Jones and Nisbett 1971). In other words, in searching for reasons for our own behavior, such as nervousness in speaking situations, we commonly attribute our unease to the situation, but when confronted with a nervous speaker we are more apt to attribute his unease as a permanent feature of his character. For this reason, attributions significantly contribute to the evaluations we make of others.

SELF-PRESENTATION

As social actors people want to convey as positive and consistent an image as they can in order to obtain social approval. We learn from a young age that consistent behavior gives actors a desirable predictability and trustworthiness that generate favorable responses from others. As strategic beings we want others to think highly of us, often because we know that positive evaluations are linked to the accomplishment of our persuasive goals. Cultivating an affinity with others is a strategic process by which actors consciously display behaviors associated with liking. For lawyers these behaviors include common courtesies, such as politeness and acting in a warm, emphathic manner (Bell and Daly 1984). Lawyers who focus solely on the issue-related objectives of a case and ignore the strategic management of impressions and affinity surrender the best position from which to advance claims. Lawyers must remember that people are driven to reduce uncertainty and take an active role in interpreting and construing their worlds. For these reasons impression management is of central concern to legal advocates.

How individuals present themselves, for the most part, is a matter of choice. By selectively choosing what information to disclose or omit and by developing this selection in congruence with persuasive goals, individuals compose a strategic self-presentation. Rather than a simulated or specious attempt at impression management, this presentation is largely a matter of emphasis and tone, tempering an image that best elicits favorable outcomes.

An individual's self-presentation strategy generally conforms to one of five distinct types, applicable to the courtroom: ingratiation, intimidation, self-promotion, exemplification, and supplication

(Jones and Pitman 1980). Attorneys and their witnesses promote these presentations as a means to influence the evaluations of other courtroom actors. By engaging in *ingratiating* behaviors such as flattery, conformity, and providing services, a communicator attempts to gain influence by establishing an affinity with the target. This strategic attempt to be liked, although highly influential, is often met with suspicion as others may interpret compliments and favors as strategically motivated and insincere. Conversely, an *intimidation* strategy is to appear dangerous, so much so that the target will perceive the agent as unpredictable, even irrational, if crossed. By engaging in behaviors that exhibit a stoic quality, the intimidator is seen as cold, uncompassionate, and unapproachable by common appeals. Targets comply with intimidators mostly to avoid confrontation and conflict, although individuals sometimes associate seriousness and competence with this approach. The more direct avenue to an attribution of competence is *self-promotion*. Through self-advertisement of accolades or by the proclamation of notable work, self-promoters seek to gain the respect of others by establishing their quality. As with ingratiation, the dilemma of insincere motives is sometimes a problem; it is felt that truly competent persons do not generally broadcast their competence. A more subtle approach is *exemplification*. The exemplifier attempts to evoke an image of saintly integrity. By cultivating the perception that one's morals are above all reproach, or at least that one's values are firmly on the side of moral culture, an agent influences by "exemplifying" the good and right. For example, the attorney who arrives first at the office and leaves last exemplifies dedication and the value of hard work, and influences others as a result. For those who lack the skills or resources to influence others through competence, *supplication* exerts power through helplessness or incompetence. When one appears weak or incapable, others comply out of compassion and pity, or to heighten their sense of powerfulness over the supplicator.

Attorneys do not transparently fall into the preceding categories. After all, who ever heard of a lawyer attempting to display incompetence in order to win a case? Consider, however, the courtroom strains of these methods. Lawyers commonly plead with juries, demand from juries, advertise before juries. Witnesses often appear helpless or the essence of purity. The question is not whether lawyers and other actors engage in forms of supplication and intimidation but rather when these presentational strategies are most successful. Based on experience with people and juries, lawyers maintain their own preferences and prejudices. It is not uncommon for lawyers to hold one or more of these strategies in contempt as violating their beliefs and values regarding human behavior and style. Yet each strategy has its place given the right case, the right jury, and the right circumstances. The point that must be made is that at the conclusion of a trial, an attorney's behaviors can be assessed as reflecting one of the five presentational approaches, and this assessment will be formulated by jurors from the sum total of communication the attorney engages in, from interaction with the judge, the client, the opposition, and the jury themselves. Skilled attorneys, in the argot of sales, learn to "work a jury" by strategically managing the images they present, and the critical first step in this management is to command a positive first impression.

How important is the initial presentation made before a jury? In a word—crucial. Research has demonstrated that actors use first impressions to guide and augment later impressions. Evidently, people use first impressions to shepherd subsequent impressions as a matter of convenience. The impression formation process begins as a tendency to group people according to their similarities and dissimilarities, placing them in categories or stereotypes or schemas (Cantor and Mischel 1979). By first establishing a schema from which subsequent information can be interpreted, actors provide themselves with a convenient structure around which other impressions can be organized. Significantly, once this schema is employed, individuals tend to consider information consistent with the schema and to disregard impressions inconsistent with the schema. Moreover, when asked later to recall overall impressions of the individual, persons commonly invoke the original schema, sometimes falsely recalling facts to remain consistent with this impression category (Hastie 1980). Because people play less attention to information received after they have formed an initial impression (Anderson 1974), and typically weigh first impressions more heavily than subsequent impressions when making an overall evaluation, a good first impression can result in a "halo effect," serving as a positive frame of reference from which subsequent behavior is evaluated.

One early experiment keenly shows how important initial information can be in forming an impression of another. In this experiment the researcher requested subjects to describe a person who was characterized by a list of six adjectives (Asch 1946). Half the subjects received the list starting with undesirable traits and ending with desirable attributes (envious, stubborn, critical, impulsive, industrious, intelligent), whereas the other subjects received the description with the order reversed, beginning with the positive adjectives. As expected, the subjects formed an impression based on the early adjectives and proceeded to interpret the remaining adjectives so they would fit this image. Those who received the description headed by "intelligent" described the person more positively than did those subjects who read the description beginning with "envious."

What the sum of research on impression formation suggests is that to manage others' impressions, one must start on solid ground. The centrality of initial information to subsequent impressions and evaluations cannot be overstated. Without question the public image one presents clearly affects the rewards obtained in social interaction. That public image is largely modified by what receivers come to expect.

EXPECTATIONS

Because communication is governed by social and cultural rules, people develop norms and expectations concerning the appropriate behavior and communication in given situations. As individuals gain more experience in a given context, frequent confirmation of communication rules and language norms endemic to that context firmly establish expectations which guide future communication and behavior. In the case of trial advocacy the public's vast exposure to courtroom drama on television has resulted in an anchored set of expectations regarding appropriate language and communicative behaviors for courtroom participants. When communicators in these contexts intentionally or accidentally violate the norms or expectations of communication behaviors, receptivity to their messages is greatly altered (Burgoon and Miller 1985). Violations seen as negative result in increased message resistance, while violations viewed as positive result in increased message acceptance.

When a communicator performs a behavior or uses language conforming more closely than anticipated to norms of appropriate communication, a positive expectancy violation occurs which facilitates persuasion. Because the source unexpectedly exhibits positive behaviors, receivers overestimate the favorableness of the behaviors and perceive them as more positive than they actually are. This positive violation reduces resistance to persuasion by promoting immediate positive attitude change toward the advocated position (Burgoon, Jones, and Stewart 1975; Burgoon, Cohen, Miller, and Montgomery 1978; Miller and Burgoon 1979). Persons who act out of character are thought to do so because of strong inner convictions. For this reason, in some cases a communicator who violates the expectancies associated with a specific role, such as an attorney, is seen as more sincere than a person who strictly conforms to the role

(Jones, Davis, and Gergen 1961; Jones, Worchel, Goethals, and Grumet 1971). In fact, communicators who display more socially desirable behaviors than expected tend to be evaluated more positively, sometimes to the extreme that they overcome initially negative impressions (Aboud, Clement, and Taylor 1974).

The classic study of expectancy disconfirmation investigated the influence of sources delivering unexpected messages on persuasion (McPeek and Edwards 1975). In this experiment, one group of long-haired males argued against the use of marijuana while another argued in its favor. In addition, one group of seminarians (also with long hair) argued in favor of marijuana use while another group argued against it. Unexpected sources were rated as more sincere and honest than their expected counterparts, and produced greater attitude change when the message was antimarijuana.

Several researchers have proposed that because communicators commonly argue for their vested interests, receivers develop biased expectations. When communicators appear to argue against their own interest, thus disconfirming these expectations, source credibility and message acceptance are enhanced (Eagly, Chaiken, and Wood 1981). In one study in an advertising context, subjects were exposed to advertisements in which a company spokesperson gave superior ratings on four features of a product (expectancy confirmed); another group viewed ads in which the spokesperson gave superior ratings on three features of the product but described one feature as less than superior (expectancy disconfirmed). Researchers found that those subjects who viewed ads that disconfirmed bias-related expectations were more likely to accept the content of that advertising than were those who viewed ads confirming those expectations.

Numerous other advantages exist concerning positive violations of expectations. When exposed to an unexpected event individuals exert greater cognitive effort and engage in more vigorous attributional processing (Pyszczynski and Greenberg 1981). Moreover, individuals who receive unexpected messages became more highly involved with those messages, processing the information piece by piece (Fiske 1982). Because expectation-confirming messages are less involving, and expectation-disconfirming messages require greater involvement, we can conclude that the stability of subsequent persuasion from these messages also varies. Research by Petty and Cacioppo (1984a, 1984b; Cacioppo and Petty 1984) proposes that individuals exposed to a persuasive message are bombarded with more cues than they can process, so they must choose which cues to focus upon. Two routes of cognitive evaluation are open to jurors making this choice: central and peripheral. When the quality of the information determines attitude change, the central route has been taken. The peripheral route refers, on the other hand, to a concentration on the characteristics of the process, such as who the witness is and what circumstances exist. Jurors' motivation and ability to process a message is called "elaboration likelihood." In a state of high motivation and ability (high elaboration likelihood), jurors would predictably choose a central route and focus on the content of the testimony or on the arguments made by counsel. When the elaboration likelihood is low, jurors form attitudes based upon peripheral cues, such as the status of the witness or the dress of the attorney.

According to the elaboration model, messages high in personal relevance receive more scrutiny. Jurors, therefore, will tend to use a central route when the testimony promises to be helpful in decision making or is relevant in some other way. When the testimony engages a high involvement from the jurors, then, the content of what is said will outweigh contextual factors. Furthermore, persuasion resulting from the central and elaborated route is more resistant to decay and is longer lasting (Petty and Cacioppo 1981). Since disconfirming messages require more involvement and elaboration, persuasion resulting from these messages will be prolonged.

To summarize, when processing a message, receivers discern cues and then assign the relevant features (the person, the message, the delivery) a social category or schema. These expectancies regarding communicators' beliefs and behaviors are used to make sense of the experience. The general rule is that expectancies are usually confirmed. In those cases where an individual's expectations are disconfirmed, message acceptance is altered.

Effective courtroom strategy regarding juror expectations consists of first ascertaining the general expectations of jurors and then designing messages that violate those expectations in a favorable manner. Perhaps more important, the advocate wants to avoid communication that negatively violates expectations. Without diminishing the role of creativity involved with message design, we can illustrate this strategy with a common example. It is safe to say that of the many expectations jurors possess concerning defense attorneys, they generally expect them to behave in an impersonal manner, to present the best case possible even if they believe the client is guilty, and to speak articulately. Lawyers might violate these expectations in several ways. A positive violation might consist of addressing jurors by surname during voir dire, whereas addressing them with nicknames would constitute a negative violation for most. Even though jurors expect an impersonal approach, they would probably view an attorney who treated prospective jurors as objects during voir dire as negatively violating this expectation. The all too common practice of referring to a prospective juror as "juror number four" exemplifies this violation. Lawyers who explicitly tell the jurors that they believe in their client's innocence may favorably violate expectations, while going as far as to espouse neutrality would negatively violate expectations. To maintain an even balance in this example, consider that lawyers who lack articulate expression will probably evoke an adverse expectancy reaction, while articulate lawyers simply conform to stereotypes. How might an attorney positively violate the expectation of articulateness? Perhaps by eliminating or elucidating legal jargon, rather then relying on the jurors to decipher it.

THE FOUNDATIONS OF CREDIBILITY:
INTRINSIC FEATURES

Few legal practitioners presume that messages would have the same effect regardless of who delivers them. Communicators are as vital to persuasion as the content of the messages they impart, and a litany of evidence suggests that a communicator accorded high credibility will exert more influence than will one with low credibility. Credibility refers to the persuasive influence that results from the perceived characteristics of the communicator. The critical point here is one of perception. Credibility is conferred by an audience to a communicator and is not inherently possessed. A communicator is only as credible as others are willing to believe, no matter how objectively honest or competent that person might be.

About twenty-five centuries ago Aristotle first described how perceptions of a speaker enhanced persuasion. The Greek philosopher believed that a speaker could persuade an audience by demonstrating that his personal character was beyond reproach. This image of character, or "ethos," framed the speaker as good and knowledgeable, prerequisites for moving an audience in a desired direction. For Aristotle ethos consisted of three components: good sense, good moral character, and good will. Modern-day scholarship acknowledges the wisdom of Aristotle's analysis. Although the names have changed, the concept of credibility remains essentially the same. Contemporary researchers continue to dispute the labels, but they generally agree that two main components constitute credibility: trustworthiness (also known as character and safety) and expertise (also known as authoritativeness, competence, and qualification). Communicators are considered trustworthy when observers presume they have no vested interest to lie or deceive the audience. For example, one study found that an employee who delivered a procompany speech was perceived as less trustworthy than a former employee who delivered the same speech (Dutton 1973). Communicators are viewed as expert when receivers presume their intelligence, ability, or experience relate to the issue in question. For example, message recipients consistently assign higher credibility ratings to high-status sources (Harms 1961; Simon, Berkowitz, and Moyer 1970; Moe 1972), presumably because they believe social position to reflect expertise (Berger, Fisek, Norman, and Zelditch 1977).

Research has also identified an additional dimension of credibility related to how active and potent a communicator is (Berlo, Lemmert, and Mertz 1969). Labeled "dynamism," this dimension refers to the source's energy, boldness, and aggressiveness, and is thought to intensify the other two factors. For example, high dynamism on the part of the speaker will intensify the evaluations of a speaker so as to make a communicator with moderate expertise appear more expert and one with moderate character appear more trustworthy. Other dimensions that intensify the perceptions of expertise and trustworthiness include composure and sociability. Should a courtroom actor, such as a witness or lawyer, be perceived to lack dynamism, composure, or sociability, reflected by nervous fidgeting, low voice intensity, and limited eye contact, he or she is likely to be perceived as relatively less expert and trustworthy by others.

Generally speaking, the primary dimensions of trustworthiness and expertise constitute credibility across contexts, even cultures (King, Minami, and Samovar 1985), yet specific evaluations and additional factors do vary according to the situation (Smith 1973). The actors' goals in a persuasive situation as well as the consequences at stake substantially influence what dimensions will weigh most heavily in conferring credibility (Cronkhite and Liska 1976, 1980). For example, lawyers are generally seen as highly competent but untrustworthy, undependable to tell the truth (Rotter and Stein 1971). Moreover, several additional factors work to enhance or attenuate an attorney's credibility.

Interviews with more than eleven hundred Maryland jurors after their jury service revealed that lawyers who are professional, well prepared, dynamic, and thorough were perceived as most credible (Cramer 1979). High marks were given to lawyers who gave authoritative presentations, who had command of the case, who kept the trial moving, and who provided clear and detailed opening statements. Lawyers who appeared to the jury to respect and believe in their clients and who made successful objections were also accorded higher ratings. Among the factors detracting from credibility were informality, interruptions, and slang. What is apparent from these findings is that message style plays a central role in perceived effectiveness.

MESSAGE STYLE.   From the criteria communicators find useful in evaluating messages a consistent pattern emerges. Receivers attribute credibility to those sources who employ a persuasive message style that they perceive to be effective. A communicator's message is perceived as more persuasive when he or she is more logical, more predictable, more factual, more emotional, more assertive, and less ambiguous (Hazelton, Cupach, and Liska 1986).

A long-standing criticism of low credibility messages is that the source often emulates a dense written style more than a conversational or oral style. One experimental study confirmed this suspicion and provided evidence of other message features which correlate with source credibility (Carbone 1975). Specifically, messages of high credibility sources contained fewer words per sentence, fewer syllables per word, and a larger number of simple sentences, which combined to make the message more conversational and easy to listen to. Highly credible sources also used more first- and second-person pronouns ("I," "we," "you") and greater reference to experts and specific individuals, making the message more interesting. In addition, messages from credible sources used more diverse language and contained more factual statements.

SIMILARITY.   When receivers see communicators as similar to themselves in attitudes, background, and experience, they are more likely to accept messages and perceive the source as likable (Berscheid 1966). The salutary effects of perceived similarity stem primarily from the individual's need to evaluate his or her beliefs. When people are unsure about the reasonableness of their opinions regarding social issues, they seek a social comparison (Festinger 1954). Indeed, humans are driven to reduce uncertainty and doggedly pursue information that will validate their opinions and attitudes. The critical issue in this process is the source of that comparison. Research has demonstrated that individuals seek out others perceived to be similar in attributes related to the relevant opinion. Once individuals perceive another to be similar in stable attributes, such as background, experience, education, status, political affiliation, etc., they use this person or group as a frame of reference from which to evaluate the appropriateness and reasonableness of their opinions.

Because of this comparison, and because similar others are seen as more attractive, similar persons are conferred greater credibility in most situations and can exert substantial influence on matters in which the perceiver is unfamiliar.

In a classic field study in this area customers who had selected paint were stopped by a salesperson who offered advice (Brock 1965). The salesperson recommended the purchase of a different paint brand that was either more or less expensive than the one they had chosen. To support this advice, the salesperson claimed that he had finished a project two weeks earlier and had used either the same amount of paint the purchaser was carrying (similar) or had used twenty times the amount of paint the customer was carrying (dissimilar). On the basis of his experience the salesperson claimed the alternative brand was superior. Results revealed that customers bought more of the advocated paint brand when the salesperson seemed similar than when the salesperson seemed dissimilar, even when the advocated brand was more expensive than the original choice.

In a criminal trial the similarity or dissimilarity between jurors and the defendant may influence perceptions of guilt and jury verdicts. Several studies indicate that jurors with attitudes similar to the defendant's rate the defendant as less guilty and recommend shorter sentences (Dane and Wrightsman 1982). Although attitude similarity unquestionably affects juror evaluations, attitude dissimilarity may produce a more pronounced effect on judgment. One scholar goes as far as to contend that attitude dissimilarity between jurors and defendant is the single most influential factor in the treatment of black defendants (Bell 1973). Research reveals that jurors with dissimilar attitudes are more likely to convict a defendant and recommend harsher sentences (Shepherd and Sloan 1979). In one study subjects whose attitudes on several issues were dissimilar to those credited to the defendant suggested longer sentences and regarded the defendant as more guilty than did those subjects who perceived greater attitude similarity (Griffitt and Jackson 1973). Interestingly, dissimilarity may sometimes be more persuasive than similarity when individuals desire verification of what they believe are facts. When a dispute deals primarily with values or opinions where no verifiably "correct" answer exists, agreement with a similar source elevates confidence in one's position. On the other hand, when the dispute concerns verifiable facts, agreement with a dissimilar source elevates confidence (Goethals and Nelson 1973). For example, suppose opponents in a trial dispute two key issues: (1) whether the suspect was physically fit (opinion); and (2) whether or not a suspect ran to the scene of a crime (fact). In the first case, if a similar person concurs that the suspect is fit, an individual is likely to be more confident that his or her assessment was correct. But the verification by a similar person that the suspect ran to the crime scene would not increase one's confidence nearly as much as the verification by a dissimilar source. Because dissimilar sources consult different outlets of information, confirmation magnifies confidence.

CONFIDENCE.   Increased confidence in one's beliefs strengthens existing attitudes and makes one more resistant to persuasion. In the same light, the confidence exuded by a source is highly influential. When receivers perceive a source to be confident, they confer the source higher credibility. One line of research contends that persuasive effectiveness is a function of the confidence speakers have in their positions (London 1973). In legal settings, research has shown repeatedly that confident eyewitnesses are perceived to be more believable and more accurate (Whitley and Greenberg 1986). Moreover, simply by coaching witnesses attorneys can enhance witness credibility. In one study researchers found that witnesses who were briefed about an upcoming cross-examination displayed increased confidence and were accorded greater credibility by jurors (Wells, Lindsay, and Ferguson 1979).

THE COMMUNICATOR'S MOTIVES.   When receivers perceive that a communicator intends to persuade them, the source is viewed as less trustworthy and hence less credible. As a result, persuasive intent will very often reduce the likelihood of message acceptance. Several studies in the area of forewarning of a persuasive message demonstrate this effect. In these experiments, when receivers are warned that a communicator will attempt to persuade them, they generate counterarguments in anticipation of the message, resulting in increased resistance to the communication (Cialdini and Petty 1981; Petty and Cacioppo 1977; Freedman and Sears 1965). But forewarning of a persuasive message is not a necessary prerequisite to this resistance. Persuasive intent alone as perceived by message recipients inhibits influence (Petty and Cacioppo 1979; Hass and Grady 1975; Kiesler and Kiesler 1964). This is especially true when the topic is personally important to the receiver. Other dubious motives also abrogate persuasion. In one study, before exposing subjects to a message, researchers described a communicator's motives in one of two ways to subjects, as either selfish or unselfish (Pastore and Horowitz 1955). The selfish motive alone significantly diminished the persuasive effect of the message. Conversely, the absence of persuasive or undesirable motives enhances the influence of messages.

For example, researchers who contrived a situation where subjects overheard a communication not intended for the subjects found the message to be more effective than a communication that was intended for them (Walster and Festinger 1962).

NONVERBAL CUES.   At the point where overt and covert influences meet, nonverbal communication may play the most crucial role in credibility (Henley 1977). Nonverbal communication consists of those messages communicated without spoken or written words, generally referring to facial expressions, body movements, and the distance between communicators, and is commonly classified into five categories: (1) Paralanguage includes vocal qualities such as pitch, loudness, intensity, and amplitude as well as speech qualities such as stuttering, nonfluencies, pauses, and omissions. (2) Facial expressions include the many different configurations of the face. The facial musculature of humans is capable of creating over a thousand different expressions (Ekman, Friesen, and Ellsworth 1972). (3) Kinesics refers to movements and gestures of the head (but not the face), arms, legs, hands, feet, and torso. (4) Eye movement includes changes in eye characteristics such as blinking and pupil size, and visual behavior such as staring. (5) Proxemics refers to how people use space to increase or decrease distance.

Nonverbal behaviors serve several communicative functions, including providing information and feedback to others, regulating interaction, exercising social control and influence, and expressing intimacy (Patterson 1983). Germane to our discussion in this chapter is the relationship between nonverbal communication and influence. Since no one nonverbal behavior or communicative act exerts a direct influence, we must treat nonverbal communication as a composite of behaviors and turn to more interactive measures of influence, such as dominance and status. Dominance is a relational attribute stemming from one person's ability to restrict or successfully control the interactional options of another. Although sometimes used to refer to an individual's predisposition and desire to influence others, more often dominance describes the social position of any one individual in relation to other individuals in a group. Dominance in this sense is considered an emergent property of social interaction and not of individual intention (Henley 1977). We can best understand the exacting influence of nonverbal communication by assessing the nonverbal indicators of dominance as well as the attributions actors make concerning consistent nonverbal features.

Paralinguistic behavior. Paralinguistic indicators of dominance include a tendency to interrupt (Natale, Entin, and Jaffee 1979), greater speech volume, speaking first (Packwood 1974), amount of talk (Sorrentino and Boutillier 1975), and tonal suggestions of anger (Bugenthal and Love 1975). Individuals who tend to overlap their speech with others are considered to be more dominant, whereas those persons who tend not to complete their own utterances are viewed as low in dominance (Ferguson 1977). Research has repeatedly demonstrated that nonfluencies in speech attenuate ratings of credibility and competence (Miller and Hewgill 1964; Sereno and Hawkins 1967). Nonfluencies include stuttering, unintended pauses such as "ah" and "umm," the superfluous repetition of a word, and sentence corrections. Moreover, excessive pauses both within a speaker's turn and between turns results in lower evaluations of competence (Lay and Burron, 1968; Newman 1982; Scherer 1979).

Perhaps the most widely examined area of paralinguistic behavior is speech rate. Moderate to relatively faster rates have consistently been found to be more socially attractive to listeners as well as inducing higher ratings of trustworthiness and competence (Miller, Marayama, Beaber, and Valone 1976; Stewart and Ryan 1982; Street and Brady 1982). How fast is too fast? Between 195 and 325 fluent syllables per minute is considered fast and advantageous. Rates upward of 375 syllables per minute are thought to diminish in attractiveness and increase the difficulty of information processing (Street, Brady, and Putman 1983).

Facial expressions. When asked to judge photographs of people for dominance, college students rated models with lowered brows or nonsmiling mouths as more dominant (Keating, Mazur, and Segall 1977). In other words, a serious expression denotes dominance. In addition, lower status persons tend to exhibit increases in facial expressions toward higher status persons (Hottenstein 1978).

Eye movement. Longer-lasting looks are commonly directed by higher status persons toward lower status persons (Fugita 1974). High status or dominant individuals receive more gaze from others, especially when speaking, and they tend to make eye contact less when listening to subordinates (Exline, Ellyson, and Long 1975). Lower status persons tend to break eye contact first (Strongman and Champness 1968). Persons who are relatively high in status or desire for control exhibit higher visual dominance ratios of looking while speaking to looking while listening. For example, attributions of power have been found to increase with more frequent looking while speaking and to decrease with more frequent looking while listening (Dovidio and Ellyson 1985). Credible communicators excel in making direct eye contact with listeners. For example, one study found that witnessees who exhibit greater eye contact during testimony presentation were judged as more trustworthy and honest than those who engaged in lower levels of eye contact (Fromme and Beam 1974).

Kinesics. Dominance is typically displayed through body movements with behaviors implying strength, comfort/relaxation, and fearlessness, whereas submissiveness is communicated by weakness, smallness, discomfort, tension, and fearfulness (Mehrabian 1981). Postural relaxation, while the individual is either standing or sitting, is seen as an indicator of dominance. Behaviors of increased body movement (arms outstretched, active hand gestures, movement while seated) are also viewed as dominant. Conversely, constriction of movement as well as tense or rigid posture and a hunched body indicate submissiveness and exert less influence.

Proxemic behavior. When placed in new environments, dominant individuals seek out and control specific locations and furniture (Altman and Haythorn 1967). Moreover, their peers give dominant and high status individuals greater access to and control over more desirable and spacious locations (Sundstrom and Altman 1974; Hall 1966). Control is strongly associated with interpersonal touching. Dominance and status imply the ability and accessibility to touch others and an inaccessibility to the touching of oneself (Henley 1977). When touch is uninvited and nonreciprocal, it becomes a status indicator (Frieze and Ramsey 1976). Higher status individuals have been shown to touch others more frequently (Henley 1973). Persons who engage in nonreciprocal touching are perceived as more aggressive, more independent, and more confident than the recipient of the touch (Major and Heslin 1982). How people approach one another is also associated with dominance and status. Higher status persons often have greater opportunity to control the approach of others (Walker and Borden 1976; Willis and Hoffman 1975). Dominance is implied by swift and direct approaches (Mehrabian 1981).

The recurrent theme in these empirical relationships makes clear that credible communicators engage in vibrant and active nonverbal behaviors, incorporating energetic gestures and movements as well as direct eye contact with listeners.

Nonverbal cues of witnesses and lawyers. When jurors assess the credibility of witnesses during testimony, they rely heavily on both verbal and nonverbal cues. In one examination of the effect of nonverbal cues on witness credibility, researchers designed an experiment where testimony content and witness attributes, with the exception of nonverbal cues, were held constant (Miller, Bender, Boster, Florence, Fontes, Hocking, and Nicholson 1975; Miller,

Boster, Fontes, LeFebvre, and Poole 1975). In this study jurors listened to identical testimony presented by either a "strong" or "weak" witness, played by the same professional actor. Weak testimony was characterized by paralinguistic and kinesic indicators of anxiety (i.e., nervous body movements and vocal distractions). Strong testimony was portrayed by confident and assertive responses with few distractions. Miller and his associates found that the nonverbal style of the witness had an effect on both witness credibility and information retention. The strong witness was rated as more credible than the weak witness, and had more of his testimony retained by the jurors.

Researchers have also examined the nonverbal styles of attorneys. In one study subjects were exposed to defense and prosecuting attorneys using one of three distinct styles: passive, assertive, or aggressive (Sigal, Braden-MaGuire, Hayden, and Mosely 1985). A passive style consisted of a slow speech rate, low levels of eye contact, reduced gestures, and a monotone presentation with many pauses. An assertive style was reflected by a normal speech rate, expressive gestures, and moderate eye contact. Attorneys exhibiting the aggressive style used a high rate and volume of speech, emotional gestures (such as pounding a fist on the table), high eye contact, and hostile inflections. As might be expected, the passive style was found to be less effective, resulting in fewer guilty judgments and a decrease in perceived confidence. Although attorneys employing the aggressive style were perceived as more effective than actors exhibiting the other two styles, verdict judgments were the same between the aggressive and assertive styles.

NONVERBAL CUES AND DECEPTION.   Persons perceived to be intent on persuading others and confident in their positions are also judged to exhibit extroverted and involving nonverbal cues. Cues related to intention to persuade and the appearance of confidence include increased eye contact, vocal volume, speaking rate, intonation, and facial activity as well as fewer behaviors reflecting anxiety (Maslow, Yoselson, and London 1971; Mehrabian and Williams 1969; Timney and London 1973). Interestingly, research consistently shows that communicators who display the same pattern of cues exhibiting extroversion, involvement, positivity, and composure are perceived as more credible and persuasive. This match signifies that individuals, on the whole, know what nonverbal cues enhance credibility and can discern when others are attempting to persuade them. But can people detect deception? The answer is complex and first requires an understanding of how individuals attempt to detect deception.

People rely most heavily on nonverbal cues when assessing the veracity of others (Argyle, Alkema, and Gilmour 1971). Nonverbal cues such as facial expressions and body movements are generally considered good indicators of the veracity of a statement made by a witness. Although research on the use of nonverbal cues by jurors to detect witness deception is not clear-cut, this area of investigation is promising. Research by Ekman and Friesen (1974) found that people are better able to detect deception from bodily cues than from facial cues. The researchers contend that the hands and feet provide the best deception cues because they are less carefully monitored than are the face and eyes.

One study provided only partial support for this contention when researchers divided deception into two distinct types: emotional and factual (Hocking, Miller, and Fontes 1978). Subjects assessed the veracity of the answers given by a witness to questions dealing with an emotional state and to responses relevant to the events witnessed. The experiment also manipulated the types of nonverbal cues subjects could see: the body only, the head only, or the body and head. By manipulating exposure to different sections of the person, the researchers could determine which cues best revealed deception. Results revealed that emotional deception was best detected when only the body was seen by subjects, and that factual deception was best detected when subjects saw the head and body or the head only.

Although these findings provide some leads to which cues most clearly reveal deception, probably the most interesting outcome of this study was that observers were most accurate in detecting deception when they were blind to all nonverbal cues. Subjects who read only transcripts of the answers were the most accurate in detecting deception. Indeed, nonverbal behaviors may actually distract from judgments of veracity. In another study subjects were more accurate when listening to or reading an interview containing deceptive communication than when they witnessed it live (Maier and Thurber 1968). This is particularly disturbing in light of research indicating that observers are highly confident in their accuracy when they rely on nonverbal cues. For example, when their judgments were based entirely on nonverbal cues without the accompanying audio, subjects asked to rate the truthfulness of a stranger reported a confidence rating in their evaluations of 58 percent (Hocking, Miller, and Fontes 1978). With the audio portion included, subject confidence increased only a modest 6 percent. To make matters worse, researchers agree that observers are not highly accurate in detecting deception with the use of all available cues.

This inaccuracy is more shocking when one considers that verbal characteristics of deceptive messages are equally distinctive. For example, deceivers are known to use fewer words, fewer different words, fewer past-tense verbs, fewer group and self references, fewer statements of self-experiences, more allness terms (everybody, none, etc.), and more disparaging comments (Knapp and Comadena 1979). More encouraging is the finding that people are much more successful at identifying truthsayers than they are liars, and some evidence suggests they depend more on vocal cues to make these veracity judgments (DePaulo, Rosenthal, Eisenstat, Rogers, and Finkelstein 1978). For example, when attempting to assess truthfulness rather than deception, subjects rely primarily on fluency, spontaneity, and enthusiasm as well as on features of the speaker's treatment of the subject matter (Cahn 1985).

The fact remains, however, that although observers are known to encode those cues that reflect deceptive behavior, remarkably they are not very accurate in detecting deception perpetrated by strangers. Several studies have demonstrated that observers succeed in identifying deceptive communicators only 50 percent of the time (Miller and Burgoon 1982). This unusual inability to detect deception can best be explained by the degree of contact between parties. Although liars often use a higher vocal pitch and more nonfluencies ("uh," "um," etc.) and anxiety-expressive behaviors such as random body movements, frequent leg crossing, and the fondling of objects (Ekman and Friesen 1969, 1974; Ekman, Friesen, and Scherer 1976; Knapp, Hart, and Dennis 1974; Streeter, Krauss, Geller, Olson, and Apple 1977), lying is best characterized by a deviancy from the communicator's normal response pattern. The communicator intent on deception will commonly exaggerate pleasant facial expressions and change normal body movements and speaking rate (Mehrabian 1971, 1972). Because juries are not typically familiar with a witness' normal nonverbal behavior, they are at a distinct disadvantage in assessing veracity. Yet many witnesses spend a good deal of time on the stand, and, assuming that deception occurs in only a part of the testimony, juries often have enough time to assess changes in behavior.

EXTRINSIC FEATURES OF CREDIBILITY

The verbal and nonverbal characteristics related to judgments of credibility discussed so far can be considered intrinsic features endemic to individuals. In addition to these characteristics courtroom actors carry with them an assortment of extrinsic factors—such as status, sex, physical appearance, age, and general reputation—that influence credibility judgments.

SOCIAL POWER. Power refers to the ability to control another person's behavior as a result of external forces, most typically the ability to punish or reward that person. Because the target does not internalize the message and act favorably upon it but rather responds to the external force of the communicator who limits the freedom to choose, scholars generally consider this influence as markedly different from persuasion and credibility. At least five sources or bases of a communicator's power exist (French and Raven 1959; Raven 1965). Coercive power is based upon the ability of the agent to punish another, whereas reward power is the influence resulting from the ability of the agent to reward another. When others believe the agent has a social or cultural right to influence them, as is commonly the case with judges, legitimate power exists. Expert power is based upon the target's belief that the agent possesses expertise relevant to the domain of influence. Finally, information power refers to the influence exerted by the content of a message. In each case power is a function of the target's perceptions of the agent's abilities. These perceptions are largely shaped by the physical and social resources available to the agent. Extrinsic features of a source, such as education, race, status, attractiveness, etc., as well as social skills, such as gregariousness, articulateness, etc., constitute an infinite set of possible resources from which an agent may draw or may be perceived to possess. When influence is a result of the perceived possession or the external promise or threat to use a resource, a communicator is said to be powerful. Although this power does not necessarily make a source more believable, the resulting influence stems from perceived characteristics of the source and falls under the rubric of credibility. Because power is dependent on the perceptions of the receiver, it is important to keep in mind that no objective standard of power exists.

Power is negotiated through communication. In other words, a person is now powerful unless others confer power upon him. For example, imagine the highly coercive scene where a hoodlum holds a citizen at gunpoint while demanding money. A first impression indicates that the gun makes the hoodlum powerful and allows him to control the other's behavior. But think again. Is it the gun or the citizen's belief that the hoodlum will use the gun that makes him powerful? We can make the same point in the courtroom. Although a lawyer holds the legitimate power and ability to castigate witnesses by demanding they follow the rules of examination, this influence occurs only if the witness believes the attorney will employ this sanction or if, in the course of examination, the attorney does indeed publicly admonish the witness for breaking the rules. Consider, however, the common act of denial where a witness violates a rule: say, she asks the attorney a question, and the attorney fails to chastise the witness but instead answers the question. If this pattern repeats itself in other forms, who, in the eyes of the jury, is powerful? Quite obviously the witness holds power, and will be afforded higher credibility as a result. The lawyer, on the other hand, by giving up legitimate power through interaction severely diminishes his own credibility.

ATTRACTIVENESS AND PHYSICAL APPEARANCE.   All other factors held constant, physically attractive people are more influential than their less attractive counterparts. Research confirms that good-looking people are perceived to possess greater social skills and to be more friendly, likable, and interesting (Berscheid and Walster 1974). In one experimental study in this area, after rehearsing a persuasive message, subject-sources stopped campus pedestrians to ask if they would complete a survey (Chaiken 1979). If passersby agreed, the sources instructed them to complete the questionnaire and then requested that they sign a petition related to the survey. Attractive sources elicited greater agreements, as reflected by the questionnaire, and educed more petition signatures.

What is it that makes physically attractive sources so appealing? Beauty, of course, but mainly an association between attractiveness and a multitude of desirable attributes, including intelligence, gregariousness, and unselfishness. Because attractive communicators also think more positively about themselves, others are motivated to identify with and to seek approval from them. Agreeing with an attractive person is one way of saying, "I am similar to an attractive person." Attractive courtroom actors appear to benefit from this identification. For example, limited evidence suggests that attractive litigants win their civil cases more often than less attractive litigants (Snyder 1971). The influence of attractiveness also extends to how we evaluate defendants.

Research confirms what legal practitioners suspect in regard to the physical attractiveness of the defendant. Physically attractive persons receive less severe punishment than do defendants perceived to be unattractive (Dion 1972; Efron 1974; McFatter 1978). This leniency, however, is affected by the type of crime committed. In a crime unrelated to physical attractiveness, such as robbery, attractive defendants tend to receive less severe punishments. When the crime is associated with attractiveness, such as larceny or embezzlement, the attractive defendant tends to receive a more severe punishment (Sigall and Osgrove 1975). Jurors are also more certain of the guilt of physically less attractive defendants (Berg and Vidmar 1975). In one study subjects were exposed to case materials containing information reflecting either positive traits of the defendant, positive and negative traits, negative traits, or no information (Kaplan and Kemmerick 1974). As defendant attractiveness decreased in these descriptions, ratings of guilt increased. In another study interviews with jurors from seven criminal cases revealed that jurors who vote for acquittal tend to view defendants and their attorneys as personable and attractive while seeing the prosecutors as less physically attractive and less personable (McLaughlin 1979).

The limitations of these findings are obvious. By itself, no one attribute, such as physical attractiveness, among the hundreds of personal, social, and legal attributes at work can reasonably be expected to determine legal outcomes. Rather, these attributes work together to influence legal and judgmental processes. For example, in one experimental study researchers exposed subjects to a series of trials involving accidents and found that the effect of physical attractiveness on verdict was mediated by perceptions of the seriousness of the accident (Kulka and Kessler 1978). As the seriousness of the accident increased, the effect of physical attraction on verdict lessened. Similarly, another study demonstrated that the quality of evidence reduces the effect of defendant attractiveness on sentencing (Baumeister and Darley 1982). When subjects read weak evidence concerning a defendant's drunk driving charge, an attractive defendant received a more lenient driving suspension (21.1 months) than an unattractive defendant (48.3 months). Subjects exposed to strong evidence against either an attractive or unattractive defendant, however, recommended harsh suspensions for both.

The general physical appearance of a defendant may also influence attributions of guilt (Shoemaker, South, and Lowe 1973). Jurors hold stereotypic notions about the appearance of criminals and generally assume that people who commit crimes maintain similar appearances, usually possessing aberrant features. Research shows that people believe an abnormal appearance to be indicative of abnormal behavior and personality (Secord 1958). For example, in one study facial disfigurement substantially influenced attributions (Bull 1979). Specifically, persons with facial scars were judged less attractive, less sincere, less affectionate, and less truthful than persons without scars.

STATUS AND GENDER.   As social actors people play a number of work- and group-related roles as they perform the functions of everyday life. The prestige associated with a role determines the status of that role. Status is an individual's relative position in a prestige hierarchy. People learn through everyday experiences that certain characteristics are associated with status, and as a result they develop expectations that affect behavior even in situations where status is not an issue (Berger, Rosenholtz, and Zelditch 1980). Status fluctuates as cultural values change. For example, presently most Americans believe a United States senator is of higher status than a mayor of even a large metropolitan city. But what of the status of a military officer, a craftsperson, or even a professor in today's society? As times and political events have changed, so has the prestige associated with many occupational roles. Most scholars agree that status is highly influential, primarily because of its relationship to power and dominance (Patterson 1985). In addition, although there is not a direct link between status and credibility, persons of high status are generally rated higher in credibility than are low status persons. Research in the legal area confirms this influence. Not surprisingly, one researcher found that a defendant described as an architect was viewed as more trustworthy than one described as a janitor (Shaw 1972). Persons low in socioeconomic status are also considered more blameworthy of the crimes they commit, resulting in longer sentences in mock jury studies (Gleason and Harris 1976; Rumsey 1976).

Because women have been held to be socially powerless, they are commonly viewed as low in status, and they experience the same credibility bias as other low status persons (O'Barr 1982). Despite the fact that women are not more susceptible to persuasive messages than are men, there exists a stable perception that women are less believable. This results from prejudicial stereotypes that cast women as inaccurate observers because of an emotional nature or as sly, manipulative persons who are vindictive and therefore untrustworthy. To combat this problem many states have established panels to study the gender bias present in their courts. Most conclude that women litigants are indeed accorded less credibility by judges, lawyers, and juries.

The reason for the credibility bias against low status and female persons can, in part, be explained by the expectations receivers hold concerning influence style. Receivers expect high status persons to employ a more direct and impolite influence strategy. In other words, high status communicators are expected to employ more commands and fewer polite phrases such as "please" and "thank you." Conversely, receivers expect lower status persons to engage in more indirect and polite influence attempts (Steffen and Eagly 1985). Because women generally occupy lower status roles, they are expected to be more polite and less direct than men (Newcomb and Arnkoff 1979). Violations of these expectancies result in negative evaluations for low status persons and females (Burgoon, Dillard, and Doran 1983). For example, when low status witnesses use direct or impolite styles, which they inevitably do during a hostile cross-examination, they will be perceived as less persuasive and likable. Lawyers and high status witnesses, however, are free to use direct and impolite styles without suffering negative consequences. In fighting against gender bias, it is important for counsel to provide status cues for female witnesses. When jurors have more definitive information about status than apparent gender, such as an occupational title, this information will often outweigh beliefs about influence style (Eagly and Steffen 1984).

One question that invariably arises during a discussion on gender bias is that of the effectiveness of female attorneys. Are female attorneys as effective as male attorneys? The evidence suggests that women are every bit as effective as men. In one study subjects viewed either a male or a female prosecuting attorney in a simulated courtroom robbery trial (Sigal, Braden-MaGuire, Hayden, and Mosely 1985). No difference in verdicts was found between male and female attorneys even when the females engaged in highly aggressive and assertive styles. In addition, subjects did not rate males as more effective than females regardless of the styles they employed. The reason for this correspondence appears to relate to the occupational role of lawyering. Job role requirements and not sex role stereotypes most strongly determine evaluations of lawyers. In other words, women engaged in occupations where they are expected to engage in aggressive behavior are not evaluated negatively when they fulfill their role obligations.

This does not mean that women and men are perceived identically. For example, although gender was found not to affect juror perceptions of effectiveness in an experimental study, females attorneys using a dynamic speaking style were perceived as more persuasive than females using a conversational style (Barge, Schlueter, Pritchard, and Rowland 1987). Conversely, male attorneys were perceived as more persuasive in the conversational mode than in the dynamic style. Stated another way, female attorneys may need to overcome competency biases by exhibiting behaviors more closely related to the stereotypic role of a lawyer and display more confident and aggressive behaviors.

AGE AND THE BIAS AGAINST CHILDREN.   As one might conclude from our earlier discussion on the effects of similarity, individuals tend to confer more credibility to same-age peers than to persons dissimilar to themselves in age (Cantor, Alfonso, and Zillman 1975). This tendency is particularly noteworthy to lawyers given the dramatic increase in testimony by child witnesses. In recent years the courts have become more willing to qualify children as competent witnesses. This is due, in part, to the court's dependence on children's testimony in cases involving children. In some instances children may be even more credible than adults because of their deficiency in social knowledge. For example, young children who testify in sexual abuse cases are typically thought incapable of producing details about which they have no basis of experience or knowledge. Yet despite the fact that children may sometimes be more credible than adults, a credibility bias exists against children. Jurors are commonly instructed that children are less credible witnesses than adults because they are more suggestible.

In general, jurors do not believe children as witnesses. When asked about the reliability of a hypothetical eight-year-old witness, less than 50 percent of potential jurors and legal professionals believed the child would respond accurately (Yarmey and Jones 1983). In one study subjects read trial descriptions or watched a videotaped mock trial which varied the age of an eyewitness whose testimony was pivotal to the case (Goodman, Golding, Helgeson, Haith, and Michelli 1987). In three different experiments subject-jurors judged children to be significantly less credible than adults. This credibility decrease was particularly pronounced for children as young as six years. The primary reason for this credibility bias is a belief by jurors that children may remember less than adults and may be easily manipulated into giving false accounts, although evidence suggests that this is not always the case (Goodman and Reed 1986). As long as this bias exists, however, attorneys should be aware that it may be virtually impossible to obtain convictions when a child provides the key testimony in a criminal trial.

REFERENCES

Aboud, F. D.; Clement, R.; and Taylor, D. M. (1974). Evaluative reactions to discrepancies between social class and language. *Sociometry* 37: 239–50.

Altman, I., and Haythorn, W. (1967). The ecology of isolated groups. *Behavioral Science* 12: 169–82.

Anderson, N. H. (1974). Cognitive algebra: integration theory applied to social attribution. In L. Berkowitz (ed.), *Advances in experimental social psychology,* vol. 7. New York: Academic Press.

Argyle, M.; Alkema, F.; and Gilmour, R. (1971). The communication of friendly and hostile attitudes by verbal and non-verbal signals. *European Journal of Social Psychology* 1:385–402.

Asch, S. (1946). Forming impressions of personality. *Journal of Abnormal and Social Psychology* 41: 258–90.

Barge, J. K.; Schlueter, D. W.; Pritchard, A.; and Rowland, R. C. (1987). The jury as audience: the impact of gender and delivery style upon jurors' perceptions. Paper presented at the convention of the Central State Speech Association, St. Louis.

Baumeister, R. F., and Darley, J. M. (1982). Reducing the biasing effect of perpetrator attractiveness in jury simulation. *Personality and Social Psychology Bulletin* 8: 286–92.

Bell, D. A., Jr. (1973). Racism in American courts: cause for black disruption or despair? *California Law Review* 61: 165–203.

Bell, R. A., and Daly, J. A. (1984). The affinity-seeking function of communication. *Communication Monographs* 51: 91–114.

Berg, K. S., and Vidmar, N. (1975). Authoritarianism and recall of evidence about recall behavior. *Journal of Research in Personality* 9: 147–57.

Berger, J.; Fisek, M. H.; Norman, R. Z.; and Zelditch, M. (1977). *Status characteristics and social interaction.* New York: Elsevier.

Berger, J.; Rosenholtz, S. J.; and Zelditch, M., Jr. (1980). Status organizing processes. *Annual Review of Sociology* 6: 479–508.

Berlo, D.; Lemmert, J.; and Mertz, R. (1969). Dimensions for evaluating the acceptability of message sources. *Public Opinion Quarterly* 33: 563–76.

Berscheid, E. (1966). Opinion change and communicator-communicatee similarity and dissimilarity. *Journal of Personality and Social Psychology* 4: 670–80.

Berscheid, E., and Walster, E. (1974). Physical attractiveness. In L. Berkowitz (ed.), *Advances in experimental social psychology,* vol. 7. New York: Academic Press.

Brock. T. C. (1965). Communicator-recipient similarity and decision change. *Journal of Personality and Social Psychology* 1: 650–54.

Bugenthal, D. B., and Love, L. (1975). Nonassertive expression of parental approval and disapproval and its relationship to child disturbance. *Child Development* 46: 747–52.

Bull, R. (1979). The influence of stereotypes on person identification. In D. P. Farrington, K. Hawkins, and S. Lloyd-Bostock (eds.), *Psychology, law and legal processes.* Atlantic Highlands, NJ: Humanities Press.

Burgoon, M.; Cohen, M.; Miller, M. D.; and Montgomery, C. L. (1978). An empirical test of a model of resistance to persuasion. *Human Communication Research* 5: 27–39.

Burgoon, M.; Dillard, J. P.; and Doran, N. E. (1983). Friendly or unfriendly persuasion: the effects of violations of expectations by males and females. *Human Communication Research* 10: 283–94.

Burgoon, M.; Jones, S. B.; and Stewart, D. (1975). Toward a message-centered theory of persuasion: three empirical investigations of language intensity. *Human Communication Research:* 240–56.

Burgoon, M., and Miller, G. R. (1985). An expectancy interpretation of language and persuasion. In H. Giles and R. N. St. Clair (eds.), *Recent advances in language, communication, and social psychology.* Hillsdale, NJ: Erlbaum.

Cacioppo, J. T., and Petty, R. E. (1984). The elaboration likelihood model of persuasion. *Advances in Consumer Research* 11: 673–75.

Cahn, D. D. (1985). Telling it exactly like it is: an experimental study of oral truth cues. *Communication Research Reports* 2: 86–89.

Cantor, J.; Alfonso, H.; and Zillman, D. (1975). The persuasive effectiveness of the peer appeal and a communicator's first-hand experience. *Communication Research* 3: 293–310.

Cantor, N., and Mischel, W. (1979). Prototypes in person perception. In L. Berkowitz (ed.), *Advances in experimental social psychology,* vol. 12. New York: Academic Press.

Carbone, T. (1975). Stylistic variables as related to source credibility: a content analysis approach. *Speech Monographs* 42: 99–106.

Chaiken, S. (1979). Communicator physical attractiveness and persuasion. *Journal of Personality and Social Psychology* 37: 1387–97.

Cialdini, R. B., and Petty, R. E. (1981). Anticipatory opinion effects. In R. E. Petty, T. M. Ostrom, and T. C. Brock (eds.), *Cognitive responses in persuasion.* Hillsdale, NJ: Erlbaum.

Cramer, M. M. (1979). A view from the jury box. *Litigation* 6: 65–66.

Cronkhite, G., and Liska, J. R. (1976). A critique of factor analytic approaches to the study of credibility. *Communication Monographs* 43: 91–107.

Cronkhite, G., and Liska, J. R. (1980). The judgment of communicant acceptability. In M. E. Roloff and G. R. Miller (eds.), *Persuasion: new directions in theory and research.* Beverly Hills, CA: Sage.

Dane, F. C., and Wrightsman, L. S. (1982). Effects of defendants' and victims' characteristics on jurors' verdicts. In N. L. Kerr and R. M. Bray (eds.), *The psychology of the courtroom.* New York: Academic Press.

DePaulo, B. M.; Rosenthal, R.; Eisenstat, R. A.; Rogers, P. L.; and Finkelstein, S. (1978). Decoding discrepant nonverbal cues. *Journal of Personality and Social Psychology* 36: 313–23.

Dion, K. (1972). Physical attractiveness and evaluation of children's transgressions. *Journal of Personality and Social Psychology* 24: 207–13.

Dovidio, J. F., and Ellyson, S. L. (1985). Patterns of visual dominance behavior in humans. In Ellyson and Dovidio (eds.), *Power, dominance and nonverbal behavior.* New York: Springer-Verlag.

Dutton, D. G. (1973). The maverick effect: increased communicator credibility as a result of abandoning a career. *Canadian Journal of Behavioral Science* 5: 145–51.

Eagly, A. H.; Chaiken, S.; and Wood, W. (1981). An attributional analysis of persuasion. In J. H. Harvey et al. (eds.), *New directions in attributional research.* Hillsdale, NJ: Erlbaum.

Eagly, A. H., and Steffen, V. J. (1984). Gender stereotypes stem from the distribution of women and men into social roles. *Journal of Personality and Social Psychology* 46: 735–54.

Efron, M. E. (1974). The effect of physical appearance on the judgment of guilt, interpersonal attraction, and severity of recommended punishment in a simulated jury task. *Journal of Research in Personality* 8: 45–54.

Ekman, P., and Friesen, W. V. (1969). Nonverbal leakage and clues to deception. *Psychiatry* 32: 88–106.

Ekman, P., and Friesen, W. V. (1974). Detecting deception from the body or face. *Journal of Personality and Social Psychology* 23: 288–98.

Ekman, P.; Friesen, W. V.; and Ellsworth, P. (1972). *Emotions in the human face: guidelines for research and an integration of the findings.* New York: Pergamon.

Ekman, P.; Friesen, W. V.; and Scherer, K. R. (1976). Body movement and voice pitch in deceptive interaction. *Semiotica* 16: 23–27.

Exline, R. V.; Ellyson, S. L.; and Long, B. (1975). Visual behavior as an aspect of power role relationships. In P. Pliner, L. Krames, and T. Alloway (eds.), *Nonverbal communication of aggression,* vol. 2. New York: Plenum.

Ferguson, N. (1977). Simultaneous speech, interruptions, and dominance. *British Journal of Social and Clinical Psychology* 16: 295–302.

Festinger, L. (1954). A theory of social comparison processes. *Human Relations* 7: 117–40.

Fiske, S. (1982). Schema-triggered affect. In M. S. Clark and S. T. Fiske (eds.), *Affect and cognition: the 17th annual Carnegie symposium.* Hillsdale, NJ: Erlbaum.

Freedman, J. L., and Sears, D. O. (1965). Warning, distraction, and resistance to influence. *Journal of Personality and Social Psychology* 1: 262–66.

French, J. R. P., and Raven, B. (1959). The bases of social power. In

D. Cartwright (ed.), *Studies in social power.* Ann Arbor, MI: Institute for Social Research.

Frieze, I., and Ramsey, S. (1976). Nonverbal maintenance of traditional sex roles. *Journal of Social Issues* 32: 133–41.

Fromme, D. K., and Beam, D. C. (1974). Dominance and sex differences in nonverbal responses to differential eye contact. *Journal of Research in Personality* 8: 76–87.

Fugita, S. S. (1974). Effects of anxiety and approval on visual interaction. *Journal of Personality and Social Psychology* 29: 586–92.

Gleason, J. M., and Harris, V. A. (1976). Group discussion and the defendant's socioeconomic status as determinants of judgments by simulated jurors. *Journal of Applied Social Psychology* 6: 186–91.

Goethals, G. R., and Nelson, R. E. (1973). Similarity in the influence process: the belief-value distinction. *Journal of Personality and Social Psychology* 25: 117–22.

Goodman, G. S.; Golding, J. M.; Helgeson, V. S.; Haith, M. M.; and Michelli, J. (1987). When a child takes the stand: jurors' perceptions of children's eyewitness testimony. *Law and Human Behavior* 11: 27–40.

Goodman, G. S., and Reed, R. S. (1986). Age differences in eyewitness testimony. *Law and Human Behavior* 10: 317–32.

Griffitt, W., and Jackson, T. (1973). Simulated jury decisions: the influence of jury-defendant attitude similarity-dissimilarity. *Social Behavior and Personality* 1: 1–7.

Hall, E. T. (1966). *The hidden dimension.* Garden City, NY: Doubleday.

Harms, L. S. (1961). Listener judgments of status cues in speech. *Quarterly Journal of Speech* 47: 164–68.

Hass, R. G., and Grady, K. (1975). Temporal delay, type of forewarning and resistance to influence. *Journal of Experimental Social Psychology* 11: 459–69.

Hastie, R. (1980). Memory for behavioral information that confirms or contradicts a personality impression. In Hastie et al. (eds.), *Person memory: the cognitive basis of social perception.* Hillsdale, NJ: Erlbaum.

Hazelton, V., Cupach, W. R., and Liska, J. (1986). Message style: an investigation of the perceived characteristics of persuasive messages. *Journal of Social Behavior and Personality* 1: 565–74.

Henley, N. M. (1973). Status and sex: some touching observations. *Bulletin of the Psychonomic Society* 2: 91–93.

Henley, N. M. (1977). *Body politics: power, sex, and nonverbal communication.* Englewood Cliffs, NJ: Prentice-Hall.

Hocking, J. E.; Bauchner, J. E.; Kaminski, E. P.; and Miller, G. R. (1975). Detecting deceptive communication from verbal, visual, and paralinguistic cues. Unpublished manuscript, Department of Communication, Michigan State University.

Hocking, J. E.; Miller, G. R.; and Fontes, N. E. (1978). Videotape in the courtroom: witness deception. *Trial* 14: 52–55.

Hottenstein, M. P. (1978). An exploration of the relationship between age, social status, and facial gesturing. Unpublished doctoral dissertation, University of Pennsylvania.

Jones, E. E.; Davis, K. E.; and Gergen, K. J. (1961). Role playing variations and their informational value for person perception. *Journal of Abnormal and Social Psychology* 63: 302–10.

Jones, E. E., and Nisbett, R. E. (1971). The actor and the observer: divergent perceptions of the causes of behavior. In Jones et al. (eds.), *Attribution: perceiving the causes of behavior.* Morristown, NJ: General Learning Press.

Jones, E. E., and Pitman, T. S. (1980). Toward a general theory of strategic self-presentation. In J. Suls (ed.), *Psychological perspectives on the self.* Hillsdale, NJ: Erlbaum.

Jones, E. E.; Worchel, S.; Goethals, G. R.; and Grumet, J. (1971). Prior expectancy and behavioral extremity as determinants of attitude attribution. *Journal of Experimental Social Psychology* 7: 59–80.

Kaplan, M. F., and Kemmerick, G. (1974). Juror judgment as information integration: combining evidential and non-evidential information. *Journal of Personality and Social Psychology* 30: 493–99.

Keating, C. F.; Mazur, A.; and Segall, M. H. (1977). A cross cultural exploration of physiognomic traits of dominance and happiness. *Ethology and Sociobiology* 2: 41–48.

Kiesler, C. A., and Kiesler, S. B. (1964). Role of forewarning in persuasive communications. *Journal of Abnormal and Social Psychology* 68: 547–49.

King, S. W.; Minami, Y.; and Samovar, L. (1985). A comparison of Japanese and American perceptions of source credibility. *Communication Research Reports* 2: 76–79.

Knapp, M. S., and Comadena, M. E. (1979). Telling it like it isn't: a review of theory and research on deceptive communication. *Human Communication Research* 5: 270–85.

Knapp, M. S.; Hart, R. P.; and Dennis, H. S. (1974). An exploration of deception as a communication construct. *Human Communication Research* 1: 15–29.

Kulka, R. A., and Kessler, J. B. (1978). Is justice really blind? the influence of litigant physical attractiveness on judicial judgment. *Journal of Applied Social Psychology* 8: 366–81.

Lay, C. H., and Burron, B. F. (1968). Perception of the personality of the distant speaker. *Perceptual and Motor Skills* 26: 951–56.

London, H. (1973). *Psychology of the persuader.* Morristown, NJ: General Learning Press.

McFatter, R. M. (1978). Sentencing strategies and justice: effects of punishment philosophy on sentencing decisions. *Journal of Personality and Social Psychology* 36: 1490–5000.

McLaughlin, M. T. (1979). Juror perceptions of participants in criminal proceedings. *Journal of Applied Communication Research* 7: 91–102.

McPeek, R. P., and Edwards, J. D. (1975). Expectancy disconfirmation and attitude change. *Journal of Social Psychology* 96: 193–208.

Maier, N. R. F., and Thurber, J. A. (1968). Accuracy of judgments of deception when an interview is watched, heard and read. *Personnel Psychology* 21: 23–30.

Major, B., and Heslin, R. (1982). Perceptions of cross-sex and same-sex nonreciprocal touch: it is better to give than to receive. *Journal of Nonverbal Behavior* 6: 148–62.

Maslow, C.; Yoselson, K.; and London, H. (1971). Persuasiveness of confidence expressed via language and body language. *British Journal of Social and Clinical Psychology* 10: 234–40.

Mehrabian, A. (1971). Nonverbal betrayal of feeling. *Journal of Experimental Research in Personality* 5: 64–73.

Mehrabian, A. (1972). *Nonverbal communication.* Chicago: Aldine-Atherton.

Mehrabian, A. (1981). *Silent messages.* Belmont, CA: Wadsworth.

Mehrabian, A., and Williams, M. (1969). Nonverbal concomitants of perceived and intended persuasiveness. *Journal of Personality and Social Psychology* 13: 37–58.

Miller, G. R.; Bender, D. C.; Boster, F. J.; Florence, B. T.; Fontes, N. E.; Hocking, J. E.; and Nicholson, H. E. (1975). The effects of videotape testimony in jury trials: studies on juror decision-making, information retention, and emotional arousal. *Brigham Young University Law Review* 27: 331–73.

Miller, G. R.; Boster, F. J.; Fontes, N. E.; LeFebvre, P. J.; and Poole, M. S. (1975). Jurors' responses to videotaped trial materials—some further evidence. *Michigan State Bar Journal* 54: 278–82.

Miller, G. R. and Burgoon, J. K. (1982). Factors affecting assessments of witness credibility. In N. L. Kerr and R. M. Bray (eds.), *The psychology of the courtroom.* New York: Academic Press.

Miller, G. R., and Hewgill, M. A. (1964). The effect of variations in nonfluency on audience ratings of source credibility. *Quarterly Journal of Speech* 50: 36–44.

Miller, M. D., and Burgoon, M. (1979). The relationship between violations of expectations and the induction of resistance to persuasion. *Human Communication Research* 5: 301–13.

Miller, N.; Marayama, G.; Beaber, R. J.; and Valone, K. (1976). Speed of speech and persuasion. *Journal of Personality and Social Psychology* 34: 615–24.

Moe, J. D. (1972). Listener judgments of status cues in speech: a replication and extension. *Speech Monographs* 39: 144–47.

Natale, M.; Entin, E.; and Jaffee, J. (1979). Vocal interruptions in dyadic communication as a function of speech and social anxiety. *Journal of Personality and Social Psychology* 37: 865–78.

Newcomb, N., and Arnkoff, P. B. (1979). Effects of speech style and sex of speaker on person perception. *Journal of Personality and Social Psychology* 37: 1293–1303.

Newman, H. M. (1982). The sounds of silence in communicative encounters. *Communication Quarterly* 30: 142–49.

O'Barr, W. M. (1982). *Linguistic evidence: language, power and strategy in the courtroom.* New York: Academic Press.

Packwood, W. T. (1974). Loudness as a variable in persuasion. *Journal of Counseling Psychology* 21: 1–2.

Pastore, N., and Horowitz, M. (1955). The influence of attributed motive on the acceptance of statement. *Journal of Abnormal and Social Psychology* 51: 351–62.

Patterson, M. L. (1983). *Nonverbal behavior: a functional perspective.* New York: Springer-Verlag.

Patterson, M. L. (1985). Social influence and nonverbal exchange. In S. L. Ellyson and J. F. Dovidio (eds.), *Power, dominance, and nonverbal behavior.* New York: Springer-Verlag.

Petty, R. E., and Cacioppo, J. T. (1977). Forewarning, cognitive responding and resistance to persuasion. *Journal of Personality and Social Psychology* 35: 645–55.

Petty, R. E., and Cacioppo, J. T. (1979). Effects of forewarning of persuasive intent and involvement on cognitive responses and persuasion. *Personality and Social Psychology Bulletin* 5: 173–76.

Petty, R. E., and Cacioppo, J. T. (1981). *Attitudes and persuasion: classic and contemporary approaches.* Dubuque: W. C. Brown.

Petty, R. E., and Cacioppo, J. T. (1984a). Source factors and the elaboration likelihood model of persuasion. *Advances in Consumer Research* 11: 668–72.

Petty, R. E., and Cacioppo, J. T. (1984b). The effects of involvement on responses to argument quantity and quality: central and peripheral routes to persuasion. *Journal of Personality and Social Psychology* 46: 69–81.

Pyszczynski, T. A., and Greenberg, J. (1981). Role of disconfirmed expectancies in the instigation of attribution processing. *Journal of Personality and Social Psychology* 40: 31–38.

Raven, B. H. (1965). Social influence and power. In I. D. Steiner and M.

Fishbein (eds.), *Current studies in social psychology* New York: Holt, Rinehart.

Rotter, J. B., and Stein, D. (1971). Public attitudes toward trustworthiness, competence and altruism of twenty selected occupations. *Journal of Applied Social Psychology* 1: 334–43.

Rumsey, M. (1976). Effects of defendant background and remorse on sentencing judgments. *Journal of Applied Social Psychology* 6: 64–68.

Scherer, K. R. (1979). Personality markers in speech. In K. R. Scherer and H. Giles (eds.), *Social markers in speech*. Cambridge: Cambridge University Press.

Secord, P. (1958). Facial features and inference processes in interpersonal perception. In R. Tagiuri and L. Petrullo (eds.), *Person perception and interpersonal behavior*. Stanford, CA: Stanford University Press.

Sereno, K. K., and Hawkins, G. J. (1967). The effects of variations in speakers' nonfluency upon audience rating of attitude toward the speech topic and speakers' credibility. *Communication Monographs* 34: 58–64.

Shaw, J. I. (1972). Reactions to victims and defendants of varying degrees of attractiveness. *Psychonomic Science* 27: 329–30.

Shepherd, D. H., and Sloan, L. R. (1979). Similarity of legal attitudes, defendant social class, and crime intentionality as determinants of legal decisions. *Personality and Social Psychology Bulletin* 5: 245–48.

Shoemaker, D.; South, D.; and Lowe, J. (1973). Facial stereotypes of deviants and judgments of guilt or innocence. *Social Forces* 51: 427–33.

Sigal, J.; Braden-MaGuire, J.; Hayden, M.; and Mosely, N. (1985). The effect of presentation style and sex of lawyer on jury decision-making behavior. *Psychology* 22: 13–19.

Sigall, H., and Osgrove, N. (1975). Beautiful but dangerous: effects of offender attractiveness and nature of the crime on juridic judgment. *Journal of Personality and Social Psychology* 31: 410–14.

Simon, H. W.; Berkowitz, N.; and Moyer, J. R. (1970). Similarity, credibility, and attitude change: a review and theory. *Psychological Bulletin* 73: 1–16.

Smith, R. (1973). Source credibility context effects. *Speech Monographs* 40: 303–09.

Snyder, E. C. (1971). Sex role differential and juror decisions. *Sociology and Social Research* 55: 442–48.

Sorrentino, R. M., and Boutillier, R. G. (1975). The effect of quantity and quality of verbal interaction on ratings of leadership ability. *Journal of Experimental Research in Personality* 11: 403–11.

Steffen, V. J., and Eagly, A. H. (1985). Implicit theories about influence style: the effects of status and sex. *Personality and Social Psychology Bulletin* 11: 191–205.

Stewart, M. A., and Ryan, E. B. (1982). Attitudes toward younger and older adult speakers: effects of varying speech rates. *Journal of Language and Social Psychology* 1: 91–110.

Street, R. L., and Brady, R. M. (1982). Speech rate acceptance ranges as a function of evaluative domain, listener speech rate, and communication context. *Communication Monographs* 49: 290–308.

Street, R. L.; Brady, R. M.; and Putman, W. B. (1983). The influence of speech rate stereotypes and rate similarity on listeners' evaluations of speakers. *Journal of Language and Social Psychology* 2: 37–56.

Streeter, L. A.; Krauss, R. M.; Geller, V.; Olson, C.; and Apple, W. (1977). Pitch changes during attempted deception. *Journal of Personality and Social Psychology* 35: 345–50.

Strongman, K. T., and Champness, B. G. (1968). Dominance hierarchies and conflict in eye contact. *Acta Psychologica* 28: 376–86.

Sundstrom, E., and Altman, I. (1974). Field study of territorial behavior and dominance. *Journal of Personality and Social Psychology* 30: 115–24.

Timney, B., and London, H. (1973). Body language concomitants of persuasiveness and persuasibility in dyadic interaction. *International Journal of Group Tensions* 3: 48–67.

Walker, J. W., and Borden, R. J. (1976). Sex, status, and the invasion of shared space. *Representative Research in Social Psychology* 7: 28–34.

Walster, E., and Festinger, L. (1962). The effectiveness of overheard persuasive communications. *Journal of Abnormal and Social Psychology* 65: 395–402.

Wells, G. L.; Lindsay, R. C. L.; and Ferguson, T. J. (1979). Accuracy, confidence, and juror perceptions in eyewitness identification. *Journal of Applied Psychology* 64: 440–48.

Whitley, B. E., and Greenberg, M. S. (1986). The role of eyewitness confidence in juror perceptions of credibility. *Journal of Applied Social Psychology* 16: 387–409.

Willis, F. N., Jr., and Hoffman, G. (1975). Development of tactile patterns and relation to age, sex, and race. *Developmental Psychology* 11: 866.

Yarmey, A. D., and Jones, H. P. T. (1983). Is eyewitness testimony a matter of common sense? In S. Lloyd-Bostock and B. R. Clifford (eds.), *Witness evidence: critical and empirical papers*. New York: Wiley.

Chapter 7

EVIDENCE AND TESTIMONY

The amount of information during a trial is often staggering. Even a simple trial produces a transcript that may be more than a hundred pages in length. This wealth of information often defies coherency, thereby requiring the jury to decipher confusing and often contradictory testimony. Only industry enables these actors to consider the implications of physical and demonstrative evidence, organize and interpret two competing stories, and then translate the testimony to decide which story is most probable.

Scholars have conducted extensive research into these trial complexities in order to assess the relative impact of the many variables on jury decisions. The result is a plethora of legal and extralegal factors which, under the right conditions, influence the way juries decide. But time and time again the research has supported precisely what the legal system has claimed for thousands of years: The single most powerful determinant of trial outcome is evidence (Reskin and Visher 1986; Saks and Hastie 1978; Visher 1987). The sheer quantity of prosecution evidence increases the likelihood of conviction (Ostrom, Werner, and Saks 1978). This comes as no surprise to practicing lawyers.

Trial lawyers have reported for years that evidence, both admissible and inadmissible, plays the central role in the courtroom drama. What they have not fully grasped is that jurors discriminate between evidence on the basis of testimony presentation. Recent research on the effects of different types of evidence as well as investigations into how that evidence is presented paints a highly insightful picture.

EYEWITNESS TESTIMONY

Eyewitnesses identify causal agents and testify about the objects, physical relationships, and temporal sequences related to the criminal or civil episode in question. This testimony depends entirely on the ability of the actor to retrieve from memory, sometimes years later, an accurate portrayal of events. Recalling accurately and precisely—what events took place, who was involved, how the action unfolded—is an interpretive process of give and take. The recall of an event and its elements is highly selective regardless of the role actors play in the action. Actors use impressions and interpretations of elements important to them as an aid to filling in those elements they don't recall as well. This interpretive process, performed by persons with differing abilities of sense-making and sensory prowess, results in biased recall. In fact, research has shown that reconstructions of events, even by eyewitnesses, are often laced with inaccuracies (Clifford and Scott 1978; Loftus 1974, 1979). Because judges and jurors are generally unaware of the sources of error in eyewitness testimony, they invariably place undue faith in its veracity (Brigham and Bothwell 1983). This becomes especially problematic when one considers that jurors regard eyewitness evidence as highly persuasive. For example, one study showed that subjects were more likely to render a guilty verdict with eyewitness corroboration, even when the eyewitness was challenged on the basis of being legally blind (Loftus 1975).

As an illustration of this fallacy, consider the following sources of eyewitness error as indicated by experimental research and the contrary common beliefs held by laypersons. Research indicates that eyewitnesses under stress are more likely to perceive events erroneously (Buckhout 1975). Yet laypersons and attorneys believe that memory for stressful events is better than memory for nonstressful events (Brigham 1981; Yarmey and Jones 1983). Laypersons are also unaware that eyewitnesses tend to overestimate the length of time involved in a crime, and that early identification from photographs increases the likelihood of identification of the same person in a lineup regardless of guilt. In addition, although research reveals law officers are not as accurate as civilian eyewitnesses, laypersons believe just the opposite to be true (Yarmey and Jones 1983). While research also confirms that memory for faces decreases significantly over time, many laypersons believe such memory would be more than 90 percent accurate several months after first observing the face. The most curious fallacy, however, regards the relationship between perceived eyewitness confidence and eyewitness accuracy.

Although eyewitness confidence exhibits little correspondence with accuracy in identifying perpetrators and reconstructing events (Deffenbacher 1980; Leippe 1980; Wells and Murray 1984), observers of eyewitnesses believe the contrary. Research has consistently demonstrated that jurors attribute greater accuracy to confident witnesses. Recent work indicates that perceived confidence has its strongest effect on the perceived accuracy of the witness' general account of events, while expertise (the ability of a witness, such as eyesight, to have seen what is claimed to have been seen) most strongly affects perceptions of identification accuracy (Whitley and Greenberg 1986). These judgments, in turn, influence jurors' beliefs. Perceived witness confidence has also been found to lead to higher witness credibility ratings by jurors (Wells, Lindsay, and Ferguson 1979). In one series of experimental studies individuals witnessed staged thefts and were then presented with a lineup task (Lindsay, Wells, and Rumpel 1981; Wells, Ferguson, and Lindsay 1981; Wells, Lindsay, and Tousignant 1980). Those persons who made identifications were questioned by an agent who was unaware of the accuracy of their selections. Subjects who observed only this questioning procedure were found to be much more likely to believe confident than diffident eyewitnesses.

Not only jurors believe confident witnesses. Attorneys and law officers also believe that confident witnesses are accurate witnesses (Brigham and Wolfskiel 1983). A recent survey indicates more than 70 percent of prosecutors and law officers believe that witnesses who are more certain are also more accurate. Defense attorneys, however, are more skeptical; only 40 percent believe in this relationship. Even the U.S. Supreme Court has twice endorsed the view that witness confidence is an indicator of testimonial accuracy (Manson v. Brathwaite 1977; Neil v. Biggers 1972). Concern over this belief is compounded by research showing that inaccurate eyewitnesses are typically as confident as accurate eyewitnesses (Leippe, Wells, and Ostrom 1978; Lindsay and Wells 1980).

Not surprisingly, many scholars contend that the confidence fallacy profoundly influences the decision of law officers to investigate cases or of prosecutors to plea bargain or even to prosecute. Considering that less than 35 percent of all reported crimes are investigated (Greenwood, Chaiken, Petersilia, and Prusoff 1975) and less than 45 percent of all felony arrests are actually prosecuted as felonies (Ebbesen and Konecni 1982), many judicial critics advocate that the fallacy be explained to law officers, attorneys, and jurors. As a result of this attention eyewitness researchers are frequently asked to give expert testimony regarding the reliability of eyewitnesses.

EXPERT TESTIMONY.   In a free society erroneous convictions as a result of inaccurate eyewitness identification are considered by some to be among the most serious and alarming of all judicial errors. To protect against such errors jurors frequently hear expert testimony warning of the possible errors made by eyewitnesses. By making jurors aware of the shortcomings of eyewitness testimony without eradicating such evidence, expert witnesses hope to provide a safeguard for the system.

Several studies have demonstrated that expert psychological testimony on the unreliability of eyewitness identification significantly reduces jurors' belief in eyewitnesses (Hosch, Beck, and McIntyre 1980; Loftus 1980; Wells, Lindsay, and Tousignant 1980). In a recent study in this area 360 subjects read one of two criminal court cases where eyewitness identification represented critical evidence in the case (Maass, Brigham, and West 1985). Half of this group was exposed to additional testimony by an expert criminologist with particular expertise in eyewitness identification. This expert testimony was also varied along a causal dimension. Half of the expert testimony group read testimony stating only the probability of eyewitness misidentification (45 percent), while the other half read testimony by the expert which offered several causal explanations for eyewitness inaccuracy.

Results of the study confirmed that expert testimony affects the credibility of eyewitnesses in the minds of jurors. Subjects exposed to the expert testimony made more lenient judgments and were more likely to acquit the offender, indicating they assigned less weight to eyewitness identifications, although they did not completely discount eyewitness testimony. These potential jurors were also found to be more influenced by expert testimony which incorporated causal reasons for eyewitness inaccuracy than by expert testimony providing only the probability of misidentification.

Although the bulk of the research supports the influence of expert testimony, the degree to which jurors discount eyewitness testimony is unclear. In another recent experiment subjects were found to be less responsive to expert testimony (Fox and Walters 1987). After viewing expert psychological testimony, and in spite of three separate warnings by the expert against relying upon eyewitness confidence, jurors continued to use eyewitness confidence to assess accuracy. Expert testimony exhibited a greater impact on eyewitness credibility when the eyewitness was less confident. The researchers also found a difference between general and specific expert testimony. General expert testimony points only to the unreliability of the eyewitness, whereas specific expert testimony (similar to the causal testimony in the Maass et al. study) includes factors jurors should take into account when assessing eyewitness accuracy. Subjects exposed to specific expert testimony exhibited a greater reliance on the psychologist's testimony and were more confident in their decisions.

These findings support the view that expert testimony may only increase juror skepticism while failing to improve the ability of jurors to assess the accuracy of the testimony (McCloskey and Egeth

1983a, 1983b). If future research adds credence to this position, experts may find themselves in a precarious dilemma. An ongoing debate among psychologists already exists concerning whether researchers know enough about eyewitness reliability and memory to do anything more than provide additional bias to already murky waters. On one side of the polemic researchers argue that it is their ethical duty to debase inaccurate eyewitness identification that might lead to the conviction of innocent parties (Loftus 1983). After all, what good is psychology if it cannot be of service in ameliorating a real-world problem. The opposition contends that the evidence on eyewitness accuracy is incomplete and that researchers are over-generalizing and jumping to conclusions (McCloskey and Egeth 1983b). To present oneself as both a partisan and scientist, these scholars contend, is a conflict of interests. Despite this debate experts continue to testify in America's courts, and generally their impact is substantial.

EYEWITNESS NONIDENTIFICATION.   Eyewitnesses are usually called upon to make positive identifications, and only occasionally are they asked to tell the court who didn't commit a criminal act (for example, "The defendant is not the man I saw"). More common is conflicting testimony between multiple witnesses who cannot agree on identification (Sanders and Warnick 1982). In either case, scholars remain split as to the potency of such nonidentifications in determining the innocence or guilt of a suspect.

Eyewitness identification indicating a defendant's guilt is clearly negative information about the defendant, whereas nonidentification is indisputably positive information. Since negative information is known to have a greater influence on person perception than positive information (Kanouse and Hanson 1972), researchers expect jurors to weigh identification evidence heavily and to underrate nonidentification evidence. Some findings support this contention (Brandon and Davies 1973).

In one recent experimental study researchers found eyewitness identifications to be more influential than eyewitness nonidentifications (McAllister and Bregman 1986). This effect was so strong that when identification and nonidentification evidence conflicted, subjects ignored the nonidentification evidence. In fact, only when there were nonidentifications by multiple witnesses did this evidence equal the effect produced by single identifications. The researchers corroborated this finding with fingerprint identifications. Positive identification of the defendant's fingerprints by an expert produced significantly higher sentences and perceptions of guilt from subject-jurors than did fingerprint nonidentification.

Another study, however, revealed opposite results (Leippe 1985). In two experiments guilty judgments were dramatically reduced when subjects read a case summary containing eyewitness nonidentification testimony. This effect occurred even when the nonidentification was countered by two positive identifications of the defendant. The second experiment revealed that the exonerating influence of nonidentification is dependent on actual testimony. When the defense lawyer merely reported the fact that a witness was unable to make an identification, perceptions of guilt increased. To explain these results the author proposed that nonidentification may represent the ideal instance of reasonable doubt in the minds of jurors. This doubt will occur, however, only when the witness insists in court that the defendant is not the culprit.

Because of inconsistent findings the sum of these studies fails to clarify trial strategy regarding eyewitness nonidentification. If jurors do indeed underweigh nonidentification evidence, then attorneys using identification evidence (typically the prosecution) maintain a distinct advantage. This advantage is inherently increased given that prosecution evidence is always presented first, thereby reducing nonidentification evidence to the weaker role of disconfirmation. Research has shown that individuals underutilize disconfirming information and are more influenced by confirming information when both types are available (Ross 1977; Snyder and Swann 1978). To offset this bias defense attorneys should, when possible, corroborate nonidentification evidence with multiple witnesses, and avoid merely reporting nonidentification. If jurors perceive nonidentification evidence as reasonable doubt of the defendant's guilt, prosecutors are best advised to address this perception in arguments before the court.

EYEWITNESS STRATEGY.   What sense can practicing attorneys make of the research on eyewitness and related testimony? Strategically, attorneys can easily capitalize on the confidence/accuracy fallacy by doing everything possible to enhance the confidence and highlight the expertise of their eyewitnesses. Remarkably, lawyers who brief and prepare eyewitnesses for questioning enjoy an advantage, since research indicates that confidence inevitably increases when witnesses prepare for cross-examination (Wells, Ferguson, and Lindsay 1981). Opposing attorneys are best advised to undermine eyewitness confidence and debase expertise when possible. Cogent testimony by psychology experts who can explain the inaccuracy of eyewitnesses constitutes an excellent vehicle for this impeachment. Experts are best advised, however, to incorporate causal reasons and factors why eyewitnesses may be inaccurate. In the case of eyewitness nonidentification, attorneys should offset the possible underutilization of this evidence by corroborating nonidentification evidence with multiple witnesses. In both cases lawyers should avoid merely reporting nonidentification or the probability of eyewitness inaccuracy, as jurors do not respond to this evidence.

CONFESSION EVIDENCE

Confession evidence is introduced more frequently than most nonlawyers realize. An early survey of deputy district attorneys in Los Angeles County revealed that confessions were given in more than 45 percent of the four thousand cases reported (Younger 1966). Such frequency alone warrants considerable attention, but most intriguing is the apparent impact confessions have on juror judgments. Undoubtedly confessions play an important role in the determination of guilt. Perhaps no single stroke can change the direction of a trial more quickly than evidence of a defendant's confessions. But the complexities surrounding the use of confessions raise far more questions than is generally realized.

Confession evidence is largely misunderstood because of our stereotypes regarding the factual nature of evidence. Confessions are by no means open and shut. Although there is little question as to the impact confessions have on verdicts, one cannot assume either empirically or intuitively that defendants who confess are indeed guilty or will be viewed as guilty by jurors. In one experimental study (Miller and Boster 1977) subjects read a description of a murder trial that included one or more of the following: (a) only circumstantial evidence, (b) eyewitness testimony from a stranger, (c) eyewitness testimony from an acquaintance, or (d) testimony alleging that the defendant had confessed to the police. Subjects who received confession evidence were most likely to view the defendant as guilty, even more so than those provided with eyewitness identification. Perhaps just as interesting is the finding that even with confession evidence, the conviction rate was only 80 percent. Contrary to popular belief, confessions do not equate necessarily with guilt. Remember that these subjects, as is the case in many trials, did not have the opportunity to scrutinize the defendant. Perhaps because of this omission or other factors, 20 percent of the subjects did not render a guilty verdict. Some jurors' reluctance to convict because of confession evidence may be, in part, because they know of the fallibility of social reality. For example, historically we know that juror judgments resulting from confessions can be erroneous. Several authors have written about cases where uncorroborated confessions resulting in convictions later proved to be false (Frank and Frank 1957; Borchard 1932). A more probable explanation, however, is the degree to which jurors believe confessions are voluntary. Recent research confirms this suspicion.

In one study subjects read one of four versions of a trial consisting of opening statements, the examination of three witnesses, closing arguments, and jury instructions from the judge (Kassin and Wrightsman 1980). The versons differed as to whether the defendant confessed and under what constraints he confessed. In the no constraint version the defendant confessed on his own initiative. In the positive constraint version the defendant confessed after being promised probable leniency by the judge. The negative constraint version had the defendant confess after being threatened by probable harshness by the judge. The last version contained no confession by the defendant.

The conviction rate for the defendant was highest (56 percent) by subjects who read the no constraint version and lowest (19 percent) in the no confession group, supporting the supposition that jurors weigh heavily confession evidence. Subjects who received the negative constraint version rendered only slightly more guilty verdicts than the no confession group (25 percent). The group reading the positive constraint version rendered a significantly greater number of convictions (38 percent). The researchers found this same positive coercion bias in two later studies focusing on the limiting effect of jury instructions on constrained confession evidence (Kassin and Wrightsman 1981; Kassin, Wrightsman, and Warner 1983).

We can surmise from this research that confessions induced by promises carry more weight in reaching guilty verdicts than their threat-oriented counterparts. But why? The authors concluded that postively constrained confessions are seen as more voluntary and therefore exert a greater impact than negatively constrained confessions. A subsequent experiment supported this conclusion. In the follow-up experiment the authors essentially replicated the first experiment with one exception. They asked subjects in the three confession groups to indicate whether they believed the defendant had confessed voluntarily. Although the conviction rates followed the same pattern as revealed in the first experiment, the judgments of voluntariness were not as neatly symmetrical. The results revealed that although 94 percent of the subjects in the no constraint group perceived the confession as voluntary, only 39 percent of the positive constraint group and 22 percent of the negative constraint group believed the confession to be of free will. Later work consistently demonstrated that subjects perceive the degree of exerted pressure to be greater in negative constraint confessions than when confessions result from promises (Kassin and Wrightsman 1981). A probable explanation is that people regard promises of reward as weaker inducements than threats of punishment (Wells 1980). This explanation further supports the contention that positively constrained confessions will be viewed as more voluntary.

To encapsulate the research in this area, we can posit two claims. First, when collated with other evidence, confession evidence is most salient to jurors, leading more frequently to conviction. Second, whether a confession is weighted heavily is due in part to the jurors' perception of confession voluntariness by the defendant. When jurors perceive that defendants were induced to make a confession, the importance of this evidence decreases. This was found to be notably more so for confessions resulting from threats than from confessions prompted by promises.

Trial strategy based on these conclusions seems limpid. Defense attorneys should question the hearer of confessions with the goal of exposing constraints upon the confession, especially those involving negative sanctions. Other factors reducing perceptions of defendant voluntariness, such as deception, conditions of detention, and mental state, should also be explored. Prosecutors confront the opposite task of strengthening belief about the free volition under which confessions were obtained.

Because the legal test for the determination of voluntariness remains broad, factors possibly relevant to both sides in limiting confession evidence include characteristics of the defendant (intelligence, literacy, mental or physical disability), state of the defendant at the time of confession (intoxication, angst), conditions of detention (inaccessibility to counsel, time), and the manner of interrogation (mental or physical abuse, threats, deception).

THE DEFENDANT'S TESTIMONY

One of the hardest choices defense attorneys must make regards defendant testimony. Should counsel have the defendant testify on his or her own behalf? There are no easy answers, and research in the area only confuses matters. On the one hand, limited evidence suggests that defendants who testify damage their cases because jurors discount a defendant's denial as self-serving and ingratiating.

For example, a study of 201 criminal jury trials in Indiana revealed that the defendant's testimony best predicted trial outcome (Myers 1979). Defendants who testified were more likely to be convicted than were defendants who did not take the stand. This finding is corroborated by several mock jury experiments. In one of these experiments subjects recommended harsher sentences when the defendant, rather than an impartial witness, testified as to mitigating circumstances surrounding a plagiarism offense (Frankel and Morris 1976).

Evidence also supports the position that defendant testimony exerts a neutral or positive influence on juror decision making. An analysis of 206 actual criminal cases in Utah revealed that acquittal was more likely when defendants testified (Werner, Strube, Cole and Kagehiro 1985). Still other research indicates that mitigating testimony reduces mock jury sentences regardless of whether the defendant or an impartial witness describes the events (Suggs and Berman 1979).

Although the general impact of a defendant's testimony is in dispute, lawyers agree that if the defendant testifies, he or she should deny any criminal offense. While this appears to be sound advice, research to date implicates the adverse effects of a strident denial by the defendant. In other words, an outburst of self-proclaimed innocence may sometimes do more harm than good. A defendant who protests his or her innocence too boisterously is more likely to be judged guilty than is a defendant who eschews such an approach (Yandell 1979). This supports nonjudicial research demonstrating that the greater the effort one exerts when withholding information, the stronger the assumed connection between withholder and the probable implications of the information withheld (Becker and Brock 1966).

WHEN THE DEFENDANT PLEADS THE FIFTH.   A criminal defendant is guaranteed the right to decline to testify by the Fifth Amendment to the Constitution. This amendment protects the defendant from self-incrimination, and by law juries and judges may not draw negative inferences from the invocation of this privilege. Yet critics of the plea contend that jurors cannot avoid drawing adverse inferences about defendants who refuse to testify. Presumably an innocent party would not withhold exonerating information, and jurors react upon this presumption.

In a series of experiments in this area mock jurors read and reacted to versions of a case transcript in which a male defendant was accused of armed robbery and murder of a storekeeper and his granddaughter (Shaffer, Sadowski, and Hendrick 1978; Shaffer and Sadowski 1979). The varying transcripts included eyewitness testimony by a store clerk, testimony by a police ballistics expert, and testimony by either the defendant or a friend of the defendant when the accused refused to testify. The prosecution presented five pieces of circumstantial evidence, but under cross-examination the defendant or his friend provided a plausible explanation for each. The researchers varied the testimony by exposing subjects to different invocations of the Fifth Amendment, by having the defendant either decline to take the stand or refuse to answer one or more questions during cross-examination.

Results indicate that when defendants invoke the Fifth Amendment in response to a potentially incriminating question, jurors are more likely to judge them guilty and deserving of conviction. Moreover, as the number of invocations of the Fifth increase, so too do the jurors' inferences about guilt (Shaffer, Case, and Brannen 1979). Jurors were also more likely to convict the accused when defendants invoked the Fifth Amendment by declining to take the witness stand, even when the judge affirmed the defendant's right to do so and warned jurors not to draw inferences of guilt from the invocation (Shaffer and Case 1982). The recordings of the mock jury deliberations during one experiment also revealed that more than 75 percent of the comments offered about the defendant's refusal to testify were negative in nature.

If these findings extend to actual trials, then defendants who testify are best advised to avoid the invocation of the Fifth Amendment when possible and to deny—though not too vociferously—guilt. Because some defendants may possess very poor self-presentational skills or potentially confusing information, attorneys may choose not to have the accused testify. But in more typical cases, especially those with evidence evenly balanced, the best rule appears to be to allow the defendant to testify.

THE DEFENDANT'S PRIOR RECORD.   The likelihood of a jury to discount a defendant's testimony is linked with the jury's perception of the defendant's credibility as a witness. The defendant's prior record represents a key factor in determining this credibility. For this reason information regarding the defendant's prior record is inadmissible unless the defendant elects to testify. When the defendant testifies, his or her background and criminal record may be introduced for the limited purposes of impeachment or establishing motive. Despite instructions from the court to use this evidence only for these purposes, legal practitioners and scholars conclude that jurors draw damaging inferences from evidence concerning the defendant's guilt.

One analysis of actual jury trials revealed that conviction rates were more than 20 percent higher in cases where the defendant's prior record was introduced (Kalven and Zeisel 1966). Should this record contain a criminal conviction, the defendant is at an even greater disadvantage. A review of experiments in this area indicates that jurors are more likely to convict a defendant if they hear testimony about previous convictions (Penrod and Borgida 1983). Apparently when jurors discuss a defendant's prior conviction during deliberation, they commonly infer that the defendant is the type of person who is capable of committing the offense in question (Shaffer 1985).

POLYGRAPH EVIDENCE

Although the accuracy, reliability, and credibility of polygraph tests are hotly contested, their use as evidence spans several jurisdictions. States remain divided on the issue, with more than half ruling that polygraph findings are inadmissible as evidence. In those states where polygraph evidence is admissible, polygraph examiners testify as expert witnesses and present the results of what is commonly called a "lie detection" test. Several types of polygraph tests exist, but all involve physiological measurements of breathing movements, blood pressure, and electrical charges in the skin. Examiners base their conclusions on discernible changes in these measures, assigning numerical scores to charted responses to questions. The proponents of the polygraph system contend that current techniques are upward of 90–95 percent accurate, and taken with other information are virtually conclusive. Opponents point out that because the choice of questions can determine the test outcome, the same individual can pass one test and fail another on the same issue.

While critics argue that polygraph results are largely a matter of chance, the fact that jury verdicts tend to coincide with the results of lie detection tests is not a coincidence (Roper 1975). Research indicates that when other evidence is not conclusive, polygraph evidence can swing the outcome in either direction.

In two studies subjects read case summaries of actual murder cases and then rendered a verdict (Cavoukian and Heslegrave 1980). Those subjects whose summary contained the actual evidence as well as a polygraph testimony in favor of the defendant were more likely to vote not guilty than were subjects who read only the evidence. Indeed, less than half (48 percent) of the subjects reading only the evidence summary voted not guilty, whereas 72 percent of the subjects who read that the defendant had passed a polygraph test voted not guilty.

In another study, where the evidence was heavily in the favor of the defendant, subjects read a four-page case summary and then participated in a discussion about the case with other subject-jurors (Markwart and Lynch 1979). Over 85 percent of the subjects who read the summary without polygraph testimony voted for acquittal after group discussion. Subjects exposed to evidence including testimony that the defendant had failed the polygraph test acted dramatically different. More than 65 percent voted for conviction after group discussion.

These findings crystallize the tremendous impact polygraph evidence has on jurors' decisions. Lawyers practicing in those states where polygraph results are admissible evidence should consider the use of such tests as standard fare for persuading juries about the guilt or innocence of clients.

WITNESS SPEECH STYLE

Testimony is more than a series of probative statements. Evidence is ineluctably shaped by the language and style witnesses use to communicate. How evidence is presented is often as influential as the type or quality of the content. Research shows not only that jurors discriminate among evidence on the basis of testimony presentation, but that testimony style greatly affects how jurors respond to witnesses, evidence, and influence attempts by lawyers. Language style used strategically captures attention, illustrates arguments, and coaxes the listener to make favorable inferences about the speaker. The most notable research program in this area began at Duke University with the work of William O'Barr and his associates (Conley, O'Barr, and Lind 1978; Erickson, Lind, Johnson, and O'Barr 1978; Lind, Erickson, Conley, and O'Barr 1978; Lind and O'Barr 1979; O'Barr 1982). In an attempt to investigate the effects of various styles of testimony delivery, these researchers analyzed over 150 hours of taped testimony. These analyses served to identify four distinct witness speech styles and the social contexts with which they were correlated.

POWERFUL VERSUS POWERLESS SPEECH STYLE.   A powerless speech style, as described by O'Barr, is characterized by the frequent use of words and expressions that convey a "lack of forcefulness in speaking." The abundant use of hedges, hesitation forms, polite forms, and question intonations combine to comprise this style of delivery during testimony. Because the incidence of use of this style was found to be more common among those witnesses with little social power (females, the poor, and the uneducated), the authors labeled this style "powerless." Testimony that did not exhibit the frequent usage of these features was thought to be more straightforward and was termed a "powerful" style. An empirical test of the reception of each style during testimony as perceived by subject-jurors resulted in clear patterns of testimony style influence. In a comparison between testimony styles subject-jurors listening to powerful style testimony found the witness more believable, more convincing, more competent, more intelligent, and more trustworthy. The authors concluded that for both male and female witnesses the use of a powerless style produces less favorable reactions to a witness than does the use of a powerful style.

Research has classified several elements exemplifying powerless speech styles, including overly polite forms ("madam," "please"), empty adjectives ("divine," "cute") and adverbial intensifiers ("very," "absolutely," "surely"). The speech elements receiving the most research attention are hedges and hesitation forms. Hedges and qualifiers, such as "I think," "I guess," "sort of," qualify statements so as to detract from their certainty and have been linked to low status courtroom sources. Similarly the use of hesitation forms, such as "uh," "ah," "well," "um," and "you know," makes speakers appear powerless and ineffective (Bradac and Mulac 1984a; Ragan 1983).

Although subsequent research corroborates the persuasive influence of powerful language, not all researchers share the belief that powerless langauge is a reflection of social class. Several scholars contend that the language of powerful people is perceived as powerful because these actors are socially powerful, possessing valuable resources and roles of high status (Hopper 1982). From this view receivers cast males and females employing powerful speech as dominant and effective (Bradac and Mulac 1984a).

In an experiment where status of the source was controlled, the use of powerful, straightforward speech (the absence of hesitations, hedges, and "you know") resulted in higher credibility ratings and persuasiveness (measured by donations following the message) for high and low status sources of both sexes (Johnson and Vinson 1987). Conversely, the use of powerless speech attentuated the witness' credibility evaluations and persuasiveness. When female witnesses of low social standing use more powerful speech, they are more positively evaluated. These favorable impressions are often magnified when evaluators are of the same gender as the source (Erickson et al. 1978; Bradac and Mulac 1984b).

HYPERCORRECT SPEECH.   O'Barr and his colleagues observed that most of the testimony examined was considerably more formal than everyday conversation. They noticed that when witnesses attempted to speak in this more formal style, they committed frequent errors in grammar and vocabulary. The authors termed this style "hypercorrect" speech. In a test between the use of a hypercorrect versus a standard speech style in testimony, the researchers found that witnesses using the standard style were rated as significantly more convincing, more competent, more qualified, and more intelligent than those who used the hypercorrect style. The authors reasoned that jurors must rapidly develop expectations about a witness' behavior on the basis of what they infer about his background and social status. They argued that when these expectations were violated by the witness in attempting to speak in a hypercorrect and more formal style, the jurors' reactions were punitive.

In a related study Parkinson (1979) found that defendants who were more polite and who answered in grammatically complete sentences were acquitted more often than defendants who did not.

NARRATIVE VERSUS FRAGMENTED STYLES OF TESTIMONY.   O'Barr and his associates reasoned that because narrative and fragmented styles entail differences in the speech behavior of lawyers as well as of witnesses, judges and jurors might interpret the use of a narrative or fragmented style of testimony by the witness as indicating the lawyer's own evaluation of the witness. The authors hypothesized that when the witness used a fragmented style, the lawyer would be thought to consider the witness as less competent than when the witness used a narrative style.

In a test of the hypothesis the researchers had subject-jurors listen to tape-recorded reenactments of direct testimony in a criminal trial. The testimony presented the same substantive evidence but varied in presentation of narrative style or fragmented style. The authors concluded that the use of narrative style or fragmented style did lead to significant differences in estimates of how competent the lawyer thought the witness to be in the eyes of prospective jurors, as well as in how competent the jurors themselves thought the witnesses to be. As hypothesized, the narrative style led to more favorable responses than did the fragmented style.

INTERRUPTIONS AND SIMULTANEOUS SPEECH.   In another study of the effects of stylistic differences in witness testimony O'Barr and his associates focused on the acts of simultaneous speech and interruptions during cross-examination. During cross-examination the researchers observed frequent verbal clashes between the examiner and the witness, resulting in interruptions and simultaneous speech. Both counsel and witness appeared "to vie for control of the testimony." The researchers argue that simultaneous speech was an attempt at control that was reduced to "which speaker could persevere longer."

In an examination of the effects of interruptions and simultaneous speech on jurors' perceptions of both witness and lawyer, subject-jurors listened to several testimonies containing variations of these elements and then completed a questionnaire in which they were asked: (1) the extent to which the lawyer controlled the testimony; (2) the extent to which the witness had an opportunity to present his evidence; and (3) the extent to which the lawyer was fair to the witness. The authors found that different versions of the testimony did indeed affect the jurors' perceptions. Two significant findings were clear. First, when counsel and witness engaged in simultaneous speech, counsel was considered to have less control. This was true for all versions of testimony where simultaneous speech occurred, and also regardless of whether the lawyer or the witness dominated the simultaneous speech. Second, when counsel engaged in simultaneous speech, she or he was seen as giving the witness less opportunity to present evidence and as being less fair to the witness.

Not surprisingly, related research reveals that when witnesses initiate simultaneous speech (begin talking while counsel is talking), lawyers perceive the act as an encroachment on the power and control guaranteed them by the court (Walker 1982).

VIVIDNESS EFFECTS.   A witness' response to a question from counsel may or may not be restricted by the question itself. For questions restricting behavioral options, such as Yes and No structured questions, the witness cannot easily elucidate or provide details or background. Other questions, however, leave the amount of detail in the answer up to the witness. In such cases detailed answers are typically considered more persuasive than their curt counterparts. Empirical evidence exists for the premise that vivid information is more persuasive than dry or pallid information in trial testimony. In the research conducted by Reyes, Thompson, and Bower (1980) in a simulated trial, subjects read testimony of a man accused of drunk driving. One group of subjects read pallid prosecution testimony and vivid (more detailed) defense testimony, while another group read vivid and detailed prosecution testimony and pallid defense testimony. Facts in the testimony remained constant except for their detailed description.

Those subjects exposed to vivid prosecution testimony were significantly more likely to render a guilty verdict, while those subjects exposed to vivid defense testimony were significantly more likely to render an acquittal. Based upon this finding and empirical research conducted in other settings, Nisbett and Ross (1980) concluded that vivid information may have a disproportionate impact on beliefs and inferences. They argue that vivid information is more easily remembered and thus more readily available for use in the decisionmaking process. Although more recent research has indicated that the power of vivid information may be much weaker than Nisbett and Ross have proposed (Taylor and Thompson 1982), the explanation provided by Nisbett and Ross fits comfortably within the storytelling framework. Detailed and vivid information allows for greater clarity and emphasis in the telling of stories. The impact of stories containing greater detail should have a more powerful impact on reconstructing the larger story of the trial and thus on the trial outcome. This is especially noteworthy considering evidence that jurors often assume a witness who does not provide details does not, in fact, remember or know them (Wells and Leippe 1981).

According to vividness research, information can be characterized as vivid to the extent it is concrete, image provoking, emotionally interesting, and personally relevant (Nisbett and Ross 1980); but the feature of concreteness, defined as the degree to which testimony contains specific details, has been the most popular avenue of investigation.

Testimony can vary in detail in several ways (Bell and Loftus 1985). Pallid statements may be elaborated with details that replace or add words already in the statement. For example, the descriptor "Chevy" can be inserted in the statement, "They jumped into the hotrod," to qualify the vehicle. The same statement may also be vividly embroidered by adding the additional statement, "A strong smell of gasoline permeated the car." In addition, statements may be vividly elaborated by adding irrelevant details to the testimony. For example, the witness might add, "Twenty-four hours earlier, I was playing racquetball at the Omni Club with my best friend." In each case the specificity of the information is increased, making the testimony more vivid.

Inconsistent research findings have been troublesome. Although case histories have been shown to be more persuasive than statistical information (Hamill, Wilson, and Nisbett 1980; Nisbett and Borgida 1975), other studies viewing concreteness differently have yielded mixed results. These range from vividness effects on immediate judgments (Bell and Loftus 1985), to effects on delayed judgment only (Reyes, Thompson, and Bower 1980), to no effects on judgment at all (Borgida 1979; Gottlieb, Taylor, and Ruderman 1977). The differences appear to stem mainly from research designs. When vividness is operationalized as the degree of detail in a statement, and when pallid evidence versus vivid evidence is contradictory, vividness affects the judgments of listeners (Bell and Loftus 1985).

Generally scholars agree that vivid information is more influential than pallid information because listeners spend more time in thought and with greater attention as a result of the increased specificity of the information (Nisbett and Ross 1980). Since research has revealed that concrete sentences are better remembered than abstract sentences (Berg and Paivio 1969; Holms and Langford 1976), it is reasonable that vivid information is also more memorable. Moreover, vivid testimony is generally believed to have a greater ability to excite the imagination, leading to more emotional responses.

LANGUAGE INTENSITY.   Testimony also varies as to the degree of intensity it exudes. Language intensity refers to the degree to which language deviates from affective neutrality. "Hate" is more intense than "dislike"; "horrified" more intense than "scared"; "completely overwhelmed" more intense than "influenced," and so on. Intense language enhances messages for which receivers are already favorable, but may hinder influence of messages directed at audiences unfavorable to the positions advocated (Bradac, Bowers, and Courtright 1979). If we assume that jurors are neutrally predisposed to the testimony they hear, then witnesses who use more intense language will be conferred higher credibility and considered more persuasive (Burgoon, Jones, and Stewart 1975). Some evidence suggests, however, that low credible sources and females are more persuasive when they use low intensity language, primarily because of the expectations receivers hold.

Although the general persuasive strategy is for witnesses to use more intense language in their testimony, special forms of intense language, such as obscene language, are often viewed as inappropriate and impinge negatively on the receiver. Studies demonstrate that speakers who use profanity in their persuasive appeals are less influential and are perceived negatively (Bostrom, Basehart, and Rossiter 1973; Mulac 1976).

OPINIONATED LANGUAGE.   We already know that confident witnesses, especially those who directly observed events important to a case, are more influential than are diffident or less confident wit-

nesses. But how does a witness exude confidence? What characteristics of speech direct receivers to evaluate speakers as confident?
One answer to these questions is opinionated language.

Opinionated language is a persuasive technique emphasizing the
social consequences of support or opposition to the speaker's position (Rokeach 1960). Nonopinionated statements indicate only the
communicator's attitude toward a particular idea or concept,
whereas opinionated statements indicate both the communicator's
attitude toward the idea and the communicator's attitude toward
those who agree or disagree with him. For example, "I support new
legislation on clean air" is a statement expressing the communicator's attitude only about the legislation and is considered nonopinionated language. By contrast, the statement, "Intelligent
human beings support clean air legislation," expresses not only an
attitude about the legislation but also an attitude toward others who
agree or disagree. This opinionated acceptance or rejection of others
is considered opinionated language.

In one study in this area researchers found that highly credible
sources were more effective when they used opinionated language
(Miller and Lobe 1967). Both open-minded and closed-minded receivers, as determined in the study, were more influenced by opinionated than nonopinionated language. In a subsequent study results
revealed that when the source was initially perceived as trustworthy,
opinionated language was more effective than nonopinionated language (Miller and Basehart 1969). Similarly, when the source was
initially judged as untrustworthy, a nonopinionated message produced less attitude change than an opinionated one. Yet another
study revealed that receivers with a high need for social approval
were more susceptible to messages containing opinionated language
than were people with low social approval needs (Basehart 1971).

In the minds of many lawyers the very nature of being a juror
requires a high need for social approval. After all, each juror knows
that deliberation is a social activity where persons must exchange
differing viewpoints in order to render a verdict, which itself must be
socially acceptable. In this light, opinionated language carries significant influence with jurors.

LANGUAGE IMMEDIACY AND DIVERSITY.   Speakers who directly associate themselves through language to the audience or topic at hand
possess verbal immediacy (Wiener and Mehrabian 1967). The psychological closeness of immediacy is demonstrated by the speaker's
use of specific language, indicating spatial and temporal proximity
("here" rather than "there"; "now" rather than "then"). Increased

use of pronouns indicating inclusion ("we" versus "I" or "you") signals involvement between speaker and receiver. For example, the statement, "We should go to dinner tonight," is far more immediate than the statement, "You and I should make dinner plans soon."

A speaker who uses greater verbal immediacy is seen as more credible and competent and generally exerts greater persuasive influence than do speakers low in verbal immediacy (Conville 1975). In addition, receivers interpreting messages high in verbal immediacy tend to see themselves as more similar to the speaker (Bradac, Bowers, and Courtright 1980).

Lexical diversity refers to the range of a speaker's vocabulary. Researchers commonly calculate lexical diversity by computing the ratio between the number of different words spoken and the total number of words employed. High lexical diversity is the obverse of redundancy, as the speaker who repeats the same words exhibits low lexical diversity. Speakers rich in lexical diversity are consistently judged as more competent, of higher social status, and more persuasive than their low diversity counterparts (Bradac, Bowers, and Courtright 1979). When speakers are known to be of high status, lexical diversity further enhances message influence (Bradac, Bowers, and Courtright 1980). In addition, listeners perceive moderate to high diversity sources as more similar to themselves (Bradac, Desmond, and Murdock 1977).

STRATEGIC LANGUAGE.   The research on the influence of language style is clear-cut. People discriminate on the basis of perceived differences about how speakers communicate. In order to arrive at accurate judgments, observers make inferences based on the information available to them, most notably language features. Because stylistic features of language vary from person to person, observers use these features as markers signaling characteristics inherent in the individual, such as confidence, competence, credibility, and status. If we assume that, in part, the advocate's role is to enhance the credibility and persuasive power of his or her witnesses, then the task at hand becomes one of strategically managing language style.

The ideal witness, one who is highly persuasive, presents testimony in a vivid and narrative style. Lawyers should coach witnesses to describe events in detail and avoid fragmented responses to questions. The ideal witness establishes confidence through opinionated language, and avoids the negative inferences associated with powerless and hypercorrect language. Attorneys can encourage opinionated language simply by requiring witnesses to respond as if no one believed them. The ideal witness also arouses jurors with moderate to intense language. The common practice of rehearsing testimony enables counsel to assess and make recommendations concerning intensity. Finally, the ideal witness generates interest with verbal immediacy and lexical diversity. Since listeners perceive themselves as more similar to sources who use verbally immediate and lexically diverse language, defense lawyers can capitalize on this inference by encouraging defendants to use a higher degree of verbal immediacy and lexical diversity in their testimony. Lawyers already presume that similarity between courtroom actors increases affinity and reduces the likelihood of conviction. In this light, jurors who perceive themselves as more similar to the defendant because of language immediacy and diversity should be less likely to render guilty verdicts in many cases.

REFERENCES

Basehart, J. R. (1971). Message opinionation and approval-dependence as determinants of receiver attitude change and recall. *Speech Monographs* 38: 302–10.

Becker, L. A., and Brock, T. C. (1966). Prospective recipients' estimates of withheld evaluation. *Journal of Personality and Social Psychology* 4: 147–64.

Bell, B. E., and Loftus, E. F. (1985). Vivid persuasion in the courtroom. *Journal of Personality Assessment* 49: 659–65.

Berg, L., and Paivio, A. (1969). Concreteness and imagery in sentence meaning. *Journal of Verbal Learning and Verbal Behavior* 8: 827–31.

Borchard, E. M. (1932). *Convicting the innocent: errors of criminal justice*. New Haven: Yale University Press.

Borgida, E. (1979). Character proof and the fireside induction. *Law and Human Behavior* 3: 189–202.

Bostrom, R. N.; Basehart, J. R.; and Rossiter, C. M. (1973). The effects of three types of profane language in persuasive messages. *Journal of Communication* 23: 461–75.

Bradac, J. J.; Boers, J. W.; and Courtright, J. A. (1980). Lexical variations in intensity, immediacy, and diversity: an axiomatic theory and causal model. In R. N. St. Clair and H. Giles (eds.), *The social and psychological contexts of language*. Hillsdale, NJ: Erlbaum.

Bradac, J. J.; Bowers, J. W.; and Courtright, J. A. (1979). Three language variables in communication research: intensity, immediacy, and diversity. *Human Communication Research* 5: 257–69.

Bradac, J. J.; Desmond, R. J.; and Murdock, J. I. (1977). Diversity and density: lexically determined evaluative and informational consequences of linguistic complexity. *Communication Monographs* 44: 273–83.

Bradac, J. and Mulac, A. (1984a). A molecular view of powerful and powerless speech styles: attributional consequences of specific language features and communicator intentions. *Communication Monographs* 51: 307–19.

Bradac, J. J. and Mulac, A. (1984b). Attributional consequences of powerful and powerless speech styles in a crisis-intervention context. *Journal of Language and Social Psychology* 3: 1–19.

Brandon, R., and Davies, C. (1973). *Wrongful imprisonment*. London: Allen and Unwin.

Brigham, J. C. (1981). The accuracy of eyewitness evidence: how do attorneys see it? *Florida Bar Journal,* 714–21.

Brigham, J. C., and Bothwell, R. K. (1983). The ability of prospective jurors to estimate the accuracy of eyewitness identifications. *Law and Human Behavior* 7: 19–30.

Brigham, J. C., and Wolfskiel, M. P. (1983). Opinions of attorneys and law enforcement personnel on the accuracy of eyewitness identifications. *Law and Human Behavior* 7: 337–49.

Buckhout, R. (1975). Nearly 2000 witnesses can be wrong. *Social Action and the Law Newsletter* 2: 7.

Burgoon, M.; Jones, S. B.; and Stewart, D. (1975). Toward a message-centered theory of persuasion: three empirical investigations of language intensity. *Human Communication Research* 1: 240–56.

Cavoukian, A., and Heslegrave, R. J. (1980). The admissibility of polygraph evidence in court. *Law and Human Behavior* 4: 117–31.

Clifford, B. R., and Scott, J. (1978). Individual and situational factors in eyewitness testimony. *Journal of Applied Psychology* 63: 352–59.

Conley, J. M.; O'Barr, W. M.; and Lind, E. A. (1978). The power of language: presentational style in the courtroom. *Duke Law Journal* 6: 1375–99.

Conville, R. (1975). Linguistic nonimmediacy and self-presentation. *Journal of Psychology* 90: 219–27.

Deffenbacher, K. A. (1980). Eyewitness accuracy and confidence. *Law and Human Behavior* 4: 243–60.

Ebbesen, E. B., and Konecni, V. J. (1982). Social psychology and the law: a decision-making approach to the criminal justice system. In Konecni and Ebbesen (eds.), *The criminal justice system: a social-psychological analysis*. San Francisco: Freeman.

Erickson, B. E.; Lind, E. A.; Johnson, B. C.; and O'Barr, W. M. (1978). Speech style and impression formation in a court setting: the effects of powerful and powerless speech. *Journal of Experimental and Social Psychology* 14: 266–79.

Fox, S. G., and Walters, H. A. (1987). The impact of general versus specific expert testimony and eyewitness confidence upon mock juror judgment. *Law and Human Behavior* 10: 215–28.

Frank, J., and Frank, B. (1957). *Not guilty*. Garden City, NY: Doubleday.

Frankel, A., and Morris, W. N. (1976). Testifying in one's own defense: the ingratiator's dilemma. *Journal of Personality and Social Psychology* 34: 475–80.

Gottlieb, D. E.; Taylor, S. E.; and Ruderman, A. (1977). Cognitive bases of children's moral judgments. *Developmental Psychology* 13: 547–56.

Greenwood, P. W.; Chaiken, J. M.; Petersilia, J.; and Prusoff, L. (1975). *The criminal investigation process*. Vol 3. *Observations and analysis*. Santa Monica, CA: Rand Corporation.

Hamill, R.; Wilson, T. D.; and Nisbett, R. E. (1980). Insensitivity to sample bias: generalizing from atypical cases. *Journal of Personality and Social Psychology* 39: 578–89.

Holms, V. M., and Langford, J. (1976). Comprehension and recall of abstract and concrete sentences. *Journal of Verbal Learning and Verbal Behavior* 15: 559–66.

Hopper, R. (1982). Power is as power speaks: linguistic sex differences revisited. In L. Larmer and M. K. Badami (eds.), *Communication, language and gender*. Madison: University of Wisconsin Extension Press.

Hosch, H. M.; Beck, E. L.; and McIntyre, P. (1980). Influence of expert testimony regarding eyewitness accuracy on jury decisions. *Law and Human Behavior* 4: 287–96.

Johnson, C., and Vinson, L. (1987). Damned if you do, damned if you don't: status, powerful speech and evaluation of female witnesses. Paper presented at the annual convention of the Western Speech Communication Association, Salt Lake City.

Kalven, H., Jr., and Zeisel, H. (1966). *The American jury*. Boston: Little, Brown.

Kanouse, D. E., and Hanson, L. R. (1972). Negativity in evaluations. In E. E. Jones et al. (eds.), *Attribution: perceiving the causes of behavior*. Morristown, NJ: General Learning Press.

Kassin, S. M., and Wrightsman, L. S. (1980). Prior confessions and mock juror verdicts. *Journal of Applied Social Psychology* 10: 133–46.

Kassin, S. M., and Wrightsman, L. S. (1981). Coerced confessions, judicial instruction, and mock juror verdicts. *Journal of Applied Social Psychology* 11: 489–506.

Kassin, S. M.; Wrightsman, L. S.; and Warner, T. (1983). Confession evidence: the positive coercion bias, judicial instruction, and mock jury verdicts. Unpublished Manuscript.

Leippe, M. R. (1980). Effects of integrative memorial and cognitive processes on the correspondence of eyewitness accuracy and confidence. *Law and Human Behavior* 4: 261–74.

Leippe, M. R. (1985). The influence of eyewitness nonidentifications on mock-jurors' judgments of a court case. *Journal of Applied Social Psychology* 15: 656–72.

Leippe, M. R.; Wells, G. L.; and Ostrom, T. M. (1978). Crime seriousness as a determinant of accuracy in eyewitness identification. *Journal of Applied Psychology* 63: 345–51.

Lind, E. A.; Erickson, B. E.; Conley, J. M.; and O'Barr, W. M. (1978). Social attributions of conversation style in trial testimony. *Journal of Personality and Social Psychology* 36: 1558–67.

Lind, E. A., and O'Barr, W. M. (1979). The social significance of speech in the courtroom. In H. Giles and R. N. St. Clair (eds.), *Language and social psychology*. Baltimore: University Park Press.

Lindsay, R. C. L., and Wells, G. L. (1980). What price is justice? exploring the relationship of lineup fairness to identification accuracy. *Law and Human Behavior* 4: 303–13.

Lindsay, R. C. L.; Wells, G. L.; and Rumpel, C. (1981). Can people detect eyewitness identification accuracy within and across situations? *Journal of Applied Psychology* 66: 79–89.

Loftus, E. F. (1974). Reconstructing memory: the incredible eyewitness. *Pyschology Today* 8: 116–19.

Loftus, E. F. (1975). Eyewitness testimony: does the malleable human memory interfere with legal justice? *Social Action and the Law Newsletter* 2: 5.

Loftus, E. F. (1979). *Eyewitness testimony*. Cambridge: Harvard University Press.

Loftus, E. F. (1980). Impact of expert psychological testimony on the unreliability of eyewitness identification. *Journal of Applied Psychology* 65: 9–15.

Loftus, E. F. (1983). Silence is not golden. *American Psychologist* 38: 564–72.

Maass, A.; Brigham, J. C.; and West, S. G. (1985). Testifying on eyewitness reliability: expert advice is not always persuasive. *Journal of Applied Social Psychology* 15: 207–29.

McAllister, H. A., and Bregman, N. J. (1986). Juror underutilization of eyewitness nonidentifications: theoretical and practical implications. *Journal of Applied Psychology* 71: 168–70.

McCloskey, M. M., and Egeth, H. E. (1983a). Eyewitness identification: what can a psychologist tell a jury. *American Psychologist* 38: 550–63.

McCloskey, M. M., and Egeth, H. E. (1983b). A time to speak, or a time to keep silent? *American Psychologist* 38: 573–75.

Manson v. Brathwaite, 432 U.S. 98 (1977).

Markwart, A., and Lynch, B. E. (1979). The effect of polygraph evidence on mock jury decision-making. *Journal of Police Science and Administration* 7: 324–32.

Miller, G. R., and Basehart, J. (1969). Source trustworthiness, opinionated statements, and response to persuasive communication. *Speech Monographs* 36: 1–7.

Miller, G. R., and Boster, F. J. (1977). Three images of the trial: their implications for psychological research. In B. Sales (ed.), *Psychology in the legal process.* New York: Halsted.

Miller, G. R., and Lobe, J. (1967). Opinionated language, open- and closed-mindedness and response to persuasive communications. *Journal of Communication* 17: 333–41.

Mulac, A. (1976). Effects of obscene language upon three dimensions of listener attitude. *Communication Monographs* 43: 300–307.

Myers, M. A. (1979). Rule departures and making law: juries and their verdicts. *Law and Society Review* 13: 781–97.

Neil v. Biggers, 408 U. S. 198 (1972).

Nisbett, R. E., and Borgida, E. (1975). Attributions and the pyschology of prediction. *Journal of Personality and Social Psychology* 32: 932–43.

Nisbett, R. E., and Ross, L. (1980). *Human inference: strategies and shortcomings of social judgment.* Englewood Cliffs, NJ: Prentice-Hall.

O'Barr, W. M. (1982). *Linguistic evidence: language, power and strategy in the courtroom.* New York: Academic Press.

Ostrom. T. M.; Werner, C. M.; and Saks, M. J. (1978). An integration theory analysis of jurors' presumptions of guilt or innocence. *Journal of Personality and Social Psychology* 36: 436–50.

Parkinson, M. (1979). Language behavior and courtroom success. Paper presented at the International Conference on Language and Social Psychology, Bristol, England.

Penrod, S., and Borgida, E. (1983). Lay rules and legal inference. In L. Wheeler and P. Shaver (eds.), *Review of personality and social psychology* vol. 4. Beverly Hills, CA: Sage.

Ragan, S. (1983). A conversational analysis of alignment talk in job interviews. In R. Bostrom (ed.), *Communication Yearbook 7.* Beverly Hills, CA: Sage.

Reskin, B. F., and Visher, C. A. (1986). The impacts of evidence and extralegal factors in jurors' decisions. *Law and Society Review* 20: 423–38.

Reyes, R. M.; Thompson, W. L.; and Bower, G. H. (1980). Judgmental biases resulting from differing availabilities of arguments. *Journal of Personality and Social Psychology* 39: 2–12.

Rokeach, M. (1960). *The open and closed mind*. New York: Basic Books.

Roper, R. J. (1975). The search for truth at trial: an argument against the admission of polygraph test results at trial. *Polygraph* 4: 130–38.

Ross, L. (1977). The intuitive psychologist and his shortcomings: distortions in the attribution process. In L. Berkowitz (ed.), *Advances in experimental social psychology,* vol. 10. New York: Academic Press.

Saks, M. J., and Hastie, R. (1978). *Social psychology in court*. New York: Van Nostrand.

Sanders, G. S., and Warnick, D. H. (1982). Evaluating identification evidence from multiple witnesses. *Journal of Applied Social Psychology* 12: 182–92.

Shaffer, D. R. (1985). The defendant's testimony. In S. Kassin and L. S. Wrightsman (eds.), *The psychology of evidence and trial procedure*. Beverly Hills, CA: Sage.

Shaffer, D. R., and Case, T. (1982). On the decision to testify on one's own behalf: effects of withheld evidence, defendant's sexual preferences, and juror dogmatism on juridic decisions. *Journal of Personality and Social Psychology* 42: 335–46.

Shaffer, D. R.; Case, T.; and Brannen, L. (1979). Effects of withheld evidence on juridic decisions: amount of evidence withheld and its relevance to the case. *Representative Research in Social Psychology* 10: 2–15.

Shaffer, D. R., and Sadowski, C. (1979). Effects of withheld evidence on juridic decisions II: locus of withholding strategy. *Personality and Social Psychology Bulletin* 5: 40–43.

Shaffer, D. R.; Sadowski, C.; and Hendrick, C. (1978). Effects of withheld evidence on juridic decisions. *Psychological Reports* 42: 1235–42.

Snyder, M., and Swann, W. B., Jr. (1978). Hypothesis-testing in social interaction. *Journal of Personality and Social Psychology* 36: 1202–12.

Suggs, D., and Berman, J. J. (1979). Factors affecting testimony about mitigating circumstances and the fixing of punishment. *Law and Human Behavior* 3: 251–60.

Taylor, S. E., and Thompson, S. C. (1982). Stalking the elusive "vividness" effect. *Psychological Review* 89: 155–81.

Visher, C. A. (1987). Juror decision making: the importance of evidence. *Law and Human Behavior* 11: 1–17.

Walker, A. G. (1982). Patterns and implications of cospeech in a legal setting. In R. J. DiPietro (ed.), *Linguistics and the professions*. Norwood, NJ: Ablex.

Wells, G. L. (1980). Asymmetric attributions for compliance: reward vs. punishment. *Journal of Experimental Social Psychology* 16: 47–60.

Wells, G. L., and Leippe, M. R. (1981). How do triers of fact infer the accuracy of eyewitness identifications? using memory for peripheral detail can be misleading. *Journal of Applied Psychology* 66: 682–87.

Wells, G. L.; Lindsay, R. C. L.; and Ferguson, T. J. (1979). Accuracy, confidence, and juror perceptions in eyewitness identification. *Journal of Applied Psychology* 64: 440–48.

Wells, G. L.; Ferguson, T. J.; and Lindsay, R. C. L. (1981). The tractability of eyewitness confidence and its implications for triers of fact. *Journal of Applied Psychology* 66: 688–96.

Wells, G. L.; Lindsay, R. C. L.; and Tousignant, J. P. (1980). Effects of expert psychological advice on human performance in judging the validity of eyewitness testimony. *Law and Human Behavior* 4: 275–86.

Wells, G. L., and Murray, D. M. (1984). Eyewitness confidence. In G. L. Wells and E. F. Loftus (eds.), *Eyewitness testimony: psychological perspectives*. New York: Cambridge University Press.

Werner, C. M.; Strube, M. J.; Cole, A. M.; and Kagehiro, D. K. (1985). The impact of case characteristics and prior jury experience on jury verdicts. *Journal of Applied Social Psychology* 15: 409–27.

Whitley, B. E., and Greenberg, M. S. (1986). The role of eyewitness confidence in juror perceptions of credibility. *Journal of Applied Social Psychology* 16: 387–409.

Wiener, M., and Mehrabian, A. (1967). *Language with language: immediacy, a channel in verbal communication*. New York: Appleton-Century.

Yandell, B. (1979). Those who protest too much are seen as guilty. *Personality and Social Psychology Bulletin* 5: 44–47.

Yarmey, A. D., and Jones, H. P. T. (1983). Is eyewitness testimony a matter of common sense? In S. Lloyd-Bostock and B. R. Clifford (eds.), *Witness evidence: critical and empirical papers*. New York: Wiley.

Younger, E. J. (1966). Interrogation of criminal defendants: some views on Miranda v. Arizona. *Fordham Law Review* 35: 255–62.

Chapter 8

WITNESS EXAMINATION

The popular image of witness examination is one of orchestrated conflict, a pyrotechnic struggle of colorful language and aggressive personalities. Thanks to the likes of Perry Mason and "L. A. Law," we readily expect a blustering attorney shouting pointed questions at a passive witness ready to break down and confess. Although the reality of examination doesn't do justice to this image, the questioning of witnesses is fundamental to the trial process as a means both to uncover pertinent information and to display the character of actors upon whom life-decisions depend.

During direct examination the focus of the courtroom is on the witness and the testimony that witness provides. Observers search in the heap of testimony and behavior for clues of veracity or bias. They evaluate whether the witness is composed or anxious, whether answers ring true or sound hollow. During cross-examination this attention shifts to the attorney and the questions this attorney designs. The tone of the examination, the power of the attorney, the fairness of the questions—all contribute to influence observers and the judgments they make. What makes this conglomerate of behaviors and judgments so complex is that each judgment is consciously formed and each behavior strategically chosen. What results is a choreographed collage of behaviors dependent upon the theory of the case and the general goals of examination.

Direct and cross examination are like two sides of a coin. During direct examination counsel is charged with the tasks of establishing the credibility of each witness and eliciting testimony that, when woven with other evidence, will combine to create a consistent and coherent story. Attorneys generally believe that if the direct examination is properly and skillfully conducted, the impression made by a witness is more lasting than any argument presented by counsel. Conversely, the objective of cross-examination entails impeachment and inconsistency. The cross-examiner's task is to impeach the witness; that is, to discredit the witness and the testimony given during the direct examination. Moreover, when a witness testifies to material facts that injure an advocate's position, it becomes the advocate's duty to "break the force of it." (Laird 1982). To break the force of the direct examination the cross-examiner must expose evidence that shows the story created by the opponent to be improbable and the elements of that story to be inconsistent. In addition, the cross-examination affords counsel the opportunity to stress evidence favorable to his or her own story and case.

Practicing attorneys generally agree on the types of questions lawyers are to use in direct and cross examination. Trial lawyers are advised to use broad, open-ended questions in direct examination to facilitate accurate descriptions, and terse, closed questions during cross-examination to bring into question the testimony elicited in the direct examination (Mauet 1980). The rationale behind allowing counsel to use leading questions in cross-examination is that testing a witness' memory, veracity, and accuracy is facilitated by the narrow and closed structure of the leading question (Marshall 1980). Lawyers readily agree that it is the direct examiner's task to allow for detailed explanations and the cross-examiner's task to control the witness so as to question the veracity and credibility of both witness and testimony.

IMPEACHING THE WITNESS

Impeaching a witness begins with the question: What qualifies the witness to give testimony? The answer, as guided by the rules of evidence, contains three parts: (1) the promise to tell the truth, as demonstrated by an oath to do so; (2) the event perceived by the witness, through his or her own senses, that pertains to the litigation; and (3) the accurate recall of the event by the witness. In order to impeach the witness, counsel designs questions that will demonstrate the oath, the perception, or the recall of the witness is suspect. As one successful trial lawyer says, "A witness cannot act credible or appear to be telling the truth under the proper questioning" (Litvin 1984).

The oath to tell the truth taken by all witnesses constitutes an important avenue for impeachment. Attorneys may assume that the majority of witnesses they confront on cross-examination have a reason to slant the truth. The lawyer's task is to uncover information and evidence displaying that the witness possesses: bias (predisposition in favor), prejudice (a predisposition against), vested interest (a stake in the outcome), or corruption (bribery or payment). By exposing the witness as having reasons for providing specious testimony, counsel successfully discredits the witness.

As a direct observer of the events in question, the witness must have been in a reasonable position and condition to perceive the events. Questions concerning both the physical and mental state of the witness at the time of the event, the location, and the ability to perceive the events clearly should be used to impeach the witness. Furthermore, other actions or objects at the time of the event, current physical or mental traits, and the time that has elapsed that may hinder memory or recall should be used to raise doubts about the accuracy of the testimony.

In some jurisdictions lawyers are entitled to impeach the witness by exposing prior wrongful acts by the witness or prior convictions of the witness. Furthermore, counsel may call another witness who will testify that the primary witness has a bad reputation for telling the truth.

The most common impeachment strategy is to show a prior inconsistent statement by the witness. This inconsistency renders the current statement incredible by exposing the witness as dishonest. In most jurisdictions the court requires that the attorney lay a foundation for the statement. That is to say, the lawyer must prompt the witness either by displaying the physical text if the statement was written or by establishing the location, time, and circumstances of the statement if it was oral. For example, imagine that a witness during direct examination says that the door to the burglarized house was open. Further suppose our investigation reveals that the door was closed. We lay the foundation: "Mr. Witness, didn't you get your hair cut last week?" "Yes." "You talked to the barber?" "Yes." "You mentioned the burglary, didn't you?" We have successfully laid the foundation and can now proceed with the impeachment question: "You told the barber the door was closed, didn't you, Mr. Witness?"

Witness responses to impeachment questions can be classified along a continuum of knowledge, from the unknown to the precisely known (Litvin 1984). Four points on the knowledge continuum represent the witness' position relative to the content of the question: (1) unknown: "I don't know"; (2) I knew once: "I don't remember"; (3) I know imprecisely: "About twenty minutes"; (4) I know precisely: "Twenty minutes." In general, we can say that the goal of direct examination is to elicit precise knowledge and to avoid movement toward limited or absent knowledge, thereby enhancing credibility. Cross-examination, on the other hand, should be designed specifically to elicit responses of limited knowledge and limited recall, thereby attentuating the witness' credibility. According to many practitioners, the more times you get the defendant to respond, "I don't know," "I don't recall," "I can't remember," the closer you are to conviction (Loftus and Goodman 1985).

CONTROLLING THE WITNESS

Impeaching the witness is only the first step toward successful cross-examination. Just as important is the ability to control the witness. Practicing lawyers know that successful impeachment depends on the explicit content of the examination. Controlling a witness translates to influencing the witness to give testimony advantageous to the case. A skilled attorney can accomplish this even when a hostile witness is determined to provide damaging testimony. Because the rules of the court state that only counsel can ask a question, and because questions can be designed in such a way as to impel agreement by the witness, the witness is at distinct disadvantage. "Capitalizing on this disadvantage, however, requires the strategic use of questions, pauses, and other devices that facilitate control. Once control is established, lawyers generally believe that observers view counsel as powerful and credible. From this view, controlling a witness by maintaining a powerful grip on both the content and rhythm of the examination is essential.

Research has revealed a host of strategies central to the process of control. The following sections survey this research with an eye toward tactics and theoretical concepts germane to the successful performance of control during examination.

SHOWING INCONSISTENCY AND CONTRADICTION.   Examination meant to display contradictory or inconsistent facts follows a particular language structure common to many conflict settings. Although this "grammar" of questioning often goes unnoticed by courtroom actors, the production of this structure is quite consistent between experienced examiners (Bleiberg and Churchill 1975). The sequence begins when the witness makes a declarative statement that counsel knows to be logically inconsistent or contradictory to earlier testimony by the witness or to facts already brought to light. Consider the following example.

Witness: *When I entered the room, I clearly saw the hammer on the floor.*

Attorney: *Did you or didn't you tell the police the room was very dark?*

Witness: *I did.*

Attorney: *Isn't it true that you told the police that you didn't see anything on the floor?*

Witness: *Yes.*

Attorney: *Your stories don't match, do they?*

After the declaration, the examiner asks a closed-choice question about a particular aspect of the statement. The witness responds by picking the answer that shows that the particular aspect under question is an exception to the previous statement. This answer is followed by a second closed-choice question, the answer to which must provide yet a second exception to the first statement. The witness, faced with only a choice between yes or no, gives the contradictory answer. The sequence is typically concluded when counsel asks a rhetorical question that openly displays the contradiction.

Consider another example, where counsel uses the witness' own words in the first statement against her.

Witness: *My father doesn't care about me and has nothing to do with my life.*

Attorney: *You lived in his house?*

Witness: *Yes.*

Attorney: *How could your welfare not be of any importance to your father?*

Notice that this question sequence follows a funnel-like pattern where the questions and answers become more precise. Since it is the witness who supplies the answers which contradict the initial statement, the inconsistency carries more force. The rhetorical question is used to heighten the inescapable logic of the questioning. We should note that several practitioners warn attorneys not to use rhetorical questions during examination (Younger 1976). The reason for this advice is the unpredictability of the witness. Logic, these practitioners contend, is only inescapable for those who think logically. And restraint is the better part of the examiner's valor.

REPETITION AND LOOPBACK QUESTIONS.   A common strategy to elicit supportive testimony is the employment of loopback questions. When an attorney chooses to repeat part or all of the answer elicited from a previous question in a new question, the question is labeled a loopback question. The function of such a loopback question is straightforward and clear: It can produce a repetition of specific points so as to ingrain those points within the memory of jurors. If remembered and then recalled later, the evidence or fact in question may play an important role in the decision-making process. As will be discussed in more detail in the next chapter, repeated statements are judged as more truthful than are new statements (Bacon 1979).

One legal theorist suggests that loopbacks are useful in regaining control of a witness who is "slipping away" (Kestler 1982). He argues that the loopback question enables the examiner to refer to a question which the witness answered favorably and to continue the questioning from that point. Perhaps more convincing is the fact that by repeating a previous answer, the attorney restricts the witness to constructing a response from that vantage or denying the earlier answer or its restatement. By not refuting the earlier answer or questioning its restatement, the witness is now forced to work from its premises, guiding both the construction and content of his or her answer.

SEMANTIC CONTAGION.   Events and objects can be described in indefinite ways and by using any number of terms or labels. Since language is the vehicle by which social reality is constructed in the courtroom, it seems only reasonable that the use of certain words or phrases would have a considerable impact on how jurors and other actors conceive of and create that reality. Politicians, for example, have a long history of substituting less offensive or reactive euphemisms for less distasteful words or expressions in an attempt to control how the public frames an event. Research suggests that such selection may not only produce desired attitudes but may also be contagious. That is to say, once a particular word or phrase is introduced, others will often adopt the term and its related meanings (Danet 1980). Lawyers always have the option to depict events in terms most conducive to their stories. Consider the conceptual difference between the following terms: teen-ager/youth; strike/bludgeon; house/residence; outfit/uniform; throw/hurl; bullet/projectile. The action and object terms vary in precision, intensity, and cultural association. If we keep in mind that words are symbols by which we communicate a social reality, the advantage of choosing one word over another is both clear and reasonable.

In one study of this semantic contagion in a manslaughter trial, courtroom actors used as many as forty competing terms to refer to the outcome of pregnancy, including the controversial distinction between "baby" and "fetus" (Danet 1980). Undoubtedly, the semantic contagion of either term would exert a broad influence on how jurors would interpret testimony. By using strategically chosen terms when asking questions, lawyers allow the witness to adopt the terms conducive to a particular framing of the story. The danger, of course, is that witnesses may reject these terms either directly or indirectly. In addition, jurors may perceive certain terms to be unreasonable (Loftus and Goodman 1985).

QUESTION STRUCTURE AND CONTROL.   Examiners possess a vast degree of freedom when designing questions. To marshal the designs most likely to produce desired results, the attorney must first understand the rules and structures of language which guide style and meaning. We can begin with the premise that question types vary on two dimensions: content and form. Few examiners fail to realize that the content variation of the questions they ask shapes the responses they will receive. But less obvious are the characteristics of question forms. Questions, like other linguistic strings, vary structurally. For the purposes of this discussion, we will focus on four features of this structural variation that greatly affect how questions will be received by witnesses.

The general properties of questions include considerations of negative construction, active-passive voice, the existence of tags, and leading construction.

Negative construction. A question is considered negative if a negative marker, such as the negative morpheme "n't," exists in the main clause. For example, "Didn't you walk into the house?" contains the negative unit "did not" signaling a negative construction. Questions not containing negative markers are considered affirmative structures.

The use of negative construction in question design becomes an intriguing issue in light of research on these designs. Not only are negative constructions hard to understand and more difficult to recall than questions stated in the affirmative (Mehler 1963; DeVito 1976), but negative constructions require longer periods to process than do affirmative sentences (Vosniadou 1982).

Active-passive construction. Questions, like other linguistic units, can be stated in either the active or passive voice. This is a simple variation resulting from the position of the subject and verb in the question. When the subject precedes the verb and is said to direct that verb, the question is termed active. When the subject follows the verb and hence is acted upon by that verb, the question is termed passive. For example, the question "Did the boy throw the rock?" is active because the subject (the boy) directs the verb (throw). A passive restatement of this question would be "Was the rock thrown by the boy?" In this passive question the subject is acted upon by the verb. Not only do they require more words, but passive questions are more difficult to understand than active ones (DeVito 1976).

Tag questions. Tag questions contain an additional phrase attached to the main clause which repeats the question. Generally, if the main clause is affirmative, the tag will be negative, and if the main clause is negative, the tag will be affirmative. Tags serve to create an expected answer, hence turning any nontag question into a leading question. Consider the affirmative question "The child was in the house?" This question does not suggest an answer, but the addition of a negative tag, such as "The child was in the house, wasn't she?" creates the expectation of a positive response.

Although a negative clause followed by a negative tag is not grammatically permissible, on rare occasions affirmative clauses will be followed by affirmative tags. Such structures, similar to echo questions, bait the respondent by suggesting incredulity on the part of the examiner. For example, the question and tag "The man struck the victim, did he?" suggests that the questioner will not believe the affirmative response.

Although tag questions are more difficult to understand than nontag questions, negative tags do not pose a more serious difficulty than do affirmative tags (DeVito 1976). Despite this basic difficulty, limited evidence suggests that tag questions produce greater retention by receivers, probably because increased difficulty requires more active participation by the listener (Findley and Ray 1986).

Leading questions. Any question that suggests an answer, whether that suggestion is obvious or not, is commonly considered a leading question (Ogle, Parkman, and Porter 1980). Questions containing an affirmative structure in the main clause and a negative tag, and those containing a negative structure in the main clause and no tag, expect a response of Yes. Conversely, questions containing a negative structure and an affirmative tag expect a No response. For example, questions such as "The car was red, wasn't it?" or "Wasn't the car red?" are leading questions, whereas "Was the car red?" or "The car was red?" are not. Lawyers often mistakenly assume that an affirmative structure without a tag is leading when it is not. Simply speaking in the affirmative does not suggest an expected response. The only exception to this rule is when suggestive details are embedded within a Yes or No question. For example, the question "Was the getaway car a red 1978 Firebird with whitewalls and a pair of dice hanging from the rear-view mirror?" is certainly suggestive and therefore a leading question. Note also that questions with an affirmative structure stated in the active voice create a unique leading question termed an "echo question" (Thomas 1965). For example, "The car followed the road?" will likely be spoken with a rising inflection, suggesting the questioner doubts that the affirmative response is probable. For this reason, echo questions are leading.

As we might expect, leading questions are more difficult to understand than are nonleading questions (DeVito 1976). But the influence of leading questions goes far beyond comprehension. Research into the nature of leading questions has revealed that aspects of leading questions often significantly alter witness responses.

THE EFFECTS OF LEADING QUESTIONS.   In an experiment designed to investigate how methods of direct and cross examination affect the accuracy and completeness of witness accounts, subjects viewed a film depicting a woman struck by a car, an altercation between the driver and the woman's companion, and witnesses who restrained the men (Marshall, Marquis, and Oskamp 1971, 1972). After viewing the film, subjects were interviewed in either open interrogation, consisting of open-ended questions which allowed for free report, or structured interrogation, consisting of closed, leading questions. Based on the actual events that occurred in the film, subject responses were gauged on the levels of accuracy and completeness.

Surprisingly, leading questions did not result in a decrease in accuracy of the facts recalled, calling into question the age-old belief that accuracy is improved during the open stance of direct examination. The free reports, however, were markedly less complete than responses to closed interrogation. As the specificity of the questioning increased, so too did the witness' coverage of the event.

What is it about leading questions that biases witnesses to respond differently? One group of researchers explains that jurors use their knowledge of conversational rules to infer that examiners have an evidentiary basis to include certain facts in leading questions (Swann, Guiliano, and Wegner 1982). In other words, jurors infer that lawyers ask the questions they do because of known evidence in the case. For this reason jurors accept both the validity of leading questions and the premises upon which they are grounded. This inference also affects judgments about witnesses who answer the leading questions. Because witnesses often unknowingly cooperate with examiners and supply answers consistent with the underlying suppositions of the question, jurors will often draw inaccurate inferences about the witness. Two experiments provide support for this explanation (Swann, Guillano, and Wegner 1982).

In both experiments subjects listened to audio interviews where questioners asked respondents a series of leading questions. These questions probed for evidence of personality traits displaying a propensity toward either introversion or extroversion. To suggest the respondent was introverted, questions such as "In what situations do you wish you could be more outgoing?" were asked. To probe for extroversion, questions such as "In what situations are you most talkative?" were employed. One group of subjects listened only to the questions, a second group only to the answers, and a third group to both questions and answers. After listening to the interviews, subjects rated the person as to their introversion or extroversion.

Remarkably, regardless of what information subjects listened to, they inferred that the respondent possessed the characteristics for which the examiner had probed. When subjects were informed in the second experiment that the leading questions had been drawn from a fishbowl, the effects of the leading questions alone were diminished but the influence of the responses to these questions continued to bias personality judgments. What seems clear from this research is that leading questions often imply evidence that does not exist, and that jurors will often adopt this information as factual. This inference process warrants further discussion.

IMPLICATIONS.   As we have already pointed out, in order to make sense of the vast amount of information presented during examination, jurors rely on cognitive frames, such as stories, to organize the evidence. Once a story or schema is established, new information is assimilated so as to fit consistently within the existing framework. As we might expect, inference plays an important role in this cognitive process. During examination evidence may be presented in varying degrees of detail and explicitness. Sometimes, in fact, counsel will elicit testimony that does not directly state the action in question. To integrate this information into the ongoing story jurors must make inferences between objects and actions. These inferences will often become embedded in memory as actual testimony. Of interest here is the influence of questions designed precisely with the goal of forcing inference. Questions formulated to contain or elicit implications will often lead jurors to draw inferences beneficial to counsel's story. An implication is a remark that causes the listener to believe something not directly stated in the sentence. For example, the statement "He was allowed to exceed the limit" may cause the inference that indeed the actor did exceed the limit when that is not stated. Similarly, the statement "She was wrapped in a fur coat" implies chilly temperatures when that might not be the case.

In one study in this area subjects first heard an excerpt of a mock trial and were then asked whether statements were true, false, or indeterminate based on the testimony. Subjects who were exposed to testimony where a statement was asserted indirectly and only implied action, such as "I ran up to the burglar alarm," were more likely to recall the implication (he rang the burglar alarm) as a definite fact (Harris, Teske, and Ginns 1975). This was true even when subjects were specifically warned not to regard implications as facts (Harris and Monaco 1978). Subsequent research has also confirmed that subjects draw implications regardless of syntactical design

(Wegner, Wenclaff, Kerker, and Beattie 1981), and such inferences often render a story less probable and believable (Stutman 1985, 1986a).

Clearly, the presuppositions embedded within leading questions influence both the witness' response and inferences drawn by jurors listening to that testimony.

PRESUPPOSITIONS IN QUESTION STRUCTURES.   A research program conducted by Elizabeth Loftus and her associates has provided attorneys with a wealth of knowledge regarding how presuppositions in questions influence the reconstruction of an event by an eyewitness. Much of this research has focused on the use of implicative or leading questions by attorneys during examination. In several of the studies subjects were shown a film of an automobile accident and then asked implicative questions (for example, "Did you see the broken headlight?"). Generally, those asked implicative questions were more likely to report having seen something, whether or not it was actually in the film, than were subjects who were asked disjunctive (either/or choice) questions (for example, "Did you see a broken headlight") (Loftus and Zanni 1975). Loftus (1980) explains that the structure of language often makes people presume things. When persons are exposed to questions containing presuppositions, they will tend to believe those presuppositions.

Contact verbs. In addition to influencing the objective accuracy of the reconstruction, leading questions which incorporated more intense language also affected the qualitative judgments of the events made by the witness. For example, subjects gave higher estimates of automobile speed rate when asked, "About how fast were the cars going when they *smashed* into each other?" as opposed to, "About how fast were the cars going when they *hit* each other?" (Loftus and Palmer 1974). Contact verbs are themselves premises from which the question operates.

Articles "the" and "a." When questioners used the definite article "the" versus the indefinite article "a," subjects recalled events differently. Questions using "the" produced fewer "don't know" responses and more false recognition of events. This is because people understand that the definite article "the" typically precedes a noun whose referent is presumed to exist by the speaker and the listener.

"Some" versus "any." When questions used the quantifier "some" rather than "any," subjects were more likely to answer Yes. For example, the question "Did you see *some* people watching the accident?" will result in greater agreement than will the question

"Did you see *any* people watching the accident?" Greater agreement is thought to occur because the quantifier "some" is used primarily in declarative sentences; when used in questions it conveys an invitation. Consider the difference between "Who wants any more?" and "Who wants some more?" In the latter, the speaker and listener both assume that the someone will desire more.

Leading tag and why questions. Tag questions assume that the hearer will agree, and this results in greater agreement. Compare, for example, the questions "Was the car red?" and "The car was red, wasn't it?" Similarly, why questions typically contain presuppositions. For example, "Why is the class meeting in room 8?" presupposes that the class is meeting. Loftus found that when the question presupposes the existence of some object or the occurrence of some event, the use of "why" increases the likelihood that people will think they actually perceived the object or event.

Marked and unmarked modifiers. Research related to the Loftus program has also identified modifiers as influencing event reconstruction. An unmarked modifier implies an indefinite upper limit to such properties as speed, height, or length. Contrariwise, the marked modifier carries no such implication (Harris 1973). For example, the question "How heavy was the package?" does not restrict the limit of the judgment, whereas in "How light was the package" the modifier "light" denotes a judgment. In an experimental study subjects were shown a videotape of an automobile accident and then asked to respond to questions concerning the accident. The use of unmarked adverbs resulted in higher estimates of speed, damage, personal injury and skidding (Lipscomb, McAllister, and Bregman 1985).

TESTIMONY CONTROL

Military history provides a provocative lesson for legal practitioners and theorists. For many centuries monarchs and their military strategists have reified the power of language for shaping the minds of subjects. Today most military schools continue to embrace the control of language as a primary means to maintain discipline and order among cadets. America's premier military school, West Point, is no exception. Each year thousands of high school seniors compete to enter the freshman class at West Point and begin what for most will be an arduous matriculation.

The freshmen, called plebes (short for plebeians), enter West Point six and one-half weeks before academic lessons to embark upon cadet basic training. Seniors train the freshman in the basics of their four-year career at West Point. Those basics include, among other disciplinary features, the manner in which to address a superior (for plebes, this is everyone). The freshmen are commanded to respond in one of four ways: "Yes, sir," "No, sir," "No excuse, sir," and "Sir, I do not understand." The West Point strategists know perfectly well the lessons of rhetorical theory: To control the character, mind, and mettle of a human one must control the language used by a human. This extends far beyond the jargon usage common to cohesive organizations to include the turn to talk and the narrative expression of discourse. Such control over language is highly coercive in many ways, not the least of which is to weaken resistance to the advocated viewpoint.

Cross-examination strategy and language control practiced by military schools bear great similarity, for reasons which are not coincidental. But a closer examination of West Point strategy reveals a void in legal questioning strategy. Consider that the West Point cadets are limited to four fragmented responses, none of which allows for narration. The key to control here is threefold: (1) Do not let the respondent talk. (2) When the respondent must talk, limit his or her options of discourse. (3) Design those options to leave the respondent unable to provide narrative responses. Thus, number 3 for practical purposes fulfills number 1. Studies on language and questioning strategies discussed thus far have adequately explored techniques useful in controlling *what* testimony gets told. What has been left relatively unaddressed by this literature is the influence of controlling *how* testimony gets told. This is a difference that makes a difference.

To illustrate this distinction, consider the work on leading questions discussed earlier. Loftus, among others, found that leading tag questions, such as "You didn't have the key, did you?" are more likely to result in agreement than less presumptuous questions. To continue this example, let us say that the question elicited the response "Yes, I did." If counsel had hoped in this example to get the respondent to say explicitly that he did have the key, then researchers in this paradigm would claim that counsel successfully controlled the witness. This example illustrates control as a content strategy where counsel attempts to gain the compliance of witnesses by having them respond in a manner judged useful by counsel.

Another way to view witness control is to focus on control as eliciting *how* a response is given. Control then becomes an attempt to control the testimony of the witness. The focus is on the performance of *how* testimony is told rather than on *what* that testimony is.

We term this "testimony control." Before further elucidating on this conception of testimony control, we must first understand the courtroom context as it frames this performance.

Naturally occurring conversation does not have the contextual constraints imposed by the courtroom and the rules of examination. In everyday conversation the order in which parties speak, how long they speak, and what they say during their turns are spontaneously negotiated and cannot be specified in advance. In the courtroom setting, however, both the turn order and the type of turn is fixed. The talk is restricted to two parties only. The examination is organized into a series of questions and answers. Whatever else these utterances might count as, they are always designed and interpreted as either questions or answers (Atkinson and Drew 1979). Since the rules of the court specify that counsel direct the examination and the witness be subject to that examination, the turn-taking is fixed: counsel asking questions and witness answering questions. The conversation between these two parties is restricted. Clearly, the conversation differs from that of naturally occurring talk where individuals *manage* the conversation. In addition, lawyer preparation also constrains the discourse. What occurs prior to the trial is a formulated planning of discourse for presentation. That is, lawyers typically script the examination process with their own witnesses and practice this dialogue in what is commonly referred to as witness preparation. Although this script cannot be followed exactly, the examination process is not one of unplanned discourse or even of planned interrogation. Even with the opponent's witnesses the attorney knows from depositions and other court documents how the witness will respond and can therefore plan a script around the key aspects of expected answers. The examination process, then, is one of improvisation more closely aligned with dialogue than with naturally occurring conversation. This difference between natural conversation and examination conversation is important because it signals that controlling a witness is very different from other types of control that may exist in other contexts.

The most obvious distinction of control in the courtroom is the control of turn-taking itself. Examination is designed so that after a witness provides an answer, the turn automatically reverts to counsel. Counsel can delay taking a turn without a chance of losing it. This in itself places counsel always in control. The witness really has no options other than to relinquish all rights of control or to struggle before allowing counsel again to maintain control. This struggle may take the form of extended answers or questions of clarification, but never results in control by the witness, as counsel is always in the next turn-taking position following any response. Control from this perspective is not a matter of content but rather a restriction of conversational turns, in which counsel always retains the edge by rules of the court. A less obvious but more important distinction of control is found within the interaction itself. Since certain types of questions attempt, by their wording or structure, to restrict the behavioral options of the witness, *how* a witness responds to this attempt at restriction is a struggle over control.

Control from this vantage is one of performance as to how the testimony gets told. In other words, control is the process by which counsel and witness struggle over how the testimony is narrated to the jurors or judge. Counsel, then, does not control the witness but rather controls the testimony of the witness. Keep in mind that the testimony can be told in a variety of fashions, such as vividly or vapidly, emotionally or apathetically, powerfully or powerlessly. How the testimony gets told is not defined by the rules of the court. Instead, it is performed through the question-answer interaction of counsel and witness. Questions and question structures from this vantage may be attempts to restrict the behavioral/response options of the witness or attempts to allow the witness free reign in choosing the response options. The former is a closing down of response options; the latter is an opening of these options. In this light "witness control" is a misnomer. The testimony and how it is told is what counsel may or may not successfully control.

Testimony control during cross-examination weakens the narrative probability of a story by forcing witnesses to espouse the elements of a story in such a fashion as to make those elements less consistent, both in detail and agreement, with other elements of the story. Testimony control used inadvertently during direct examination also weakens the narrative probability of the story, which is the direct opposite of what the advocate wants to do. Given two competing stories, the story that is more cohesive and consistent—with the stronger narrative probability—is considered the more acceptable or believable story.

One advantage of this control conception is stability. Whereas evidence changes from case to case, the performance of how evidence becomes presented remains constant. In other words, the underlying structure of the performance of storytelling is the testimony control performed by both attorneys and their witnesses. In relation to other empirical research on the trial process, such as storytelling, vividness, and testimony style, the usefulness of examining this performance becomes obvious.

The witness' response to a question from counsel may or may

not be restricted by the question itself. For questions restricting response, such as Yes and No structured questions, the witness will find it difficult to provide details or background. Other questions, however, leave the amount of detail in the answer up to the witness. In such cases detailed answers are typically considered more persuasive than terse responses. Moreover, detailed and vivid information allows for greater clarity and emphasis in the telling of stories. Taken together, the impact of stories containing greater detail should have a more powerful impact on reconstructing the larger story of the trial and thus on the trial outcome. Since control by counsel is an attempt to restrict options, then the successful dominance of counsel over witness during cross-examination would be to limit vivid and detailed information by asking questions which deny such explanation. During direct examination just the opposite goal would be favored. Counsel would attempt to open options so that the witness could provide detailed accounts, thus decreasing the ambiguities in the resulting testimony.

Conversely, restricting the options of the witness during direct examination might have adverse consequences. Conley, O'Barr, and Lind (1978) found that subject-jurors tended to evaluate a witness in terms of how they perceived the lawyer evaluated the witness. The subjects concluded that if the lawyer constrained the witness by asking questions which called for only brief answers, the lawyer must have had little faith in that witness. Subjects then perceived that witness as less competent, less intelligent, and less assertive. While this is the goal of the cross-examiner, to restrict a witness during direct examination is to undermine the credibility of one's own witness, whether intentionally or not.

Since control should directly affect the presentation style of the witness in terms of a fragmented or narrative style, and since Bennett's storytelling theory describes these styles as affecting the ambiguities which result in the stories constructed from testimony, these findings are thought to provide additional support for the relevance of control during examination. How fragmented and narrative styles can be produced we argue, is through testimony control during examination. When counsel attempts to control the witness by restricting response options and when the witness submits to such control, a fragmented style of testimony results. Conversely, when counsel attempts to open the response options of the witness by using question structures which enhance the telling of stories and when the witness responds by using detailed answers, a narrative style results.

In one of the few empirical examinations in this area Danet and her associates examined the use of question types as they ameliorated control (Danet, Hoffman, Kermish, Rafn, and Stayman 1980). After an analysis of the direct and cross examination in one criminal trial, the researchers developed a typology of question forms. They identified the most common question forms in the courtroom as: (1) the declarative, with or without a tag; (2) interrogative yes/no, or choice, forms; (3) interrogative—who, what where, when, why—forms; (4) requestions; and (5) imperative forms. In an examination of the same case the researchers ordered the question types according to the degree to which they believed the questions constrained or limited the witness, with declaratives as most coercive and imperative least so. They then examined the relationship between coerciveness of question form and response features for both direct and cross examination. The results indicated that of the questions cast in coercive form during direct examination, 72 percent received a short response, while of those cast in noncoercive form only 15 percent received a short response. In addition, coercive question forms were somewhat more effective than noncoercive ones in discouraging hedging or qualification of replies, during both direct and cross examination. Danet et al. concluded that coerciveness of question form does indeed influence formal features of responses.

Using the Danet et al. study as a foundation, we conducted two studies that explored the nature and influence of testimony control (Stutman 1986b). In the first study we observed fifteen trials, civil and criminal, in a U.S. District Court in northern Utah, in an attempt to design a taxonomy of questions and answers constituting testimony control. After defining attempts at control by counsel as posing question types which restrict the options of response by the witness, it was assumed that the witness had three options available in any response. First, the witness could submit to the controlling nature of the question, in which case the interact was said to exhibit testimony control, with counsel successfully controlling how the story is told. Second, the witness could deny the controlling nature of the question, in which case the interact was said to exhibit a struggle, with counsel unsuccessfully controlling the witness. Third, in those cases where counsel posted questions opening the response options of the witness, regardless of how a witness responded the interact was said to exhibit a neutral relationship. The final coding scheme, outlined below, consists of eight controlling questions forms, three open question structures, three submissive response types, six denial responses and three neutral responses. In addition, the scheme provides rules for coding simultaneous speech, interruptions, compound questions, and objections.

Control Category Scheme

Eight Controlling Question Types

1. Leading question (declarative)
   Ex.: Isn't it true that you were at the scene prior to 9 P.M.?
2. Leading Question with tag
   Ex.: The bike was red, wasn't it?
3. Negative construction leading question
   Ex.: So, there was no car, isn't that correct?
4. Loopback or repeated answer question
   Ex.: So you took the gun and walked toward the defendant?
5. Choice question (x/y choice or yes/no choice)
   Ex.: Was the car black or purple?
6. Precise imperative question
   Ex.: Do you really recall what time you saw the defendant?
7. Precise interrogative question
   Ex.: What time did you see the defendant?
8. Imperative demand or request
   Ex.: That's fine, Mr. Smith, stop right there.

Three Open Question Types

1. Imprecise interrogative question
   Ex.: About what time did you see the defendant?
2. Imperative request or question requiring elaboration
   Ex.: Tell us why you broke the glass?
3. Open-ended interrogative question
   Ex.: Would you explain to the court what happened?

Three Submissive Response Types

1. Compliance with x/y or yes/no choice
   Ex.: Q—Was the car black or purple?
   R—Black
2. No attempt to explain or provide details beyond the scope of the questioning structure.
   Ex.: Q—What color was the car that came toward you?
   R—Blue.
3. Compliance with or failure to respond to an imperative demand or request.
   Ex.: ID—Stop right there, Mr. Smith.
   R—(silence, Smith stops at request)

Six Denial Response Types

1. Deny x/y or yes/no choice questions
   Ex.: Q—Was the car black or purple?
   A—It was neither black or purple.

2. Provide details or explanation beyond questioning structure

> Ex.: Q—Isn't it true that you were at the scene prior to 9 P.M.?
> R—I was walking toward my friend's house at about 8 P.M. and as I stated earlier I then went directly home. This would place me at the scene sometime between 8:30 and 10 P.M.

3. Hedging

> Ex.: Q—Isn't it true that you were at the scene prior to 9 P.M.?
> R—I really can't say for sure.

4. Question as answer

> Ex.: Q—Isn't it true that you were at the scene prior to 9 P.M.?
> R—What is it you want me to say?

5. Clarification of question or request for repetition

> Ex.: Q—Isn't it true that you were at the scene prior to 9 P.M.?
> R—I don't understand what you are asking.

6. Failure to respond or to answer the question asked

> Ex.: Q—Isn't it true that you were at the scene prior to 9 P.M.?
> R—(silence)
> Q—Well, Mr. Jones?

Three Neutral Response Types

1. Explanation following an open question type
2. No explanation following an open question type
3. Any other response to an open question type

Simultaneous Speech and Other Cases

1. Simultaneous speech is considered a control attempt by counsel and a denial response by the witness.
2. Interruptions are considered a control attempt by counsel and a denial response by the witness.
3. Compound questions are considered two separate questions.
4. Objections by the nonexamining counsel that are sustained consequently eliminate the question or response from consideration.

When a closed question structure is followed by a submissive response, a control interact is said to exist. (The term, "interact," simply refers to the coupling of question and response.) When a closed question structure is followed by a denial response, a struggle exists, as counsel and witness are competing over the presentation of the testimony. Finally, when an open question structure is used, any response combines to create a neutral interact.

In the second study we investigated the influence of testimony control on juror evaluations of witness credibility and testimony believability. In a field study we recruited prospective jurors (six for each case), representative of actual jurors in age, occupation, and background, to listen to the testimony of 56 eyewitnesses across twelve cases in the same district court. After hearing the testimony, subject-jurors rated the witnesses and testimony for credibility.

The results of the study emphasize the distinction between direct and cross examination in regard to testimony control. Both lawyers and witnesses perform differently in direct and cross examination. During direct examination, lawyers attempt to open the response options of the witness by utilizing question structures conducive to storytelling. Direct examination contained 42.8 percent more neutral interacts and 27.66 more average words per answer than cross examination. Whether of conscious intention or not, these results support the contention that lawyers allow witnesses to narrate during direct examination. When lawyers fail to allow witnesses to narrate during direct examination, and control interacts invariably increase, there results a decrease in the authoritativeness of the witness and the believability of the testimony as perceived by jurors. This confirms the theoretical explanation that a decrease in storytelling and an increase in control over the testimony by counsel results in a less believable reality as interpreted by jurors.

As was predicted, cross-examination contained a significantly larger number of control interacts in comparison to direct examination. Specifically, cross-examination contained 38.61 percent more control interacts on average,and this increase resulted in an average word response of only 7.32, in comparison to a 34.98 average word response during direct examination. Although the use of control interacts clearly differentiates between the two examination processes, a control increase again led to a significant decrease in testimony believability as perceived by jurors. During cross-examination lawyers clearly attempt to restrict the response options of the witness by utilizing question structures which accomplish this restriction. What results is exactly what the practical literature predicts will result: controlled testimony is viewed as less believable, thus working to the opposition's advantage.

Interestingly, as control increased, the character of the witness in either direct or cross examination was unaffected. We believe this supports the usefulness of the testimony control construct over more traditional ways of viewing witness control. Testimony control is a narrative performance where structural attributes of lawyers' questions and witnesses' responses interact either to enhance or constrict storytelling. In the more traditional view control is conceptualized as something lawyers "do" to witnesses. This witness control emphasizes the effect of constraint on the witness's perceived believability.

Our study focused on the believability of the witness' testimony rather than on the witness himself or herself. The credibility variable of character stresses the effect of constraint on the witness as an honest or dishonest person. Interestingly enough, control had no significant effect on this witness characteristic, which would have supported the witness control concept, but control did indeed affect the believability of the witness' testimony. It seems reasonable to expect a restriction or control of testimony to have a significant effect on the authoritativeness of a witness, as authority is less intricately connected to the person and more interwoven with the performance of the testimony. In other words, an honest and friendly person may or may not lack the authoritativeness deemed equal to the performance of the testimony, and this feature of credibility is more likely assessed in terms of the testimony given rather than evaluatively separated, as character might be.

Only witness authoritativeness during direct examination declined as control increased. In relation to the differences between the examination processes this finding seems congruent. During direct examination counsel is a proponent of the witness; that is, counsel is working to support the witness and to make this witness' testimony appear favorable to his or her position. Reasonably, when counsel increases control during this "friendly" examination, jurors perceive such restriction as harmful to the force of the witness and the testimony given by the witness. Hence, the authoritativeness of the witness decreases in the eyes of the jurors.

During cross-examination a different relationship between counsel and witness exists. Counsel is the opponent; an adversarial relationship takes place, and is expected by jurors. It seems reasonable to speculate that as control increases during this adversarial examination, the attenuated authoritative performance of the witness is expected by the jurors and therefore results only in an insignificant decrease. Credibility does not decrease significantly because the jurors view the constraint of the question structures as justifiable considering the adversarial positions of the players. In contrast, control during direct examination is viewed as unfair and unreasonable, since the players are supposed to be on the same side.

The single most important finding was the relationship between testimony control and testimony believability. In both direct and cross examination an increase in control resulted in a significant decrease in the believability of the testimony given by the witness. Bennett's storytelling theory provides the most useful explanation of this relationship. According to Bennett's theory, the descriptive and detailed elements of the stories presented must coalesce to form a consistent and coherent framework from which jurors can construct a larger, coherent story. When these elements contradict or do no mesh together, ambiguity results, making the smaller story harder to interpret. Narration is simply impossible when witnesses conform to the controlling structures of questions. In addition, when control increased during direct and cross examination, the style of the response by the witness became more fragmented, as he or she used fewer words and thus gave fewer details. This indirectly supports Bennett's theoretical position that the decrease in testimony believability is a result of increased control, creating story ambiguity and emptiness.

CONTROL STRATEGY

Lawyers should use question structures which allow the witness to provide detailed description during direct examination in order to have this "friendly" testimony viewed as more believable and the witness perceived as more authoritative. In addition, lawyers must refrain from precise controlling questions during direct examination. Empirical research now suggests that the consequence of controlling structures during direct examination is testimony viewed as less believable by jurors. Moreover, counsel should refrain from simultaneous speech with the witness and interruptions of the testimony during direct examination, as this is a restriction of the witness' response and therefore considered a struggle for control of the testimony.

During cross-examination, lawyers should indeed use closed questions; more specifically, these questions should restrict the response options of the witness. Research clearly shows that an increase in the restriction of a witness' responses leads to a decrease in the testimony believability of the witness. Leading questions during cross-examination work to provide two effective strategies. First, leading questions restrict the response options of the witness, often to an answer of Yes or No, or Right or Wrong. When a witness responds within the limits of this structure, counsel has successfully controlled that piece of testimony. Second, leading questions provide details advantageous to the examiner's position. In other words, leading questions provide a vehicle by which lawyers can add to the details of the story.

In addition, the research indirectly suggests three other recommendations during cross-examination. First, lawyers should keep their questions simple, to promote clarity. During cross-examination, lawyers do not want the witness to ask for clarification or repetition of a question, as this is a denial of testimony control. Anything the lawyer can do to prevent such requests, such as careful pronunciation and direct question construction, will benefit the examiner. Second, when witnesses provide details beyond the scope of the question structures, counsel can control the testimony by requesting that witnesses refrain from providing unnecessary elaboration and answer only the question asked. Such testimony control will again benefit the position of the examiner. Third, leading questions which are phrased as yes/no choices are the most controlling of all structures because they are the hardest to deny; thus the use of such questions should dominate cross-examination.

We take issue with the traditional view of witnesses as passive courtroom actors. The practical and research literature repeatedly stereotypes the witness as a passive participant in an exchange controlled by lawyers. Our research contends that testimony control is negotiated by both lawyers and witnesses. Counsel cannot control the testimony of the witness unless the witness allows for that control. The witness can, and often does, provide details beyond the questioning structure posed by counsel. When witnesses deny control attempts or fail to storytell when given open question structures, they directly influence the way the story becomes constructed.

LIMITING TESTIMONY AND EVIDENCE

Observers who sit through a complete trial for the first time often report that they are amazed most by what goes unsaid. Questions not asked, witnesses not examined, arguments not pursued contribute to a feeling of puzzlement and frustration on the part of the uninitiated. What novice spectators do not immediately comprehend is that what doesn't get said is often more influential than what does get said during a trial. In other words, omitting and/or limiting evidence is a strategic and tactical call on the part of counsel. Although what to omit during a trial is case specific, both counsel and witness possess strategies at their command to limit evidence. For counsel, the most prevalent strategy is that of objecting to evidence. For the witness, limiting evidence is a conscious attempt to evade questions by providing incomplete, yet ostensibly accurate, testimony. Research regarding these strategies provides the practitioner with understanding paramount to successful examination.

OBJECTIONS.   The influence of inadmissible evidence on jury decision making is well documented. As a means of attentuating that influence, objections provide attorneys with the ability to limit inadmissible evidence; they also serve the function of disrupting examination rhythm and shifting juror focus. But although legal practitioners and scholars have discerned the functions of objections, they seldom agree as to when to raise objections or as to their effect on juror perceptions.

According to Tornquist (1983), there are two types of objections: substantive and form-of-question. Substantive objections are raised when the substance of a statement is in dispute. This includes issues of relevance, hearsay, admissibility of evidence, and competence. A form-of-question objection is raised when a question form is considered improper, including leading questions, questions that assume a fact, compound questions, narrative questions, or repetitive questions. Form-of-question objections are easily overcome by merely restating the question in an acceptable manner, whereas substantive objections are more problematic. Because their purpose is usually to keep the judge or jury from hearing inadmissible evidence, substantive objections can be made "in limine," presenting the objection before the trial actually begins.

Dombroff (1985) argues that a trial attorney should make her objections in limine whenever possible to avoid the problems inherent in an objection made in court. Most notably, if the evidence is presented, even in abbreviated form, before it is objected to, the jury will have heard the evidence despite its inadmissibility. An attorney may follow this objection with a motion to strike; if this is granted, the court may give the jury a curative instruction, usually involving instruction to disregard the evidence. But, as Dombroff and others point out, the jury is already poisoned. Dombroff also contends that a substantive objection followed by the curative instruction not only is ineffective but will focus the jury's attention on the evidence and may influence its decision to an even greater extent than if the objection had never occurred.

One experimental study provides support for this contention (Wolf and Montgomery 1977). Subjects in this study read a criminal trial transcript in which critical testimony was ruled admissible, inadmissible, or inadmissible with an admonition by the judge to disregard the evidence. Surprisingly, subjects reading the transcript where the judge specifically warned them to disregard the inadmissible evidence were most biased by that evidence. In addition, the research revealed that critical testimony had its greatest impact when it was the focus of an objection and subsequently ruled admissible. Subsequent studies have also found that when inadmissible evidence was the object of objection, there resulted an amplification of the impact of that evidence (Reinard and Reynolds 1978; Reinard 1985).

Trial manuals provide copious advice and strategy regarding objections. For example, Givens (1980) suggests that the witness' attorney may use objections to interrupt cross-examination as a means to give the witness time to gather her thoughts. Hegland (1978) advises that lawyers stand when objecting to endear themselves to the court and to divert attention away from the witness. Dombroff (1984) contends that objections focus the jury's attention on the evidence objected to, as well as disrupting the continuity of the testimony so that the evidence is more difficult to piece together. He also argues that objections create an unfavorable impression of the opposing lawyer in the eyes of the jury. Hamlin (1985) proposes that jurors interpret objections as an indication that the objecting lawyer's case is in trouble. Hamlin also suggests that since jurors detest interruptions and delays, they view objections and the lawyers who make them unfavorably.

Despite the many competing claims proposed in popular trial manuals, three issues surface repeatedly. First, lawyers believe that when they use objections, jurors will form evaluations concerning the objecting lawyer's general fairness and competence. Second, experienced lawyers believe that objections will focus the jury's attention on the evidence so that the evidence objected to will become salient in the minds of the jurors. Third, seasoned lawyers believe that objections disrupt the information processing of the jurors so that other evidence and facts will be forgotten.

In three experiments designed to investigate the influence of objections raised during examination on juror perceptions and information processing, conclusions regarding these issues were addressed (Stutman 1987). Subjects in the experiments viewed different versions of an examination videotape with varying objection sequences. The results confirmed that jurors perceive courtroom actors differently, giving higher fairness, but not competence, ratings to the objecting lawyer than to the examining lawyer during cross-examination. The consequences of objecting to evidence, however, are both positive and negative. On the negative side, attorneys can expect a less favorable evaluation of competence when he or she objects more than several times during the examination of a witness. On the positive side, when counsel increasingly objects to evidence presented by the adversary's witness, jurors' evaluations of fairness toward the adversary, at least during cross-examination, decrease. In addition, increased objections are negatively related to recall of the objected facts.

Although the primary function of objections is to prevent the trier of fact from being exposed to inadmissible evidence and to preserve the record for appeal (Dombroff 1985), objections can also be used tactically. The experiments revealed that objections influence juror information processing. Objections were found to shift jurors' attention to facts objected to. Jurors responded more actively to evidence receiving objections than to evidence not receiving objections. Because the increased elaboration contained more counterarguments, the results suggest that the effect of that focus also increases the jurors' resistance to those facts. Objections render the evidence objected to less influential.

Finally, the results indicated that jurors more accurately recall objected facts than facts not objected to. Since lawyers traditionally assume that the accuracy of recall, in turn, influences the quality of judgments and decisions made by jurors, then objections play a crucial role in subsequent testimony consideration. Jurors were also found to exhibit enhanced recall to objected facts in comparison to the recall of unobjected facts. Since lawyers also assume that during deliberation jurors can only scrutinize those facts they recall, then we can reason that objections substantially influence deliberation.

An obvious objection paradox exists for attorneys. By their objection to a particular fact or opinion which is subsequently overruled, lawyers rally jurors to respond actively to the fact when it is heard. Although this response is usually negative, involving counterarguments, the objection ensures that subsequent recall of the fact will be enhanced. This dilemma is highly disturbing. It appears that lawyers confront a judgment call concerning how damaging a fact might be and the probability that a judge will overrule their objection. Lawyers must balance the impact of negative response favorable to their case with enhanced recall of the fact during deliberation. On an encouraging note, it appears safe to say that when counsel assumes a pivotal fact will be recalled as a matter of import to the case, then an objection even one overruled, is a wise and salutary tactic.

HOW THE WITNESS CAN DENY INFORMATION.   Witnesses are often motivated to provide less than accurate portrayals of events. For reasons including credible self-presentation, fear of self-recrimination, vested interest in the trial outcome, and relationship with the litigants, witnesses often evade questions with answers that are less than complete. While deception is defined as intentionally providing false information, evasion and other forms of denial constitute a strategic choice not to reveal information unless forced. A fine line separates information denial and deception, yet we can say that a majority of witnesses engage in some form of information denial, whereas witnesses who intentionally deceive the court or suborn their testimony are far less frequent. The reason for this is a distinction in morality. Although our cultural values of honesty prohibit outright deception and prevarication, generally we believe that withholding information is not a form of lying. This belief gives us the moral flexibility to provide knowingly specious information without admitting to dishonesty. As a result, choosing not to reveal information is both an acceptable and important communicative goal of respondents.

Undoubtedly, denial strategies influence testimony presentation during a trial. For this reason alone lawyers should have a better understanding of how to circumvent attempts at denial. Indeed, a better understanding of how witnesses deny to reveal information would enable counsel to discern when witnesses employ such strategies and to design questions promoting a complete and accurate account of events. We have already seen that the denial of closed question structures disrupts attempts at testimony control, allowing the witness' testimony to be seen as more believable. In our discussion of testimony control we briefly described several response types that deny the question structure. What follows here is more detailed description of the denial strategies used by witnesses and research related to understanding how witnesses answer questions.

The extant theory on memory and information retrieval contends that people have multiple strategies for retrieving information from memory and hence have multiple strategies for answering questions (Reder 1987). Two strategies appear most prevalent. The first and most common is labeled "direct retrieval." In this strategy the respondent decodes the question by trying to find a fact which encodes the answer in memory. We can illustrate this by using a mathematics example. When confronted with a problem of multiplication, we often assess how familiar the problem is before selecting a procedure for solution. We recognize that 9×9 is stored directly in memory. This recognition and retrieval process is direct retrieval. The respondent searches the question for information that signals what memory information to retrieve. Because many of the questions we are confronted with can quickly be answered by direct retrieval, this strategy is the most commonly employed.

But there exist questions which are not as easily decoded or encoded, sometimes questions for which we have no exact information. In the math example we may be assigned the multiplication problem 9×19. In cases such as this, where we do not recognize the question or problem as directly stored, we often evaluate the question as one that should be broken down before answering. In this strategy, called "plausibility" respondents compute a plausible answer given a set of facts stored in memory. For example, consider the question "What did you eat for breakfast on this date exactly one year ago?" In a courtroom most of us would respond with "I don't recall." But if pressed, we would move to separate the components of the question in order to arrive at a plausible answer. By raising smaller questions for direct retrieval—Where was I on that date? What were my eating habits at that time? What did I usually eat for breakfast?—we could compute a plausible answer.

When respondents attempt to withhold information, they invariably employ the plausibility and not the direct retrieval strategy. In this way they are afforded the opportunity to find a plausible yet in some sense incomplete answer to the question.

Once respondents decide which answering strategy they will employ, they engage in two interpretive processes central to formulating an answer (Lehnert 1978). The first is to determine the true intention of the question asker. For example, the intention of the query "Is that a salt shaker over there?" can be interpreted in several ways, including seeking confirmation, desire for the salt shaker, or annoyance that one has been denied the shaker. Typically we recognize this question to translate as "Please pass the salt shaker," but that interpretation is entirely dependent on contextual and individual knowledge. Only when the questioner intends the query to seek confirmation is a yes or no response acceptable. When the questioner intends to receive the shaker, a yes or no response it not only a misinterpretation of this intention but can also be considered an incomplete answer. This is the second assessment process. Upon hearing a question a respondent must decide what level of answer is appropriate. In other words, how much detail is required (for example, will a Yes or No be enough?).

General denial strategies. At the initial level of processing respondents can intentionally withhold information by misinterpreting the intention and appropriate level. For example, consider common questions posed of witnesses during cross-examination. By misinterpreting the intention of the examiner in the question "You weren't comfortable staying in the same room with the defendant?" a witness is capable of withholding information with the response, "No, the room was quite cozy." In the same vein a witness can deny information yet still accurately respond to a request such as "Describe the car for the court" with the simple response "It was blue." While both of these responses are easily circumvented by counsel by further questioning, we must remember the goal of examination is to control both the witness and the testimony at all times. Prevention of such attempts at denial may be as important, or more so, than circumvention strategies.

Not surprisingly, witnesses often chose to withhold information openly. Whereas feigning poor memory is a matter of deception and not denial, witnesses are constitutionally afforded the option not to respond. Of course, witnesses must "plead the Fifth" or be held in contempt of court for not answering a question. Because of possible future legal ramifications that might ensue from this tactic witnesses are much more likely to resort to deception or other denial strategies unless advised to refuse by counsel. Research has identified other evasive strategies that also merit attention (Edwards 1986).

Literal meanings. One avenue open to respondents is to give an answer that is based on the literal meanings of words or figurative expressions. For example, the witness who wanted to deny information concerning a traffic violation might choose to interpret the following question literally: "Did the defendant race his engine?" By choosing to define "race" literally, the witness might look confused and reply, "I don't believe he raced anything." The best way to avoid this denial attempt is to choose words and expressions carefully and to clarify figurative language before the response. This advice parallels recommendations made by practitioners to avoid the use of homophones in questions. Homophones are those words that are defined and spelled differently but pronounced the same, such as bear/bare, pear/pare, two/too.

Irrelevant information. Witnesses often parry a question by providing irrelevant information pertaining to components of the question. This information is usually highly detailed and is provided as a show of honesty toward the topic at large. This strategy disrupts the examination and is often successful at denying key information. Attorneys can best prevent this attempt by asking precise and leading questions. Advice to avoid compound and narrative questions during cross-examination seems equally applicable here.

Hypothetical answers. Witnesses employ a more sophisticated evasion strategy when they provide a hypothetical response to a question. In this strategy the witness explains what might have happened rather than what actually occurred. For example, when asked why he slapped his girlfriend, a witness might answer: "People respond differently to conflict situations. I have one friend who explodes whenever his girlfriend flirts. That may have been it." Once again, precise and leading questions work to prevent such hypothetical answers.

Ambiguity. Ambiguity in communication has been addressed under a variety of labels, including unclarity (Wender 1968), indirectness (Nofsinger 1976), vagueness (Pascale and Athos 1981) and strategic closedness (Eisenberg 1984). What makes this a particularly slippery concept is the fact that ambiguity can be expressed through detailed, literal language as well as through imprecise, figurative language. Any response may entail an intention to be undetailed, unclear, vague, or indirect, though the message itself may be clear or ambiguous. In other words, actual ambiguity can be totally independent of perceived ambiguity. For this reason ambiguity is the most perfidious denial strategy an examiner confronts. The general rule for circumventing ambiguity during cross-examination is for counsel to provide the necessary precision and detail in leading questions, relying on the witness only to agree or disagree with those details. When we consider the possibility of undetected ambiguity in witness responses, it is not hard to agree with the position that counsel should ask only leading, yes/no questions during cross-examination.

REFERENCES

Atkinson, J. W., and Drew, P. (1979). *Order in the court: the organization of verbal interaction in judicial settings.* London: Macmillan.

Bleiberg, S., and Churchill, L. (1975). Notes on confrontation in conversation. *Journal of Psycholinguistic Research* 4: 273–78.

Conley, J. M.; O'Barr, W. M.; and Lind, E. A. (1978). The power of language: presentational style in the courtroom. *Duke Law Journal* 6: 1375–99.

Danet, B. (1980). "Baby" or "fetus?" language and the construction of reality in a manslaughter trial. *Semiotica* 32: 187–219.

Danet, B.; Hoffman, K. B.; Kermish, N. C.; Rafn, H. J.; and Stayman, D. G. (1980). An ethnography of questioning in the courtroom. In R. W. Shuy and A. Shnukal (eds.), *Language use and the uses of language.* Washington, DC: Georgetown University Press.

DeVito, J. A. (1976). Relative ease in comprehending yes/no questions. In J. Blankenship and H. G. Stelzner (eds.), *Rhetoric and communication.* Urbana: University of Illinois Press.

Dombroff, M. A. (1984). *On unfair tactics.* New York: Wiley.

Dombroff, M. A. (1985). *Trial objections.* Santa Ana, CA: Ford.

Edwards, R. (1986). Information denial strategies in interpersonal communication. Paper presented at the convention of the Speech Communication Association, Chicago.

Eisenberg, E. M. (1984). Ambiguity as strategy in organizational communication. *Communication Monographs* 51: 227–42.

Findley, P. L., and Ray, J. L. (1986). The effects of leading tag questions on retention, attitude change and source credibility. Paper presented at the convention of the Western Speech Communication Association, Tucson.

Givens, R. A. (1980). *Advocacy: the art of pleading a case*. New York: McGraw-Hill.

Hamlin, S. (1985). *What makes juries listen*. New York: Harcourt Brace.

Harris, R. J. (1973). Answering questions containing marked and unmarked adjectives and adverbs. *Journal of Experimental Psychology* 97: 399–401.

Harris, R. J., and Monaco, G. E. (1978). The psychology of pragmatic implication: information processing between the lines. *Journal of Experimental Psychology: General* 107: 1–22.

Harris, R. J.; Teske, R. R.; and Ginns, M. J. (1975). Memory for pragmatic implications from courtroom testimony. *Bulletin of the Psychonomic Society* 6: 494–96.

Hegland, K. F. (1978). *Trial and practice skills*. St. Paul, MN: West.

Kestler, J. L. (1982). *Questioning techniques and tactics*. New York: McGraw-Hill.

Laird, A. W. (1982). Persuasion: a tool of courtroom communication. *Psychology* 19: 50–57.

Lehnert, W. G. (1978). *The process of question answering*. Hillsdale, NJ: Erlbaum.

Lipscomb, T. J.; McAllister, H. A.; and Bregman, N. J. (1985). Bias in eyewitness accounts: the effects of question format, delay interval, and stimulus presentation. *Journal of Psychology* 119: 207–12.

Litvin, G. (1984, August). Interview with Gerald Litvin, Director of the Academy of Trial Advocacy, Philadelphia.

Loftus, E. F. (1980). Language and memories in the judicial system. In R. W. Shuy, and A. Shnukal (eds.), *Language use and the uses of language*. Washington, DC: Georgetown University Press.

Loftus, E. F., and Goodman, J. (1985). Questioning witnesses. In S. Kassin and L. S. Wrightsman (eds.), *The psychology of evidence and trial procedure*. Beverly Hills, CA: Sage.

Loftus, E. F., and Palmer, J. C. (1974). Reconstruction of automobile destruction: an example of the interaction between language and memory. *Journal of Verbal Learning and Verbal Behavior* 13: 585–89.

Loftus, E. F., and Zanni, T. (1975). Eyewitness testimony: the influence of wording of a question. *Bulletin of the Psychonomic Society* 5: 86–88.

Marquis, K. H.; Marshall, J.; and Oskamp, S. (1972). Testimony validity as a function of question form, atmosphere and item difficulty. *Journal of Applied Social Psychology* 2: 167–86.

Marshall, J. (1980). *Law and psychology in conflict*. 2nd ed. Indianapolis: Bobbs-Merrill.

Marshall, J.; Marquis, K. H.; and Oskamp, S. (1971). Effects of kind of question and atmosphere interrogation on accuracy and completeness of testimony. *Harvard Law Review* 84: 1620–43.

Mauet, T. A. (1980). *Fundamentals of trial techniques*. Boston: Little, Brown.

Mehler, J. (1963). Some effects of grammatical transformations on the recall of English sentences. *Journal of Verbal Learning and Verbal Behavior* 2: 346–51.

Nofsinger, R. E. (1976). On answering questions indirectly: some rules in the grammar of doing conversation. *Human Communication Research* 2: 172–81.

Ogle, R.; Parkman, A.; and Porter, J. (1980). Questions: leading and otherwise. *The Judges Journal* 19: 42–45.

Pascale, R. T., and Athos, A. G. (1981). *The art of Japanese management*. New York: Simon and Schuster.

Reder, L. M. (1987). Strategy selection in question answering. *Cognitive Psychology* 19: 90–138.

Reinard, J. C. (1985). The effects of witness inadmissible testimony on jury decisions: a comparison of four sources. Paper presented at the convention of the Western Speech Communication Association, Fresno, CA.

Reinard, J. C. and Reynolds, R. A. (1978). The effects of inadmissible testimony objections and rulings on jury decisions. *Journal of the American Forensic Association* 15: 91–108.

Stutman, R. K. (1985). The controlling of testimony in the courtroom. Paper presented at the convention of the Speech Communication Association, Denver.

Stutman, R. K. (1986a). Witness disclaiming during examination. *Journal of the American Forensic Association* 23: 96–101.

Stutman, R. K. (1986b). Testimony control and witness narration during courtroom examination. Paper presented at the convention of the Western Speech Communication Association, Tucson.

Stutman, R. K. (1987). The effect of objections on recall, recall accuracy, cognitive response and juror evaluations of counsel. Paper presented at the convention of the Speech Communication Association, Boston.

Swann, W. B.; Guiliano, T.; and Wegner, D. M. (1982). Where leading questions can lead: the power of conjecture in social interaction. *Journal of Personality and Social Psychology* 42: 1025–35.

Thomas, O. (1965). *Transformational grammar and the teacher of English.* New York: Holt, Rinehart.

Tornquist, L. J. (1983). A response to legal strategies, communication strategies and research needs in direct and cross-examination. In R. Matlon and R. Crawford (eds.), *Communication strategies in the practice of lawyering.* Annandale, VA: Speech Communication Association.

Vosniadou, S. (1982). Drawing inferences from semantically positive and negative implicative predicates. *Journal of Psycholinguistic Research* 11: 77–93.

Wegner, D. A.; Wenclaff, R.; Kerker, R. M.; and Beattie, A. E. (1981). Incrimination through innuendo: can media questions become public answers. *Journal of Personality and Social Psychology* 40: 822–32.

Wender, P. (1968). Communicative unclarity: some comments on the rhetoric of confusion. *Psychiatry* 31: 247–74.

Wolf, S., and Montgomery, D. A. (1977). Effects of inadmissible evidence and level of judicial admonishment on the judgments of mock jurors. *Journal of Applied Social Psychology* 7: 205–19.

Younger, I. (1976). *The art of cross-examination.* American Bar Association.

Chapter 9

THE CLOSING ARGUMENT

Despite the popular belief that jurors have solidified their positions on the case prior to the summation, the opportunity to interpret the facts for the jury has led many trial lawyers to contend that the closing argument is the performance that most determines the outcome of the case. Jurors themselves tell researchers that they believe the closing argument to be more important than the opening statement in a trial (Tarter-Hilgendorf 1986). When asked what factors most affect deliberation, jurors ranked the closing statement second only to the questioning of witnesses (Matlon, Davis, Catchings, Derr, and Waldron 1985). This may be due, in part, to the dynamic nature of the closing argument.

Counsel is not constrained as in the opening statement. An attempt to persuade the jury is not only allowed during the closing argument but is expected. The law specifies that the closing argument provide the forum for a full discussion of the facts and issues in the case. More specifically, the argument can challenge the credibility of the witnesses, the probative value of the evidence, and the probability of the events as presented in testimony. The opening statement and closing argument are best viewed as two halves of the same structure, each complementing the other. The opening sets the stage for the evidence and the closing highlights those facts in the most favorable light. A masterful attorney knows before the trial starts what it is she or he will say to the jury in summation. Everything coming before the close should support that argument.

For prosecutors in criminal trials the summation is designed to argue what the evidence shows "beyond a reasonable doubt." Although the prosecution has the burden of proof, limited evidence suggests that jurors liberally interpret "reasonable doubt," finding defendants guilty even when certainty is not guaranteed. In one study, after subjects listened to a criminal trial, half were asked to judge whether the defendant was guilty beyond a reasonable doubt, while the other half were asked to estimate the probability that the defendant had committed the criminal act. A comparison of the two groups revealed that those people who estimated a probability of at least 74 percent of criminal wrongdoing found the defendant guilty beyond a reasonable doubt (Simon 1970). This adherence to probability was also demonstrated in a British study that examined instructions to a jury (Sealy and Cornish 1973). In that study jurors returned as many guilty verdicts when they believed it was "more likely than not" that a defendant was guilty as they did when they were "sure and certain" of his guilt.

This research signifies that the closing argument is the final struggle over interpretation of the evidence, and that both sides are handicapped: the prosecution by burden of proof and the defense by liberal interpretations of guilt.

From a storytelling framework the comprehensive goals of the closing argument appear straightforward. Counsel's first and primary charge is to tell a convincing story. By repeatedly referring to specific evidence heard during examination, counsel should chronologically describe the events as they occurred. Special attention must be paid to all five elements of the narrative: the central action, all agents involved in that action, the agency or means by which the action was accomplished, the motive for each agent involved, and the scene. Successful storytellers will provide vivid details for each of these elements, taking particular care to elaborate each action in the sequence. The attorneys then can make the necessary connections and leaps of faith for the jurors, answering questions the jurors might have before they gel. Only when this story is firm in the jurors' minds is counsel ready to point out the ambiguities and incoherency in the opponent's narrative. To do so sooner would be to orient the jury's own reconstruction of the events with the opponent's story line, allowing those elements to become salient. The rebuttal of the opposing story is then accompanied by noting the inconsistencies of unfriendly witnesses and raising further suspicion as to their credibility.

Beyond meeting these general goals, practitioners are divided. We can dispense with the general advice outlined in trial manuals by summarizing the only point on which they agree: Attorneys should personalize the closing argument by expressing appreciation for the jurors' time and effort and by avoiding unnecessary jargon and legalese. Although other advice is plentiful, most practitioners disagree as to the best tactics to employ in the close. To make matters worse, research findings in the area are thin. What the research does suggest, however, is that two dimensions critical to a successful closing argument exist: argument position and strength. In the following sections we will attempt to outline the basic research related to these factors and recommend strategies dictated by this knowledge.

THE NUMBER OF ÀRGUMENTS

How many arguments can jurors process efficiently? While that question has not received extensive research attention, its answer is crucial in designing the close. All too often attorneys present jurors with too much information in the summation. Jurors, like all people, have a limited capacity to absorb and process information. When they receive too many arguments, jurors become confused and disoriented and will remember only a small number of the total number of arguments presented (Eagly 1974). So how many arguments are too many? The only study in this area provides an adequate guide.

In the study researchers exposed mock jurors to closing arguments which supported either the defense or the prosecution (Calder, Inkso, and Yandell 1974). The subjects were divided into groups that heard a different number of prosecution arguments (either one, four, seven, ten, thirteen, or seventeen) and either four or seven defense arguments. They were then asked to rate the likelihood of the defendant's guilt. Results showed that ratings of guilt increased steadily as the number of arguments for the prosecution increased, peaking at ten arguments. When the defense presented seven arguments, however, guilt ratings increased most between four and seven prosecution arguments. The researchers therefore concluded that seven arguments appear to be the optimal number of arguments during the close.

An additional touchstone for the optimal number of arguments is contained in the adage "quality over quantity." Research has repeatedly demonstrated that a smaller number of strong arguments is more persuasive than a greater number of weak arguments, especially when receivers are highly involved (Petty and Cacioppo 1979).

REPETITION

Rhetoricians as far back as Aristotle have advised speakers to repeat themselves in order to plant a point firmly in the listener's mind. The tendency to believe statements on the basis of repetition rather than on evidence irks many scholars; indeed, the philosopher Wittgenstein compared the repetition effect to buying a second newspaper to determine whether the first one was correct. Nonetheless, empirical support for the persuasive effect of repetition continues to grow. By simply repeating an argument speakers may gain a considerable persuasive advantage. For example, in one experimental study mock jurors exposed to an attorney's recommendation retained the message better and agreed more when they heard the argument three times as opposed to one time (Wilson and Miller 1968). A repetition effect generally refers to the propensity of receivers to regard repeated statements as more true than new statements. In two studies in this area subjects reported truth ratings on sets of plausible but unfamiliar statements (Hasher, Goldstein, and Toppino 1977; Hasher and Chromiak 1977). Subjects were exposed to subsequent sets of statements containing repetitious statements as well as statements not previously presented. Results firmly supported that repetition influences belief. Not only were repeated statements rated as more true than new statements, but repeated statements received higher truth ratings as the number of repetitions increased. Moreover, this effect occurred equally for objectively true and false statements.

Persuasion lore tells us to mask our repeated statements—to change the wording and style so as to avoid recognition of the repetition by the hearer—presumably because when they recognize repetition hearers will be less likely to respond favorably. A study designed to test this recognition hypothesis, however, found just the opposite to be true (Bacon 1979). In two experiments employing a multitude of trivia statements, the repetition effect occurred even when subjects were informed that repeated statements were repetitions. Support was tendered for the explanation that it is the recognition of repetition and not the repetition itself which is influential. Results revealed that statements judged to be repeated were rated as relatively true regardless of whether they were in fact repeated. These findings have broad implications for the use of repetition in persuasive situations. Since repeated statements are systematically judged truer as the frequency of these statements increases, lawyers should intentionally repeat those statements and concepts beneficial to the case. Furthermore, announcing that specific facts or statements have been repeated or suggested during a trial should also enhance attitudes toward those facts. Both tactics should be standard practice during the closing argument.

A word of warning is in order, however. A problem can arise when repetition is overused. Excessive repetition (more than three times) may be viewed as irritating or even offensive to an audience. Research has shown that while moderate levels of repetition allow receivers to cognitively elaborate message arguments, high levels of repetition promote counterarguing (Petty and Cacioppo 1979). To avoid this possibility while gaining the advantage of repetition, attorneys are best advised to repeat central arguments up to three times during the course of the summation. Although this is an arbitrary cut off, evidence suggests that as many as five repetitions result in fewer positive thoughts, more negative thoughts, and a general decrease in persuasive effect.

MESSAGE ORDERING: PRIMACY AND RECENCY

Given research on impression formation and cognitive framing, one would expect that information presented first—testimony by the first witness, the first opening statement, the first argument in the opening, etc.—will exert a greater influence on jurors than what comes later. This is termed a primacy effect. In contrast, a recency effect suggests that information presented later will have the greatest influence. Generally, theorists suggest that recency effects are a function of memory. Arguments presented early in a message or in a sequence, such as a trial, are remembered less than arguments presented later. As the time between the two arguments increases, so does the magnitude of the recency effect (Miller and Campbell 1959). Since jurors will consider those arguments they remember best, and since arguments are assumed to be forgotten at an accelerating rate with time, we can predict that closing arguments will generally be more powerful than opening statements. Moreover, the recency effect on deliberation between the order of the closing arguments will be more influential than the recency effect between the order of the opening statements. These effects diminish as the time interval between any presentation and the deliberation of that information increases.

Because of the burden of proof in a criminal trial the prosecution traditionally proceeds first and the defense then follows. This is termed the gross order in which each side presents its case. In contrast, the internal order refers to the sequence in which testimony is presented by each side within its own case. Research results from experimental studies are mixed. Regarding both the gross and the internal order of examination researchers have found both a recency effect (Walker, Thibaut, and Andreoli 1972) and a primacy effect (Pennington 1982). This is not so surprising.

Research on cognitive framing suggests that when jurors are relatively unfamiliar with the events in question, as they are at the start of a trial, they will search for ways of organizing the information presented. Because of this, arguments presented first will provide them with the point of reference necessary to digest the information efficiently. Research focusing on order effects for unfamiliar subjects confirms this primacy effect (Lana 1961). As jurors develop a sense of what a case involves, such as during the summation, more recent arguments will be better remembered and a recency effect should commonly prevail. Because experimental studies have primarily used closing arguments or combinations of arguments, it is not surprising that researchers more consistently find a recency effect (Wallace and Wilson 1969; Wilson and Miller 1968; Zdep and Wilson 1968).

Why else might researchers find a primacy effect in some cases and a recency in others? One explanation is that primacy effects are most common in trials that turn on impressions of courtroom actors, and recency effects are most likely to occur in trials that turn on beliefs and values (Lind 1982). Another researcher has suggested the length of a trial may influence the effect. Because jurors' attention diminishes over the course of a long trial, lengthy trials may promote a primacy effect (Pennington 1982).

REFUTATION: THE ADVANTAGES
OF TWO-SIDED MESSAGES

During the Second World War the U.S. War Department sought to ascertain the most expedient means of convincing soldiers that the Pacific conflict might continue for several more months. Researchers conducted a study to investigate the advantages of one-sided and two-sided messages to serve this function (Hovland, Lumsdaine, and Sheffield 1949). A one-sided message raises only arguments supporting the persuader's position, whereas a two-sided argument also raises and refutes possible objections to the persuader's position. The one-sided message in this study stressed Japan's strength and resources, while the two-sided message included the arguments used in the one-sided message but also mentioned and refuted arguments about Japan's weaknesses. The investigators found no overall difference in persuasive effectiveness between the two messages but did find differences between audience characteristics. The initial positions held by the soldiers and their knowledge and familiarity with the issues affected their response to one- or two-sided messages.

Since that study a score of experimental studies have examined the advantages of one- and two-sided messages. A recent review of these studies concluded that two-sided messages provide a strategic superiority over their one-sided counterparts (Jackson and Allen 1987). Although early studies suggested that one-sided messages were sometimes more effective when the audience was initially favorable to the position, when the audience possessed lower educational levels, and when audiences were more familiar with the issues involved, the majority ot studies support the contention that two-sided messages are generally superior to one-sided messages despite differences in audience characteristics. In addition, two-sided messages also enhance speaker credibility and produce greater resistance to subsequent persuasive messages from an opponent (McGuire and Papegeorgis 1961).

Scholars have offered several explanations for this advantage. To begin with, a persuader who presents only one side of an issue may appear biased or ignorant. As a result, receivers may discount the persuader's arguments on the grounds that the agent has not considered the weaknesses in his or her own position. Another view is that a one-sided communication may provoke receivers to rehearse arguments against the advocated position mentally. In other words, receivers commonly produce counterarguments to messages. These counterarguments may be delayed or eliminated when the persuader addresses and refutes them before the audience has a chance to.

The practical implications of this work for the closing argument appear forthright. Attorneys should not only provide arguments in support of their client's position but should also raise and refute arguments harmful to that position. Interestingly, research suggests this task is best done in a positive order (Jackson and Allen 1987). In other words, two-sided messages are most effective when the supportive arguments appear first and are then followed by refutation. This order is more effective than when the two are interwoven, which, in turn, is superior to a refutation-first ordering.

WHEN PROMISES ARE BROKEN

Attorneys are advised to preview the case during the opening statement and to explain patiently and completely what the evidence will show. Given that the testimony is yet to come, this explanation during the opening takes the form of a "promise" as to what will be told. As we have already seen, extensive case previews of what will be displayed through the testimony are more powerful than previews that provide little detail. In the course of composing such a complete preview, attorneys often consciously or unconsciously exaggerate what facts the testimony will reveal. Of concern for the closing argument is the effect these unkept promises have on jurors.

Although only one study exists in this area, its findings and implications are germane to a successful rebuttal of an opponent's case. In that study, researchers exposed mock jurors to one of three conditions: (1) an opening statement that promised more than was actually revealed by the testimony; (2) an opening statement that promised more than was delivered and a remark in the opposing counsel's summation noting the failure to keep the promise; and (3) a control condition containing the same evidence but without mention of a promise unfulfilled nor the remark by the opposing attorney (Pyszczynski, Greenberg, Mack, and Wrightsman 1981). Essentially, the researchers found that unkept promises made during the opening statement have positive effects when they do not receive attention from the opposing counsel. When counsel reminds jurors that his opponent has failed to keep his opening promises, this effect is nullified. This discrediting, however, does nothing to advance the opponent's position.

Strategically, then, it is crucial for attorneys to flag unfulfilled promises in order to cancel the effects of the information contained in these promises. A point worth highlighting is that this study further demonstrates—as one would predict from the story perspective—that orienting information, even if not proven accurate, can sway subsequent judgments.

IMAGINATION

Prosecuting and defense attorneys in the publicized criminal trial of auto magnate John De Lorean embellished their closing arguments with quotations, literary allusion, and analogy. The defense went as far as to compare the government's case to the Salem witch trials and De Lorean to the emperor who had no clothes, while the federal prosecuting attorney quoted Sir Walter Scott, "O, what a tangled web we weave, when first we practice to deceive," and closed with a lyric from Bob Dylan, "You don't need a weatherman to know which way the wind blows." Such image making has long been thought to add flare and panache to the closing argument as well as to strengthen the argument by activating the jurors' imaginations. For the literary and metaphorically inclined, it comes as no surprise that research supports the suasory effect of imagination.

Research in memory processes suggests that people often store information in images (Bower 1972). In fact, as aids to memory and recall about other people, images are most effective (Lord 1980). Evidence also suggests that when only one scenario is imagined and reimagined, the likelihood of the occurrence of the act increases (Gregory, Cialdini, and Carpenter 1982). For attorneys in the closing argument, causing jurors to imagine an event in a particular way is tantamount to leading them to think that the event is more likely. In one study subjects who imagined themselves performing a series of behaviors subsequently viewed themselves as more likely to perform the behaviors, while those who imagined themselves not performing the behaviors later claimed they were less likely to perform the behaviors (Anderson 1983). The more frequently an individual imagines himself engaging or not engaging in a set of behaviors, the more powerful this change.

Lawyers are naturally concerned whether this effect applies to the construction of social behavior similar to a criminal story. Although research has not directly examined legal events, one study confirms that imagination does influence judgments regarding the likelihood of a social event. In this study subjects who were prompted to imagine the election of a political candidate came to believe the occurrence was more likely (Carroll 1978). Lawyers have every reason to believe that having jurors imagine events in a way beneficial to the case will strengthen belief in the event as described.

The reason for this effect may be due to the competition among scenarios. When we can imagine alternative scenarios, the consequence of each sequence most informs our intentions to behave. A limited number of scenarios, however, precludes a thorough search or evaluation of alternatives, leading to an increased acceptance of those offered. When only one scenario is imagined, this conception appears most plausible. In other words, conceiving an event as occurring in a specific manner creates a cognitive frame that impairs the ability to see the event in competing ways.

While imagining an event doesn't make it so, the viability of a story is certainly enhanced through the generation of selected and consistent images. Given the research in this area, an attorney is best advised to develop one consistent image which jurors must mentally illustrate. To mix images or analogies, as in the example of the De Lorean case, is to dilute the impact of an image, perhaps to the point of confusion. This can be avoided by first selecting a coherent theme and using image-enhancing language to support this focus.

Among the rhetorical devices available to attorneys for facilitating or orchestrating the fancy of jurors are literary allusions, analogies, and allegories. As these devices operate from the same principle of substituting one concept for another, they fall generally under the rubric of metaphor.

METAPHOR

Metaphor refers to the signifying process where aspects of one object are transferred to another object so that the second object is spoken of as if it were the first (Hawkes 1972). This substitution of one concept for another takes several forms, including direct and indirect assertions. For example, students are notorious for transferring the features of school (object one) to those of prison (object two). In a direct form a speaker using this metaphor might declare that "school is prison." A more indirect form might include the assertion that the "prisoners are restless, especially during a class-room lockup." Metaphors stated indirectly require the listener to engage the concepts being substituted and to draw parallels between them. Generally, metaphors are comprehended and interpreted in a three-step sequential process: error, puzzlement-recoil, and resolution (Osborn and Ehninger 1962).

At first the listener makes the mistake of interpreting a metaphor in a literal manner. The puzzlement-recoil step occurs when the listener recognizes that the word or phrase is not being employed in its usual sense and that a reinterpretation is called for. During this step the listener suffers the agitation of uncertainty, an agitation he is motivated to resolve by solving the metaphor puzzle. Resolution occurs when the listener indeed resolves the metaphor puzzle and the message of the metaphor becomes apparent.

The three-step process also provides the means to measure the potency of a metaphor. The greater degree of surprise or shock that a listener experiences when first confronting the relation thought to exist between subject and item for association, the greater the strain placed upon the associations used to tie the divergent elements of the metaphor together. A new or radical metaphor produces a state of high tension in the listener-reader, a state that can either be resolved through solution to the metaphorical puzzle or by the metaphor falling apart as meaningless. This has important implications for attorneys. When employing metaphors in the closing argument, attorneys should generally involve associations that are easily resolved so the flow of the speech will not be interrupted by the listeners spending too much time in the puzzlement-recoil and resolution stages. When lawyers choose to use a complex metaphor, the metaphor should be followed by an extended pause or repetition to allow the listener to search and solve the puzzle.

A growing body of research demonstrates that metaphors are highly persuasive when incorporated with arguments (Reinsch 1971). In particular, the use of metaphors at the conclusion of a message is highly persuasive (Siltanen 1981).

RHETORICAL QUESTIONS

A rhetorical question is a question which assumes its own answer. In other words, a question is rhetorical when its answer is so obvious it does not require response. Such a question focuses attention by prompting the audience to respond cognitively and generate the mandated answer. For example, suppose that an attorney's case turns on the anxiety experienced by his client after an auto accident.

A rhetorical question might be: "Is it wrong to be anxious after an accident?" or "How many of you would not have been shaken by this event?"

Attorneys often employ rhetorical questions during summation to emphasize key points, and for good reason. When compared to traditional statements of introduction, rhetorical questions have been found to produce more favorable thoughts and to elicit more favorable attitudes when used in a strong message (Burnkrant and Howard 1984). In contrast, just the opposite results (less favorable thoughts and attitudes) occur when such questions are used with weak arguments that are easy to refute. It may be that rhetorical questions strengthen a persuasive message simply because an audience expects the rhetorical form to be associated with superior arguments (Zillman 1972). For example, when an attorney's summation was presented using the rhetorical question form rather than the traditional statement form in a hypothetical criminal case, subjects recommended more lenient sentences. Theorists also believe that rhetorical questions focus more attention on the arguments used, especially for issues of low personal relevance for an audience. Thus, their use with weaker arguments is risky. Furthermore, the placement of rhetorical questions also invites caution.

Rhetorical questions, like complex metaphors, may sometimes disrupt a receiver's train of thought. In the case of a strong and highly involving summation, this disruption would have an adverse effect on persuasion, whereas the disruption would benefit a weak summation by hindering the production of negative thoughts (Petty, Cacioppo, and Heesacker 1981). As a consequence, attorneys are best advised to use rhetorical questions sparingly during the body of the summation and to capitalize on their ability to capture attention by employing them in the summation's conclusion.

AVOIDING REACTANCE

Summation appeals often stress the harmful or beneficial social consequences of adopting message recommendations, namely social approval or disapproval. That others will think more positively or negatively about the receiver can have a substantial effect on behavior. In one study in this area researchers found that messages advocating voluntary blood donations to the Red Cross were most effective when they contained cues stressing social approval: that donors would be perceived as socially concerned and unselfish. Messages containing social disapproval cues (that nondonors would be perceived as socially unconcerned and selfish) were less effective, but had considerably more influence than messages void of either approval or disapproval cues (Powell and Miller 1967). This and related work demonstrates the need for attorneys to cast their normative demands (for example, the classic appeals "We cannot let the defendant free to victimize others" or "It is a miscarriage of justice to find the defendant guilty") in positive terms, stressing social approval rather than disapproval as is typically the case.

Caution must be taken, however, in the use of such social demands. When jurors perceive their choices as restricted or eliminated, they will often be motivated to regain the lost freedom and react in an unfavorable manner. Termed "psychological reactance," this need to reinstate a lost or limited freedom is well documented (Brehm 1966, 1972). Research has shown that when people believe a restriction of their behavior is necessary or justified, then no need to react exists. But when that restriction is believed to be illegitimate or unjustified, then individuals will have a strong desire to behave in the opposite manner (Grabitz-Gniech 1971). The less justification of the restriction, the greater the reactance aroused within an individual.

When attorneys make demands for a jury to side with their case, they often resort to arguments that paint events in black or white terms. Combined with an ardent display of showmanship, these arguments are sometimes perceived as demands which restrict a jury's choice. When taken like this, reactance can occur, prompting the jury to reassert their right to choose. As a result, reactance often predisposes juries against an advocated position rather than for it. Eliminating this Romeo and Juliet effect, as it has been called, requires only that attorneys explicitly justify their demands. For example, an attorney who does not justify the statement "You can only find the defendant not guilty" invites reactance. One can almost hear a juror cognitively respond, "Don't tell me what I must find." Disclaimers, such as "Given the evidence," or "In my considered opinion," do little to alleviate this perceived restriction. The key is to make the juror fully aware of the legitimate reasons for a demand and so relieve the need to rebel.

ARGUMENTATIVE STRUCTURE

In chapter 2 we described the elements of a Ciceronian oration which influence the structure of the trial: *exordium, narratio, confirmatio, refutatio,* and *peroration.* In chapter 5 we observed that the opening statement serves the function of exordium and narratio: to introduce the case and tell the story. The closing argument, from this perspective, functions as a peroration which brings together all the previous elements and drives them home with the power necessary to persuade. We further noted in chapter 5 that while a narrative structure is most appropriate for the opening statement, it is necessary to structure the closing argument in such a way as to enfold the narrative within the more traditional argumentative structure prescribed by legal practice. In chapter 10 we will describe in detail the reasons for this demand, so our summary here will be brief.

In studies of jury deliberation we find that jurors bring a version of the story with them into the deliberation room that will probably not change much. However, they do engage in extensive inferences needed to fill gaps in the evidence, and they modify their version of the story to fit verdict requirements given in the judge's instructions. So the work done in the jury room tends to focus on understanding what the law requires for various verdicts and adjusting the story to allow the verdict the majority favors.

Knowing this, lawyers preparing the closing argument begin with a traditional analysis of the issues based on what the judge will instruct the jurors and build arguments that will help the jury accept a version of the story consistent with the desired verdict (Spangenberg 1971). If, for example, the case involves a charge of burglary, the judge may instruct the jury that in order to find the defendant guilty they must conclude that (1) there was an unlawful entry into (2) a dwelling at (3) night with (4) intent to commit a felony. To prepare the closing argument, then, the lawyer would organize the argument around these essential elements or issues.

The structure would begin with a preview.

> As the judge will instruct, it will be necessary for you to answer Yes to four questions in order to find the defendant guilty of burglary. Did the defendant enter the building unlawfully? Is the building a dwelling? Did he enter at night? Did he enter with the intent to commit a felony? In this closing argument I will discuss these questions one by one in relation to the evidence you have heard. When I am done, you will be able to answer each question Yes beyond any reasonable doubt.

Arguments are then constructed around each issue. The form of the argument varies, and little research has been done to find what structure may be best for each case. We do know, however, what arguments are typically employed. In one study the transcript of closing arguments in a typical civil case was analyzed to set out a typology of arguments actually used (Sheppard and Rieke 1983). The resulting list of arguments included the following:

1. Arguments about what the law is, including
   the letter of the law in precise wording
   prescribed legal procedures

2. Jurors' obligation/responsibility to the law, including
    juror responsibilities
    jurors' obligation to adhere to the law
3. Jurors' moral obligation to careful decision making
4. Arguments on what is equitable
5. Arguments on the presence and credibility of evidence
6. Arguments about the reality of events within the narrative
7. Arguments about what society reasonably expects of individuals
8. Analogies between this case and what jurors know
9. Arguments which develop causal relationships among events

POTENTIAL OF THE CLOSING ARGUMENT

There remains considerable debate about what can be accomplished through the closing argument. The ongoing question as to whether opening statements or closing arguments are more important is probably moot. More to the point is the question about what, if anything, can be accomplished in the closing argument.

We will report in chapter 10 that basic story structures will probably exist in the jurors' minds before they get up to go into the jury room. And we will further report that what the first majority decides will probably be what the final verdict is. If these assertions are true, then we cannot help but wonder if many times the closing argument is a futile process of talking to people who have already made up their minds.

In a study of 115 mock jurors exposed to a sample trial that varied closing argument systematically—from both sides arguing, to only one side presenting an argument, to neither side arguing—no significant difference was found in verdicts regarding liability (Rieke 1971). Since this was a civil trial involving charges of negligence in an automobile accident, the study suggests that jurors had established a story of what happened and who was at fault before hearing any closing argument.

In the same study jurors were asked before deliberation to respond to a questionnaire that asked for their attitude toward the litigants and counsel. Again, attitudes did not vary from those who heard arguments to those who did not. They did not even change their attitude toward one side when they heard only that side argue.

However, when responding to a simple questionnaire that asked them to suggest what, if any, money damages should be awarded to the plaintiff (they could select an amount from zero to $12,000), significant differences were found. Specifically, the highest amounts of money were selected by those mock jurors who heard only the plaintiff give a closing argument. The lowest amounts of money were selected by jurors hearing only the defense argument. Jurors who heard both sides present closing argument tended to favor the plaintiff in money damages.

In many cases the closing argument may well not be the dramatic force that stampedes the jury from one side to the other—as it is portrayed in literature and the reminiscences of great trial lawyers. On the other hand, the opportunity to make some surgical corrections in the minds of jurors should not be taken lightly.

REFERENCES

Anderson, C. A. (1983). Imagination and expectation: the effect of imagining behavioral scripts on personal intentions. *Journal of Personality and Social Psychology* 45: 293–305.

Bacon, F. T. (1979). Credibility of repeated statements: memory for trivia. *Journal of Experimental Psychology: Human Learning and Memory* 5: 241–52.

Bower, G. H. (1972). Mental imagery and associative learning. In L. Gregg (ed.), *Cognition in learning and memory*. New York: Wiley.

Brehm, J. W. (1966). *A theory of psychological reactance*. New York: Academic Press.

Brehm, J. W. (1972). *Responses to loss of freedom: a theory of psychological reactance*. Morristown, NJ: General Learning Press.

Burnkrant, R. E., and Howard, D. J. (1984). Effects of the use of introductory rhetorical questions versus statements on information processing. *Journal of Personality and Social Psychology* 47: 1218–30.

Calder, B. J.; Inkso, C. A.; and Yandell, B. (1974). The relation of cognitive and memorial processes to persuasion in a simulated jury trial. *Journal of Applied Social Psychology* 4: 62–93.

Carroll. J. S. (1978). The effect of imagining an event on expectations for the event: an interpretation in terms of the availability heuristic. *Journal of Experimental Social Psychology* 14: 88–96.

Eagly, A. H. (1974). Comprehensibility of persuasive arguments as a determinant of opinion change. *Journal of Personality and Social Psychology* 29: 758–73.

Grabitz-Gniech, G. (1971). Some restrictive conditions for the occurrence of psychological reactance. *Journal of Personality and Social Psychology* 19: 188–96.

Gregory, W. L.; Cialdini, R. B.; and Carpenter, K. M. (1982). Self-relevant scenarios as mediators of likelihood estimates and compliance:

Does imagining make it so? *Journal of Personality and Social Psychology* 43: 89–99.

Hasher, L., and Chromiak, W. (1977). The processing of frequency information: an automatic mechanism? *Journal of Verbal Learning and Verbal Behavior* 16: 173–84.

Hasher, K.; Goldstein, D.; and Toppino, T. (1977). Frequency and the conference of referential validity. *Journal of Verbal Learning and Verbal Behavior* 16: 107–12.

Hawkes, D. F. (1972). *Metaphor*. London: Methuen.

Hovland, C. I.; Lumsdaine, A. A.; and Sheffield, F. D. (1949). *Experiments on mass communication*. New Haven: Yale University Press.

Jackson, S., and Allen, M. (1987). Meta-analysis of the effectiveness of one-sided and two-sided argumentation. Paper presented at the convention of the International Communication Association, Montreal.

Lana, R. E. (1961). Familiarity and order of presentation in persuasion. *Journal of Abnormal and Social Psychology* 62: 573–77.

Lind, E. A. (1982). The psychology of courtroom procedure. In R. Bray and N. Kerr (eds.), *Psychology in the courtroom*. New York: Academic Press.

Lord, C. G. (1980). Schemas and images as memory aids: two modes of processing social information. *Journal of Personality and Social Psychology* 38: 257–69.

McGuire, W. J., and Papegeorgis, D. (1961). The relative efficacy of various types of prior belief-defense in producing immunity against persuasion. *Journal of Abnormal and Social Psychology* 62: 327–37.

Matlon, R. J.; Davis J. W.; Catchings, B. W.; Derr, W. R.; and Waldron V. R. (1985). Factors affecting jury decision-making. Paper presented at annual convention of the Speech Communication Association, Denver.

Miller, N. and Campbell, D. T. (1959). Recency and primacy in persuasion as a function of the timing of speeches and measurements. *Journal of Abnormal and Social Psychology* 59: 3.

Osborn, M. and Ehninger, D. (1962). The metaphor in public address. *Communication Monographs* 29: 223–34.

Pennington, D. C. (1982). Witnesses and their testimony: effects of ordering on juror verdicts. *Journal of Applied Social Psychology* 12: 318–33.

Petty, R. E., and Cacioppo, J. T. (1979). Issue involvement can increase or decrease persuasion by enhancing message-relevant cognitive responses. *Journal of Personality and Social Psychology* 37: 1915–26.

Petty, R. E.; Cacioppo, J. T.; and Heesacker, M. (1981). Effects of rhetorical questions on persuasion: a cognitive response analysis. *Journal of Personality and Social Psychology* 40: 432–40.

Powell, F. A., and Miller, G. R. (1967). Social approval and disapproval cues in anxiety-arousing communications. *Speech Monographs* 34: 152–59.

Pyszczynski, T.; Greenberg, J.; Mack, D.; and Wrightsman, L. S. (1981). Opening statements in a jury trial; the effect of promising more than the evidence can show. *Journal of Applied Social Psychology* 11: 434–44.

Reinsch, N. L. (1971). An investigation of the effects of the metaphor and simile in persuasive discourse. *Communication Monographs* 38: 142–45.

Rieke, R. D. (1971). The role of argument in the trial at law. Paper presented at the convention of the Speech Communication Association, San Francisco.

Sealy, A. P., and Cornish, W. R. (1973). Juries and the rules of evidence. *Criminal Law Review* 208–23.

Sheppard, S. A., and Rieke, R. D. (1983). Categories of reasoning in legal argument. In D. Zarefsky, M. Sillars, and J. Rhodes (eds.), *Argument in transition*. Annandale, VA: Speech Communication Association.

Siltanen, S. (1981). The persuasiveness of metaphor: a replication and extension. *Southern Speech Communication Journal* 47: 67–83.

Simon, R. J. (1970). Beyond a reasonable doubt—an experimental attempt at quantification. *Journal of Applied Behavioral Science* 6: 203–09.

Spangenberg, C. (1971). What I try to accomplish in an opening statement. In G. W. Holmes (ed.), *Excellence in advocacy*. Ann Arbor, MI: Institute of Continuing Legal Education.

Tarter-Hilgendorf, B. J. (1986). Impact of opening and closing statements. *Trial,* 79–80.

Walker, L.; Thibaut, J.; and Andreoli, V. (1972). Order of presentation at trial. *Yale Law Journal* 82: 216–26.

Wallace, W., and Wilson, W. (1969). Reliable recency effects. *Psychological Reports* 25: 313.

Wilson, W., and Miller, H. (1968). Repetition, order of presentation, and timing of arguments and measures as determinants of opinion change. *Journal of Personality and Social Psychology* 9: 185.

Zdep, S., and Wilson, W. (1968). Recency effects in opinion formation. *Psychological Reports* 23: 199.

Zillman, D. (1972). Rhetorical elicitation of agreement in persuasion. *Journal of Personality and Social Psychology* 21: 159–65.

Chapter 10 ―――――――――――――――

JURY DELIBERATION

"Just tell me what goes on in the jury room," said the defense lawyer, "and I can increase my chances of winning." He was speaking to a trial consultant, and was willing to pay a high price for solid information on how juries go about the process of deliberation and decision making. In one sense he was showing his knowledge of the importance of understanding the audience to be persuaded. However, he was also expressing the frustration of a professional who daily tries to make a case to people who will decide in absolute secrecy. Lawyers have always dreamed of eavesdropping on jury deliberations, and some have done so surreptitiously.

No matter how curious lawyers have been over the centuries about the conduct of jury deliberations, serious study of the process is quite recent. This is explained in part by the role juries are expected to play in the legal process, and in part by the development of social science research in law. Juries are expected to employ standards of judgment that are not explicit, and social science research in law did not emerge until this century. These ideas will be developed further in the following discussion of theory and research in jury decision making.

THE THEORY OF JURY DECISION MAKING

No one can say precisely what it is a jury is supposed to do. There are volumes of accounts that claim to know, but disagreement abounds. Furthermore, no one can say with certainty whether juries accomplish their task, whatever it is, because juries do their work in private.

Before looking at jury deliberation from a theoretical point of view, it is useful to reconsider the discussion of dispute resolution in chapter 1. Of the innumerable differences among people that occur each day, only a tiny portion become formalized. And of those that become formalized, most are resolved without any recourse to legal procedures. Ordinary people manage to resolve their differences through negotiation, mediation, or arbitration.

Professional judges or the learned judiciary are not required for the resolution of most disputes. Lay judges (ordinary people without special training in the law or in decision making) are sufficient and even superior to the learned judiciary for deciding most human conflicts. So an important point to be made is that jurors are not so unqualified as one might suspect; they represent the group that makes most human decisions.

When both judges and juries were asked to judge the same case independently, they agreed most of the time. Kalven and Zeisel (1966) found that judges and juries agree in their decisions 75.4 percent of the time. This too suggests that juries are well qualified for their task. Of course, we have not yet explained the 24.6 percent of the cases in which judges and juries disagree, nor have we faced the question that if there is so much agreement, why not just use the single judge instead of the group of jurors. To set a framework within which to discuss these questions, let us look at two examples in which the jury disagreed with the learned judiciary.

WILLIAM PENN AND LEROY REED.   Hans and Vidmar (1986) recount the story of the trial of William Penn (who gave his name to Pennsylvania) in 1670 when he was accused of preaching before an "unlawfully and tumultuously" assembled congregation. The indictment asserted that the crowd remained for a long time and created some "terror and disturbance" among the people. The jury, after much deliberation, concluded only that Penn was guilty of preaching, and they refused to convict him of participating in an unlawful assembly. The judge refused to accept this verdict and sent the jury back to deliberate, with the announcement that English law permitted him to hold the jury until they reached a proper verdict (meaning one the judge wanted).

Even with this threat the jurors refused to find Penn guilty. So the court sent Penn to jail anyway and *sent all twelve jurors to jail as well*. Ultimately the jurors were released, and subsequently the practice of punishing jurors for bringing in a verdict not desired by the judge was ended. Who was correct in the conflict over the Penn decision, the judge or the jury? No one can say, and perhaps both were in terms of their relative perspectives. The better question is, Did the jury perform a socially valuable function?

Over three hundred years later in Milwaukee, Wisconsin, Leroy Reed was accused of owning a firearm while he was still on parole as a convicted felon (Levin 1986). Reed's case became significant because it is the first and only time the deliberations of an actual jury were legally recorded. The Public Broadcasting System presented their program "Frontline" with Judy Woodruff in which they had secured permission of the judge, the prosecutor, the defendant, and all twelve of the jurors to videotape and broadcast the deliberations.

This was an extraordinary accomplishment in view of the fact that when Kalven and Zeisel (1966) began their jury study, they were prevented from tape-recording jury deliberations, and it has been presumed since that doing so was against the law.

Leroy Reed, who was on parole, enrolled in a correspondence course for private investigators that suggested the students buy a hand gun. Reed did so, went to the police to register it, and they discovered he was on parole. They told him to go home, get the gun, and bring it back to them. He did as he was told, and when he returned to the police station with the gun, he was arrested for violating the law prohibiting convicted felons from owning a firearm.

In the trial Reed's lawyer admitted that strictly speaking Reed had done what the statute prohibited: He was a convicted felon who had bought a gun. The defense consisted of the argument that Reed was not fully competent mentally, and it was not fair to expect him to exercise the same knowledge expected of ordinary citizens. The law makes knowledge (defendant must be shown to have knowingly purchased a firearm knowing himself to be a convicted felon) an essential element.

The twelve members of the jury quickly elected a foreman, a white male employed as a toolmaker, who was sitting at the end of a rectangular table (there were two people at each end of the table and four along each side). The jury room resembled a library: relatively large, with one wall covered with bookshelves, a leather sofa, a table with refreshments, and the large library table at which the jury sat.

The jury included seven men and five women; there were two blacks (the defendant was black), and in addition to the toolmaker there were three teachers (one grade school, one high school, and one college English professor), one school psychologist, a physician, a firefighter, a production analyst, a data analyst, a food service manager, a housewife, and a laborer. They were instructed by the judge that to convict, they had to answer Yes to the following questions: (1) Is Reed a convicted felon? (2) Did he purchase a firearm: (3) Did he do so knowingly?

While the jury was absent, the defense lawyer had requested that the judge include in the instructions the fact that a jury can nullify a law in the sense that they can acquit an accused for any or no reason. The judge refused on the grounds that although it was true that once a jury leaves the courtroom they can make any decision they wish and no one will ever know why, if juries know this explicitly it might lead to anarchy. By implication the judge was saying that if a jury is to nullify a law, they must agonize their way to that conclusion and do so with the same kind of determination shown by the jury in the William Penn case.

The jury took a little over an hour to present each member's thinking before they took their first vote. The positions on one side supported the notion that clearly the three essential issues had been affirmed: Reed admitted on the witness stand that he knew he was on parole, he knew he had bought the gun, and there was no denial that he had indeed bought a gun. The decision in this sense is easy: The judge had given the jury the law. If a person is a convicted felon who purchases a firearm knowing himself to be a felon, then he is guilty of violating the law. The facts were undisputed; verdict: guilty.

On the other side were those who said they could not deny the affirmation of all three essential issues, but they did not feel Reed ought to be convicted. They concentrated on the claim that Reed was not mentally competent. They recalled the testimony of a psychologist who had said Reed had a mental age of seven years. One juror said a jury has the opportunity to consider a specific law in a specific case and make an exception when a particular defendant has the understanding of a second grader. Others said that while they felt this was a good law, it would accomplish no good for society to convict this defendant. They felt he constituted no threat, as evidenced by the fact that he went to the police to register the gun and even went back home to get it when asked to do so. They spoke of jurors not acting like computers and instead exercising a special level of conscience. They wondered if justice would be served by a guilty verdict no matter what the law says.

The vote on the first ballot was nine to three in favor of acquittal. Quickly one person changed a vote to make it ten to two for acquittal. The two guilty votes came from the toolmaker foreman and the firefighter. The remaining deliberation was directed at these two, particularly the firefighter, to bring them around to the majority position.

Arguments were generated to justify a not-guilty verdict within the limits of the law rather than blatantly choosing to ignore the law. For example, much discussion centered around the question of whether the defendant was able to "know" in the sense implied by the law considering his limited mental abilities. They used the metaphor of reality being a pinhole of light in an otherwise black background. The defendant may have been aware of being on parole and of buying the gun, but seeing reality as a pinhole of light prevented him from seeing these facts in juxtaposition. Thus he did not act knowingly in the sense of the law.

Another argument was that he lacked criminal intent. He bought and sought to license the gun openly rather than buying it secretly on the street. Several versions of the Leroy story were told characterizing him as a simple-minded and harmless guy who fantasized himself as the "Equalizer" and who innocently went to the police and even took a bus all the way home and back to fetch the gun. This story painted Leroy as one who should be helped, not convicted.

These arguments brought one more vote for acquittal, leaving only the firefighter favoring guilty. His arguments were direct: The judge told us to decide three issues and to avoid speculation. You all agree that the three issues are affirmed, but you insist on wild speculation. There is no reasonable doubt that Leroy is guilty. He said, "I probably look at this too basic, one, two, three. But when you get to reasonable doubt . . ." But the firefighter's will was weakening. He said that he would go along with the majority in order to make a unanimous decision, but he would never feel good about it. That statement brought some outbursts from others who seemed uncomfortable with the idea of merely forcing a reluctant juror to join the majority. They resumed making arguments in an effort to satisfy the firefighter's doubts.

The high school teacher, who also listed herself as a naturalist, said, "I found myself feeling real dumb last night. I thought, hey, this guy's guilty. Is there some way out of him being adjudged guilty by us? Could I live with my writing guilty for this particular person? But I mashed around with that for a while and thought if there's any justice really, it's in drawing attention to this man's limitations. Getting rid of the firearm is okay, too. But judging him not guilty, then I can believe in juries. I mean, that's where I find myself."

The firefighter never truly announced that he was satisfied with a not-guilty verdict. He seemed aware of the support he was receiving from the others, agreed that Leroy was not a threat and instead needed help, and finally just seemed to acquiesce quietly. The group continued to talk briefly after it was all over. They seemed to feel the strong cohesiveness that comes to twelve strangers who have just become a group through their common experience of difficult decisionmaking. The professor said, "I was aware of the weights on each one of us as a juror." They all agreed. They had taken their job seriously.

Two hours and twenty-eight minutes after leaving the courtroom, they returned a verdict of not guilty. They left immediately, and probably would never see each other again.

THE JURY'S TRADITIONAL ROLE AND SOCIAL SCIENCE RESEARCH. What does society expect of juries? Surely we do not expect them to nullify the law on a regular basis, for that would, as the judge said, lead to anarchy. In truth, there is more tradition than theory behind the continued existence of juries. The tradition has been well explained elsewhere (Kalven and Zeisel 1966; Hyman and Tarrant 1975; Hans and Vidmar 1986), and it is not necessary to review it in detail here. For our purposes we can note some important aspects of the tradition.

The jury system is derived from ancient traditions of lay judges: ordinary people making decisions. The jury as we know it today emerged from lay judges in England during the Middle Ages. The fact that we continue to employ juries reflects a basic commitment to the use of laypersons in the administration of justice (Kalven and Zeisel 1966). This is extraordinary: using amateurs to decide important professional issues. By contrast, consider a group of physicians presenting a critical medical issue to a group of lay judges. Consider professors calling in a group some of whom did not graduate from high school to resolve an intellectual issue. Whether one approves or disapproves of the jury system, there is general agreement that juries will at least some of the time make a decision that disagrees with that made by trained professionals.

The traditional objective of the trial is to find the truth. In the past this was expected to be accomplished through divine intervention: through oaths, witnesses, and compurgators (those who affirmed the credibility of the parties at issue), inviting God's wrath if they lied, and through ordeals (for example, carrying a pound of hot iron or thrusting a hand in boiling water) to see if God would protect the innocent from bodily harm. When these methods lost support, the truth was sought by inviting people who knew about the case to come together to tell the court what they felt to be the facts. They were called a jury, but functioned as modern witnesses. From divine intervention the courts had moved toward an empirical notion of truth: testimony on what people knew from their own sensory experience.

Gradually another function emerged. In addition to the *presenting* jury, which included those with direct knowledge of the case, there developed a *petit* jury, consisting of at least some people not familiar with the case, who would make a decision. They too were chosen from the locale in which the case occurred, on the grounds that the jury ought to represent the opinions of the community about what would be a fair and proper verdict. They would add belief and conscience to the direct knowledge brought by jurors selected from the presenting jury.

In Renaissance England it is not unlikely that the discovery of Aristotle's works had some influence on the development of juries. In the *Rhetoric* (Roberts 1954), Aristotle argued that legal decisions are made on short notice in contrast to the long deliberation in the making of laws. Moreover, legislators have a prospective and general view, whereas juries decide definite and specific cases in retrospect. Jurors, said Aristotle, often have "allowed themselves to be so much influenced by feelings of friendship or hatred or self-interest that they lose any clear vision of the truth and have their judgment obscured by considerations of personal pleasure or pain (1354b)."

When legislators make the law, they are deciding about their own vital interests, and so will use their good judgment to decide on the strength of arguments. Jurors, on the other hand, are deciding other people's affairs and lack the guidance of informed self-interest. It is possible that they can be moved simply to choose the more attractive litigant rather than make a sound judgment. From Aristotle's view, then, the jury should not include those likely to be influenced by friendship or self-interest. This supports an argument for the development of a deciding jury in contrast to a presenting jury made up of those with personal involvement in the case. Incidentally, Aristotle's argument also supports the laws of evidence which filter testimony before it goes to jurors to assure the avoidance of evidence likely to lead to choice rather than sound judgment.

In colonial America the jury became more clearly defined. The distance between England and America was great both geographically and politically. The judges and other administrators were appointed by the distant king and were responsible to him. The jurors came from among the colonists and were representative of the emerging sense of liberty and democracy. During the time prior to the American Revolution juries served to express local values in contrast to laws passed in England. The jury came to be the expression of the fundamental interests of the people in general, even when they were in conflict with law. In the American experience laws too far removed from the values and interests of the people did not deserve support. John Adams said in 1771 that the jury not only had the right but the duty to decide according to its best understanding, judgment, and conscience even if it ran in direct opposition to the instructions of the court (Hans and Vidmar 1986).

In theory a jury is still supposed to be only a fact-finding body just as it functioned six hundred years ago in England. Judges still instruct jurors that they are to decide only questions of fact and that the court, through its instructions, will decide the law. But as we saw in the case of Leroy Reed, juries continue the well-established pattern of deciding cases as a whole (combining law and fact) through their combined understanding of the facts as these were presented in court, their understanding of the law as explained in the judge's instructions, and in terms of their sense of conscience and values as fellow citizens with those involved in the trial.

Most of the time (75.4 percent, according to Kalven and Zeisel, 1966) juries decide just as judges would. In those instances in which juries disagree with judges, they are not necessarily violating explicit law or tradition. They may be expressing an instance in which the understanding, values, beliefs, or conscience of the community do not support an application of the law *in this case*. As the jury said in the Reed case, we like the law and believe it ought to be enforced, but not this time. As Aristotle said, legislators write laws in general anticipation of problems and their prevention. Today juries must decide the specific case. Legislators, said Aristotle, cannot write a law that anticipates every specific case that might emerge, no matter how hard they try. So courts are necessary to deal with individual cases, and juries continue to exist largely to provide ongoing citizen involvement in this aspect of the legal process just as they are continually involved in the legislative process through elections, referenda, and other parts of the political process.

RESEARCH IN JURY DELIBERATION

Just as churches maintain some sense of mystery and awe through the use of robes, altars, and impressive buildings, so too does the law. Part of the effectiveness of the law in maintaining public order and respect is achieved through the sense of power communicated by its processes. Many have felt that it is not healthy for the public to know too intimately the nature of the legal process. For example, many of the arguments used to oppose the requirement that police explicitly inform those accused of crime of their right to remain silent and to have an attorney present were based on the assumption that if people knew their rights, law enforcement would suffer. One of the most closely protected mysteries of the law is what goes on in the jury room. (Another mystery still not carefully explored is what goes on during the conferences of the members of the Supreme Court of the United States.)

This guarding of the mystery of the law, combined with the fact that lawyers know how to use the law to protect their interests, probably explains why serious social science research into jury deliberation did not begin until the middle of the twentieth century. When the University of Chicago Jury Project made careful arrangements to record jury deliberations, they were censured by the attorney general of the United States, they were subjected to hearings by the Senate Judiciary Committee, and many jurisdictions enacted statutes prohibiting jury tapping (Kalven and Zeisel 1966).

To study jury deliberation, then, social scientists had to develop elaborate designs of mock trials and mock juries that would replicate the real process sufficiently well to warrant the claim that what happened in mock jury deliberations also happened in real jury deliberations. Obviously this was not easy, and early efforts produced a great deal of research that has subsequently been rejected on the grounds that it was simply not a valid measure of real jury behavior. It is not unlike the physicist who, being unable to observe the actual phenomenon, studies the shadows it makes.

JUDGE–JURY DISAGREEMENT.   The major contribution of the Chicago Jury Project (Kalven and Zeisel 1966) was to characterize those instances in which juries disagree with judges. Knowing this, we can better answer the question of whether juries are worth the trouble they cause.

Juries do not disagree with judges because they fail to understand the case or to take their job seriously. There is every evidence that they follow the case and understand the facts. As fact finders, juries differ very little from judges (in addition to Kalven and Zeisel 1966, see also McCabe and Purvis 1972, 1974; Simon 1977; Bridgeman and Marlowe 1979; Hastie, Penrod, and Pennington 1983; Pettus 1986).

Value differences constitute something like two-thirds of the judge–jury disagreements. As in the case of Leroy Reed, the jury may not openly revolt against the law by imposing its own values, but it may well interpret the facts in the light of its different values: Leroy Reed, having the mentality of a second grader, did not "knowingly" commit criminal acts even though his "knowledge" was sufficient in terms of legal values.

Juries are not as rule-oriented as judges. They will try to decide a case on what they believe is equitable, not paying much attention to the legal distinction between criminal and tort issues. That is, a jury may decide that a man accused of negligent homicide has suffered enough and acquit him when they learn that his child was killed and he was crippled in the auto accident. But they are not blindly in favor of defendants. For example, in the case of Bernard Goetz, who was accused of shooting four young men who he claimed were trying to rob him, the jury found him not guilty of the assault (which he admitted but which the jury apparently felt was justified in the light of modern urban crime) but found him guilty of carrying a concealed weapon for which he was fined and sentenced to jail.

No two juries are alike. It is a mistake to presume that each jury constitutes a valid random sample of the population. Different groups will render different decisions (see Austin 1982). Finally, jury decisions are largely a function of the majority on the first ballot, and the following deliberation serves mainly to bring dissenters to the majority view (see Bridgeman and Marlowe 1979; Tanford and Penrod 1986).

Hastie, Penrod, and Pennington (1983) found, however, that the deliberation occurring after a controlling majority is reached varies significantly with the decision rule in effect. That is, if the jury must reach a twelve-person unanimous verdict, this postmajority deliberation tends to include high proportions of requests for additional instructions from the trial judge. Jurors make about a quarter of the oral corrections of errors, a third of the discussion of the beyond reasonable doubt standard, and discuss substantial amounts of trial testimony and judge's instructions during the period after a controlling majority is reached. On the other hand, if the jury is only required to achieve a vote of ten out of twelve, or eight out of twelve, the post–majority-of-eight deliberation is much less robust. Generally, the more strict the decision rule (unanimity is the most strict), the more robust will be the talk after a majority of eight appears.

In the case of Leroy Reed, the time following the first ballot was spent bringing the toolmaker and the firefighter into line. In the case of a college-age man accused of espionage, reported in the book *The Falcon and the Snowman* (Lindsey 1979), the jury's first informal vote was eight to four for conviction after several hours of deliberation. The first formal vote, coming after several more hours of deliberation, was ten to two for conviction. The two holdouts, both women, were then subjected to intense argument to change their votes. Within an hour one changed. The final holdout, a prelaw student who claimed to have reasonable doubt, was subjected to extreme pressure, including the refusal of the other eleven jurors to sit with her at lunch. She later reported,

> I wanted to hold out forever; I was under terrible pressure; you're cut off from all contact with other people; you're alone, and they refused even to listen to my arguments. They were cold and laughed at me. They just didn't understand the concept of reasonable doubt. Finally, I said, "All right, I'll say he's guilty," but I didn't think he was (p. 366).

She had stood her ground for almost three days of deliberation, and even though she finally voted with the majority, she had not changed her mind. What happened in the Reed and the Falcon and Snowman cases is typical: The minority may be brought into line with the majority to allow a verdict, but those jurors forced to change their vote do not necessarily change their minds (Hastie, Penrod and Pennington 1983).

THE ROLE OF STORIES IN DELIBERATION. Throughout this book we have suggested that the narrative or story constitutes an important conceptual focus in understanding the communication in trials. Obviously, if stories did not serve juries in making their verdicts, our previous points would be seriously undermined. There is, however, solid evidence that juries use stories in a most central way.

Theorists have suggested that the only way lay judges can make sense of the complexities of a trial is to employ the standards of judgment they have learned throughout their lives in the critical evaluation of stories (Bennett and Feldman 1981; Hutchins 1980; Pennington and Hastie 1981). Causal and intentional relations between events become the central mode of organizing the evidence and arguments presented in the trial.

Witnesses, physical evidence, documents, and lawyers' interpretations of them are highly contradictory, inconsistent, incomplete. To reach a verdict the jury must extract a single sensible whole on which to base their decision. Further, the jury must inferentially fill in gaps left from incomplete data.

The story model of jury decision making suggests that sense is made by putting together a story of what happened. As jurors listen to the trial, they try out various accounts of what happened and test their hypothetical accounts against their well-learned ideas of narrative rationality, a concept that includes the subordinate ideas of narrative coherence (the formal features of a story as a sequence of thought, whether it hangs together without contradictions) and narrative fidelity (judging the truth qualities of a story by comparing it with our own logic, experiences, and values) (Fisher 1987).

A juror may raise a question of narrative coherence and fidelity in judging a case in which a noted politician reports that he meant to take only a day cruise with a beautiful young woman and another couple consisting of his political adviser and the young woman's dear friend. But when they arrived in Bimini, they failed to clear the harbor in time and were forced to spend the night, during which time they sang and danced at a night spot and then spent the night with the women sleeping in a different boat from the men, and nothing happened that should upset the politician's wife.

From the point of view of coherence one might question whether the sequence of events hangs together to support the claim that it began as an innocent day's outing and only turned into an overnight event through inadvertence. In terms of fidelity one might question the claim that after a night of drinking, singing, dancing (and posing for pictures with arms around each other), the group truly divided men and women for sleeping purposes. Overall, fidelity might seriously challenge the claim that the two married men and the two unmarried women merely were distant political acquaintances who planned a friendly but proper day on a cruise.

Using a simulated trial in which a man was killed by a knife wound outside a bar by a man with whom he had quarreled earlier in the day, Pennington and Hastie (1986) did a content analysis of the deliberations of jurors who decided in favor of each of the following possible verdicts: first-degree murder, second-degree murder, manslaughter, and not guilty by reason of self-defense. To reach each verdict required that the jurors accept a specific version or story of the contradictory events described by the witnesses. For example, to vote for first-degree murder the jurors had to accept a story that the killing was intentional, with insufficient provocation, and without a full attempt to avoid the conflict. On the other hand, to vote for manslaughter the jurors had to believe that although the killing was deliberate, it was done in the heat of passion, with diminished mental capacity under great provocation, but still without a full attempt to avoid the conflict.

The research concluded that juror deliberations are best characterized as focusing on story structures. The stories jurors inferred involved making connections, mostly on a causal basis: "Johnson was angry, so he decided to kill him." Jurors make inferences about events that do not appear in testimony. Almost half the events mentioned by jurors involved inferences not given in witness testimony about such things as mental states, goals, and inferred actions necessary to fill the gaps left in testimony and to complete stories needed to arrive at a verdict. The stories created by jurors have a beginning, middle, and end in typical narrative style, and include embedded episodes of varying importance.

Pennington and Hastie (1986) further concluded that stories vary in structure and content for different verdicts. The main episodes of stories match the necessary requirements for the verdict. For example, if the jury decides in favor of murder in the first degree, the story they tell includes an episode in which the killer consciously goes home to get his knife and returns with the intent to kill the other man. But in the not guilty by reason of self-defense verdict, the story is that the killer always carries his fishing knife by habit and to keep it away from his children. He returned to the bar innocently and without intention of even seeing the other man.

Pennington and Hastie concluded that the story model is an appropriate concept of what jurors are actually doing when they decide a criminal case. The model includes three stages: (1) The story construction stage involves giving meaning and relevance to trial evidence by incorporating it into one or more scenarios which describe "what happened." This includes the adding of general knowledge about the structure of human action sequences described in narrative rationality. (2) In the verdict category establishment stage the defining features of each possible verdict are represented. (3) The story classification stage involves fitting the story and verdict requirements together to allow a conclusion. Different jurors reach different verdicts on the same evidence largely because stories are constructed by reasoning from world knowledge and evidence. Different people have different world knowledge and apply it in different ways by forming analogies to experienced and hypothetical episodes.

INTERACTION IN DELIBERATION.   What do jurors talk about during their deliberations? Typically, something close to half the comments made concern the testimony of witnesses (Hastie, Penrod, and Pennington 1983; Tanford and Penrod 1986). With a unanimous decision being the most strict and eight of twelve being the least, the more strict the decision rule, the more robust the discussion of trial testimony. However, with a possibility of mentioning forty-three different fact citations (with a possible fifteen key fact citations) juries averaged mentioning 85 percent regardless of the strictness of the decision rule in the Hastie, Penrod, and Pennington study.

About 25 percent of jurors' comments have to do with verdict preferences (Hastie, Penrod, and Pennington 1983; Tanford and Penrod 1986). As we have learned, majorities tend to dictate the verdict. But an individual juror's verdict preference is a stronger and more pervasive predictor of the content of deliberation than the group vote. For example, in the Leroy Reed case, from the first vote the majority favored acquittal and they got their way. But we can predict what an individual, such as the firefighter, will say by noting the individual preference. In the firefighter's case we could predict his continued resistance to sympathetic arguments and his insistence on following the judge's instructions.

Functionally, three-quarters of the communication among juries consists of statements asserting or conveying information (Hastie, Penrod, and Pennington 1983). Among those statements 1 percent are in error, some involving mistakes about testimony and more making mistakes about the judge's instructions. However, 30 to 50 percent of the erroneous statements are corrected by subsequent comments by other jurors. Other communication functions are questions and organizational directives, each of which takes up almost 10 percent of the talk. Group outbursts, when five or more jurors speak simultaneously, occur about once every three minutes (Hastie, Penrod, and Pennington 1983).

The nature of the deliberation changes during the course of the jury's interaction. At the outset most jury talk is substantive, dealing with trial testimony. This gradually drops as a proportion of total talk as time goes by (Forston 1970; Hastie, Penrod, and Pennington 1983). Toward the end of deliberation the content of talk tends to turn more toward procedural issues, particularly those related to the judge's instructions. In a civil case those juries which ultimately decide in favor of the plaintiff make more proplaintiff comments than prodefendant, and in the final phase of their deliberations this variance becomes even more pronounced. Those juries which ultimately find in favor of the defendant make increasingly more prodefendant comments throughout (Forston 1970). As deliberation goes on, statements conveying information and questions gradually decline as comments expressing verdict preferences and directing the others to action increase (Hastie, Penrod, and Pennington 1983).

The foreperson. With rare exceptions, one of the first procedural tasks for the jury is selecting a foreperson. While this proves to be an important role, the selection process is remarkably informal. Most commonly it works this way: One person speaks up and points to another saying, "You be the foreman." If that juror accepts, it is done. Once in a while the juror declines the appointment, typically by saying, "You do it." In that case, if the original speaker accepts, the foreperson is selected. A second pattern is for someone to ask, "Who has been a foreman before?" Or, "Who wants to be foreman?" In either case the first person to speak after such a question is designated foreperson. Rarely does the jury actually vote for the selection, and the whole process typically takes less than a minute (Forston 1970).

More often than not, the one selected as foreperson is a male, sitting at the end of the table, with a relatively higher socioeconomic status (Strodbeck, James, and Hawkins 1957; Hawkins 1960). Recall that in the Leroy Reed case the foreperson was a white male toolmaker sitting at the end of the table.

The foreperson role leads to a significantly high interaction rate. It is reasonable to expect this person to speak three times as much as any other juror, commenting on legal and organizational issues, but not speaking as often about possible verdicts (Hastie, Penrod, and Pennington 1983). The foreperson does a great deal of summarizing of what others have said, but this person also contributes significantly to the body of original fact-related and analytical statements.

Factions. Folklore suggests that frequently juries are such that one person—often believed to be the foreperson—can so control the others as to dictate the verdict. The story of *Twelve Angry Men* is part of this lore. It tells of one man who held out against a guilty verdict until he won the other eleven to his thinking. Judge James C. Adkins of Florida called this situation a lion among sheep.

Research suggests that contrary to folklore it is factions that control jury decision making. Forston (1970) found what he called the central work group (CWG), consisting of about six jurors who were perceived by their peers as being the most active and influential participators in the decision-making process. The other jurors Forston called peripheral observers (PO). Members of the CWG occupied about 83 percent of the talking time, and the PO spoke for only about 14 percent of the time. Educated, high-income, professional males constituted an overrepresented group in the CWG. Caucasian, male, married, wealthier, Republican, conservative, and authoritarian jurors are not only likely to appear in the CWG, they tend to participate more in deliberations and are more persuasive to other jurors (Moran and Craig 1986).

Hastie, Penrod, and Pennington (1983) grouped those jurors who indicated common verdict preferences into factions. Those who start deliberation with no clear verdict preference constitute a faction destined to disappear early, although in rules that allow eight of twelve or ten of twelve to decide the verdict, jurors are likely to remain undecided longer. This size of factions is the factor most closely associated with verdicts, and when a faction reaches eight, the verdict is usually made, although not necessarily so. When a unanimous verdict is required, the wishes of the eight-juror faction may be frustrated by a hung jury and even, rarely, by the ultimate emergence of an opposing faction which finally sets the verdict.

After initial factions are established, movement from faction to faction becomes critical. Early defections become significant. When the first juror announces, "I'm changing my mind and voting with the other group," it may signal a trend. Large factions tend to be attractive. People are less likely to leave them, and those in small factions are more likely to defect to them. The power of group pressure works to force those in small factions to speak more to defend themselves: "Why do you fail to see that the correct verdict is what *all* of us have chosen?" Furthermore, people who stay in small factions tend to be high participators who are resistant to persuasion. On the other hand, those in large factions tend not to speak as frequently as those in small factions. Large factions emerge more quickly in nonunanimous juries.

Styles of deliberation. Hastie, Penrod, and Pennington (1983) identify two quite different styles of deliberation: verdict-driven and evidence-driven. The verdict-driven style can be described as essentially argumentative. At the outset of deliberation the jury takes a public ballot, factions are identified, and a debate begins in which the factions are asked (or coerced) to create arguments for "their" side and to include evidence from trial testimony to support their position. Frequent pollings occur in the verdict-driven debate to see if and to what extent faction defections are taking place.

Evidence-driven deliberation, on the other hand, involves public voting only late in the discussion, sometimes voting only once to validate the clear deciding faction that has emerged. This style of deliberation fits a classical dialogue model in which individuals do not typically identify closely with a single verdict preference and may recall testimony in support of several possible verdicts. Evidence is discussed in general rather than in support of a verdict claim. A good deal of time is spent constructing the story that will ultimately be selected.

Hastie and his colleagues found that verdict-driven juries are more common under majority rule than unanimity, they reach their verdict more quickly, and they rated themselves lower in persuasiveness and openmindedness. Evidence-driven juries showed more activity in either fact–issue pairings or a more thorough development of connections between testimony and judge's instructions. Evidence-driven jurors rated themselves higher in the seriousness of deliberation and the perceived pressure from other jurors.

PRACTICE AND JURY DELIBERATION

At the start of this chapter we quoted the lawyer who wanted to know what goes on in the jury room so he could increase his chances of winning. Now that we know fairly well what happens in deliberation, how can our lawyer use that knowledge?

Clearly, lawyers will be wise to concentrate on the development of a solid narrative justification of their case. They will consider the implications of narrative rationality, test their case for coherence and fidelity, and incorporate that narrative structure in their opening and closing statements.

Hastie, Penrod, and Pennington (1983) say that the three-stage story model that characterizes deliberation is a recapitulation of what occurs in the mind of each individual juror before deliberation. As individual jurors enter the deliberation, they have already combined their world knowledge and values with trial testimony to build a story of what "happened." They have listened to the judge and used that information to relate their story to a verdict category, so that as deliberation begins and initial factions form, these pre-deliberation judgments will be critical. Lawyers, then, will seek to send as many favorable jurors as possible (ideally as many as eight in a twelve-member jury) into the jury room. Once a juror establishes a story of what happened, it is unlikely that story will be significantly changed in deliberation.

How, then, do changes in factions occur? Almost always jurors justify their changes by acknowledging some change in interpretation of the law or jury procedures (Hastie, Penrod, and Pennington 1983). Since instructions are often confusing and produce misunderstanding during deliberations (Kessler 1975; Pettus 1986), lawyers may need to pay more attention to what the judge will instruct the jurors and seek to clarify this in favorable directions. In opening and closing comments lawyers will be wise to focus on legal rather than evidentiary issues, as we have discussed in chapters 5 and 9. Throughout the trial lawyers should keep in mind what is currently presented in movies and television so that these stereotypes which are most likely in jurors' minds can be related to the specific case at hand (Pettus 1986). The interpretation of evidence and law will probably be influenced by current media representations.

As we explained in chapter 4, years of social science research have failed to reveal a pattern of scientific jury selection that will significantly increase the effectiveness of lawyers' persuasion. Our knowledge of human persuasion does not even theoretically support the idea that all one needs is specific information about individuals in order to guarantee persuasion. On the other hand, there is substantial evidence that knowledge of how groups of people selected from the same population as the jury will deliberate on the trial stories will be valuable in preparing the most effective case (Hastie, Penrod, and Pennington 1983).

This knowledge of jury deliberation has a clear implication for practice: Lawyers should try out their cases on panels of mock jurors and listen to the deliberation. By hearing how the mock jurors deal with case elements, lawyers can revise their cases to increase the likelihood that favorable stories will be constructed and connected with favorable verdict choices. Lawyers will be cued to look for both styles of deliberation: verdict-driven and evidence-driven. Each style of deliberation may reveal different types of weaknesses in case preparation. For the verdict-driven deliberation, weaknesses may appear in evidentiary support for the desired verdict. Lawyers must realize that they will send into the jury room advocates for their position, and they must supply their advocates enough ammunition to build their faction to the determining size.

For evidence-driven deliberation, lawyers may see critical story elements that are missing or are misunderstood. They can revise their presentation to increase the likelihood that a desired story will be constructed.

REFERENCES

Austin, A. D. (1982). Jury perceptions on advocacy: a case study. *Litigation* 8: 15.

Bennett, W. L., and Feldman, M. S. (1981). *Reconstructing reality in the courtroom*. New Brunswick, NJ: Rutgers University Press.

Bridgeman, D. L., and Marlowe, D. (1979). Jury decision making: an empirical study based on actual felony trials. *Journal of Applied Psychology* 64: 94.

Fisher, W. R. (1987). *Human communication as narration*. Columbia: University of South Carolina Press.

Forston, R. F. (1970). *How the jury decides*. Des Moines: Iowa State Bar Association.

Hans, V. P. and Vidmar, N. (1986). *Judging the jury*. New York: Plenum.

Hastie, R.; Penrod, S.; and Pennington, N. (1983). *Inside the jury*. Cambridge: Harvard University Press.

Hawkins, C. H. (1960). Interaction and coalition realignments in consensus-seeking groups: a study of experimental jury deliberations. Unpublished doctoral dissertation, The University of Chicago.

Hutchins, E. (1980). *Quality and inference*. Cambridge: Harvard University Press.

Hyman, H. M., and Tarrant, C. M. (1975). Aspects of American jury history. In R. Simon (ed.), *The jury system in America*. Beverly Hills, CA: Sage.

Kalven, H., Jr., and Zeisel, H. (1966). *The American jury*. Boston: Little, Brown.

Kessler, J. B. (1975). The social psychology of jury deliberations. In R. J. Simon (ed.), *The jury system in America*. Beverly Hills, CA: Sage.

Levin, A. (1986). Inside the jury room; broadcast on "Frontline" with Judy Woodruff. Boston: WGBH Educational Foundation. Wisconsin v. Leroy Reed, case number L0855.

Lindsey, R. (1979). *The Falcon and the Snowman*. New York: Pocket Books.

McCabe, S. and Purvis, R. (1972). *The jury at work*. Oxford: Basil Blackwell.

McCabe, S., and Purvis, S. (1974). *The shadow jury at work*. Oxford: Basil Blackwell.

Moran, G., and Craig, J. (1986). Neither "tentative" nor "fragmentary": verdict preference of impaneled felony jurors toward capital punishment. *Journal of Applied Psychology* 71: 146–55.

Pennington, N., and Hastie, R. (1981). Juror decision-making models: the generalization gap. *Psychological Bulletin* 89: 246–87.

Pennington, N., and Hastie, R. (1986). Evidence evaluation in complex decision making. *Journal of Personality and Social Psychology* 51: 242–56.

Pettus, A. B. (1986). An investigation of jury decision making based on posttrial interviews. Unpublished doctoral dissertation, Department of Communication, University of Utah.

Roberts, W. R. (trans.) (1954). *The Rhetoric of Aristotle*. New York: Random House.

Simon, R. J. (1977). The American jury: instrument of justice or of prejudice and conformity? *Sociological Inquiry* 47: 254–93.

Strodbeck, F. L.; James, R. M.; and Hawkins, C. H. (1957). Social status in jury deliberations. *American Sociological Review* 22: 713–18.

Tanford, S., and Penrod, S. (1986). Jury deliberations: discussion content and influence processes in jury decision making. *Journal of Applied Social Psychology* 16: 322–47.

Name Index

Aaronson, D., 13
Aboud, F., 114
Adams, J., 225
Adkins, J., 223
Adler, F., 74
Adorno, T., 74
Ajzen, I., 106
Allen, M., 15
Altman, I., 123
Anderson, C., 210
Anderson, N., 112
Aquinas, Thomas, 35–36
Argyle, M., 125
Aristotle, 30–32, 34, 35, 40, 44, 116, 224–225
Asch, S., 112
Atkinson, J., 182
Auerbach, J., 13
Augustine, 34–35
Austin, A., 228
Austin, W., 72, 75

Bacharach, S., 11
Bacon, F., 205
Balch, R., 71
Barge, J., 131
Barraclough, R., 106
Basehart, J., 160
Baumeister, R., 129
Becker, L., 151
Bell, B., 158, 159
Bell, D., 119
Bell, G., 13
Bell, R., 110
Bennett, W., 47, 48, 49, 98–101, 229
Benoit, W., 92
Berscheid, E., 118, 128
Berg, K., 74, 129
Berg, L., 159
Berger, J., 117, 130

Berlo, D., 117
Bleiberg, S., 172
Boehm, V., 74
Borchard, E., 149
Borgida, E., 159
Bostrom, R., 159
Bower, G., 209
Bradac, J., 155, 156, 159, 161
Brandon, R., 146
Bray, R., 74
Brehm, J., 213
Bridgeman, D., 227, 228
Brigham, J., 143, 144
Brock, T., 119
Broeder, D., 56, 69
Bronson, E., 75
Brooker, G., 69
Buchanan, R., 58
Buckhout, R., 143
Bugenthal, D., 122
Bull, R., 129
Bullis, C., 7
Burgoon, M., 105, 113, 131, 159
Burnkrant, R., 212
Burr, Aaron, 67

Cacioppo, J., 114
Cahn, D., 126
Calder, B., 204
Calhoun, L., 72
Cantor, J., 112
Cantor, N., 132
Caplan, H., 33
Carbone, T., 118
Carroll, J., 210
Cavoukian, A., 153
Chaiken, S., 128
Chang, M., 70
Charrow, R., 58
Christie, R., 75

238

Subject Index

adjudication, 3
administrative hearing, 4, 19–21
adversarial models, 54–55
advocacy, 34–36, 39
alternative dispute resolution (ADR), 3
American Bar Association: Special Committee on Dispute Resolution, 14, 17; American Law Institute, 37
arbitration, 3, 5, 21–24; American Arbitration Association, 21–23; Better Business Bureau, 21, 22; Federal Arbitration Act, 22; Magnuson-Moss Act, 22
argument, 11–12; number of, 204; repetition, 204–206; structure, 213–215
attorneys' "promises," 208–209
attitudes of judges, 59
attractiveness, 128–129
attribution, 76–77, 109–113
authoritarianism, 74–75
avoidance, 3–5

BATNA (best alternative to a negotiated agreement), 12
bias: children, 131–132; gender, 129–131; racial, 72–73; trial, 55–58, 66–67, 69

capital punishment, 75–76
child witnesses, 131–132
Citizen Settlement Program, Miami, 17–19
Civil Rights Act of 1964, 13
closing argument: goals of, 202–203; limits of, 215–216; metaphors, 210–211; promises, 208–209; reactance to, 212–213
commitment, 9–10
communicator motives, 120–121
compensation, 77
composure, 117
confessions, 148–150
confidence fallacy, 143–144
confidence of source, 120
confirmatio, 34

credibility, 116–118, 152
cross examination, goals of, 169–171

deception, 124–126
denial, 194–198
direct examination, goals of, 169–171
discovery, 43
dispute, 2
dogmatism, 74–75
dynamism, 117

elaboration likelihood, 114–115
empirical science, 41–42, 47
empiricism, 30–31
enthymeme, 31–32
episode schema, 101
essential elements, 36–38
ethos, 104, 116
evasion, 194–198
evidence, 43–45; confession, 148–150; impact of, 142; inadmissible, 56–58; polygraph, 153–154
exemplification, 111
exordium, 33, 88
expectations, 113–116
expertise, 116–118
expert testimony, 144–146
eye movement, 122
eyewitness: confidence, 143–144; nonidentification, 146–147; testimony, 142–144; survey data, 62

facial expressions, 122
facts, 30, 33, 34, 44, 47, 88, 93, 95, 227
fairness: trial outcomes, 53; procedural, 53–55
fifth amendment: in the courtroom, 73–74; procedural, 53–55
forepersons, 232–233
fragmented speech, 156–157, 184

243